# DRYBONE
### A HISTORY OF
### FORT FETTERMAN, WYOMING

ALSO BY TOM LINDMIER (with Steve Mount):

*I See by Your Outfit:*
*Historic Cowboy Gear of the Northern Plains*

# DRYBONE
## A HISTORY OF
### FORT FETTERMAN, WYOMING

Tom Lindmier

*with a foreword by*
*Douglas C. McChristian*

*To: Gene Partner*
*Hope you enjoy the*
*book.*
*Best Wishes —*
*Tom Lindmier*

HIGH PLAINS PRESS

The cover art is from
the December 16, 1876, issue of *Harper's Weekly.*

Copyright © 2002 Tom Lindmier
Printed in the United States of America
10 9 8 7 6 5 4 3 2 1

Library of Congress Cataloging-in-Publication Data

Lindmier, Tom, 1951-
Drybone: a history of Fort Fetterman, Wyoming / Tom Lindmier ; with a
foreword by Douglas C. McChristian.
        p. cm.
Includes bibliographical references and index.
ISBN 0-931271-65-7 (Hardcover, limited edition : alk. paper)
ISBN 0-931271-66-5 (Trade paperback : alk. paper)
1. Fort Fetterman (Wyo.)--History. 2. Frontier and pioneer
life--Wyoming--Fort Fetterman Region.   I. Title.
F769.F58 L46 2002
978.7'95--dc21

                                        2002008174

For a catalogue or information contact:
HIGH PLAINS PRESS
P.O. Box 123
Glendo, Wyoming 82213
Ph. 1-800-552-7819

I dedicate this book to those who have, over the thirty years of my research and writing, encouraged and given me the capabilities to accomplish this project.

To my parents Bill and Irene Lindmier who taught me that hard work and perseverance is the key to success;

And also to three men who guided and assured me that I could successfully publish this historic study: the late Edward Rowley who took the time to excite a fledgling history student; Russ Broderdorp, my favorite high school instructor, who tried to help me get a better grasp of the English language; and finally the late Dr. T. A. Larson, without doubt Wyoming's most honored historian and my favorite college instructor.

Without these individuals this book would have never been written.

# Contents

*Foreword: Hardship and Hard Luck
    by Douglas C. McChristian* **ix**

1. Opening the Bozeman Trail **15**

2. Building a Post 1867–1869 **23**

3. Transportation and Communications **35**

4. The Peace Treaty of 1868 and Its Aftermath **49**

5. Fort Fetterman and the Centennial Campaigns **69**

6. Garrison Life at Fort Fetterman **89**

7. Expanding the Fort 1870–1881 **115**

8. Fort Fetterman Becomes a Town 1882–1885 **145**

9. The Rise and Fall of "Drybone" 1885–1890 **159**

   *Appendices:*

      *A. Biographies of Prominent Fort Fetterman Citizens* **191**

      *B. Children Born at Fetterman as a Military Post* **201**

      *C. Companies and Post Commanders Stationed at Fort Fetterman* **203**

      *D. Biographies of Selected Officers at Fort Fetterman* **205**

   *Notes* **217**

   *Bibliography* **237**

   *Index* **243**

# Hardship and Hard Luck

The story of Fort Fetterman is one of hardship and hard luck, but it is also the story of a frontier military post too tough to die, at least for a while. Throughout its active life, location worked both for and against it, too often the latter. Like most frontier army posts, the government established Fetterman to satisfy immediate military needs aimed at the eventual subjugation of the Plains Indians. The discovery of gold in the Beaverhead country of western Montana created a need for a shorter, more direct route from the States to that region. In 1863, one of those prospectors, John Bozeman, explored a feasible route from the Oregon Trail on the North Platte northward across what is today central Wyoming. Problem was, it passed through the heart of the last great buffalo hunting ground. With the Crows and the Sioux already fighting over the disputed area, white incursions via the Bozeman Trail only fueled the conflict.

Following the Civil War, the U.S. Congress officially recognized the Bozeman Trail by appropriating funds to build two additional forts on the middle, and most dangerous, portion of the trail. Fort Phil Kearny was situated on Piney Creek, at the eastern base of the Big Horns, while Fort C.F. Smith was positioned north of the range on the Bighorn River. The protection these forts promised, though their garrisons were besieged most of the time, attracted heavy emigration over the road to Montana in 1866.

The next year witnessed the completion of the transcontinental railroad across southern Wyoming territory, a development that sounded the death knell of the old Oregon Trail along the Platte. Suddenly, eager prospectors could ride the cars west to Cheyenne, the new jumping-off point to the northern gold camps.

Following the abandonment of the old Oregon emigrant road, it was quickly apparent to the army that a garrison would be advantageously situated near Bridger's Ferry, where the new trail crossed the North Platte. Troops from Fort Laramie were dispatched to the area in summer 1867 to

9

select a location for the new fort. With negotiations then underway to affect a new treaty with the Sioux, one that would recognize the vast region north of the North Platte as an "unceded" hunting territory, the army had the foresight to choose a site on the south bank. Accordingly, Fort Fetterman was situated just outside the boundary of lands designated for Indian use alone.

Nevertheless, the location was to prove a curse for the post. The barren wind-swept plateau made human habitation there a challenge throughout most of the year with searing summer heat contrasted with ferocious winter blizzards and sub-zero temperatures. Despite those environmental handicaps, the troops carried out their mission of protecting the road, and by their presence, promoted white settlement in the region south of the river. In less than a year, however, Oglala chief Red Cloud compelled the government to surrender the Bozeman road and the three northern forts. It was a hollow victory. The completion of the railroad to Salt Lake City made possible a shorter route from that point to western Montana.

The closing of the Bozeman Trail left Fort Fetterman with little purpose, other than acting as a buffer between the Indian hunting lands and the increasingly settled regions south of the North Platte. The presence of the army allowed ranching to flourish in what had formerly been a dangerous region. That was, in perspective, the fort's most significant contribution to Wyoming's development.

Fort Fetterman is perhaps best remembered for its role as the base of operations for Brigadier General George Crook's 1876 campaigns against the Indians, in concert with other columns converging from Montana and Dakota Territory. Three times that year Crook launched expeditions northward from the post. Those efforts contributed significantly to the army's success in eventually wearing down the hostile factions. Indeed, the Sioux War marked Fetterman's zenith as a military installation.

As early as 1866, General of the Army William T. Sherman envisioned a plan to confine the Indians on defined reservations, where they could be watched over by a few perimeter posts. The bulk of the army would be consolidated in fewer posts along the railroads. There, the troops could be supplied more economically, yet be readily dispatched to trouble spots. Fort Fetterman was among those posts that lay in the hinterlands—far off the railroad and too distant from the Sioux reservations in Dakota to be of much use. Five years after the Sioux War, Fetterman was dropped from the army inventory. The only surprise was that it lasted as long as it did.

Unlike most abandoned frontier posts, however, Fort Fetterman refused to die. Therein lies the truly fascinating chapter in its history. In the years following the army's exodus, the post underwent a phoenix-like transformation into a rural town. Civilians in the area, already accustomed to the place, immediately moved into the buildings. That alone was not unusual—local citizens frequently took up temporary residence at abandoned forts all across the West—but what was different is that so many businesses sprang up at Fetterman. Within only a few years, it offered everything a cowboy could want—saloons, a general store, post office, hotel, even a restaurant—and of course no self-respecting cow town was replete without a bawdy house. Eventually Fetterman boasted its own doctor and a community hospital!

But, bad luck plagued the place. A railroad extending west from Nebraska was surveyed to strike the North Platte several miles below the old fort. Adding to Fetterman's woes, the hopefuls who had purchased the buildings neglected to consider that the surrounding land was still owned by the government. Although the railroad secured a right-of-way for the track, the government withheld permission for a town site. Consequently, a town development company cooperating with the railroad fixed the station at a new place just outside the military reservation. Had it not been for that oversight, we would see "Fetterman, Wyoming" on today's road maps, rather than Douglas. The final insult came when the rails bypassed the old fort by a mile, and only then did the government declare the military reservation open to homesteading. But, it was too late.

Fort Fetterman has long warranted a detailed examination. Although many authors have referred to the fort tangentially with regard to the Bozeman Trail and the 1876 Sioux War, little else has been written about it until now. Tom Lindmier is superbly qualified to do that, having dual interests in frontier military and Wyoming cowboy history. A native of Douglas, he became curious about the place in his youth and spent many hours poking around the site. It was a lasting attachment. Over a long period, Tom applied his academic training to amassing a trove of primary documentation and, in the process, acquired a more intimate knowledge of the fort's history than perhaps any other person. In this comprehensive volume, he shares his knowledge and enthusiasm for one of the West's important, but heretofore neglected forts.

DOUGLAS C. McCHRISTIAN
*The U.S. Army in the West 1870-1880: Uniforms and Equipment*

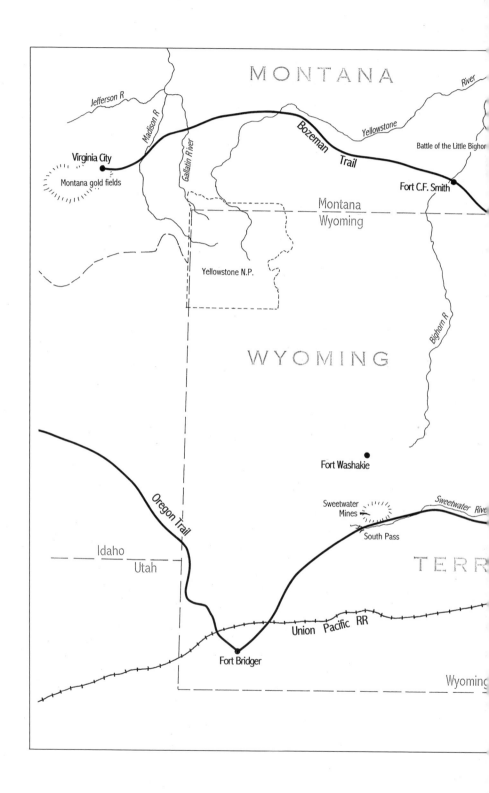

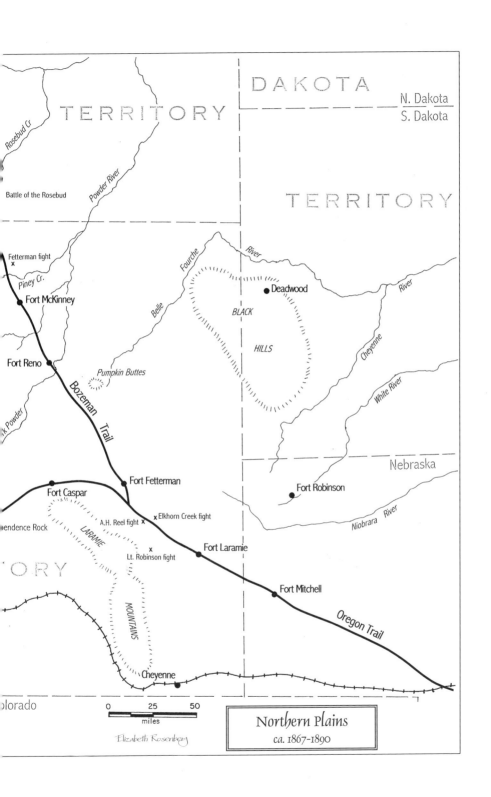

DAKOTA

N. Dakota

S. Dakota

TERRITORY

TERRITORY

Rosebud Cr

Powder River

Battle of the Rosebud

Fetterman fight
x

Piney Cr.

Fort McKinney

Belle

Fourche

River

River

Deadwood

BLACK

HILLS

Cheyenne River

Fort Reno

Bozeman Trail

Pumpkin Buttes

White River

k Powder

Fort Fetterman

Nebraska

Fort Caspar

Fort Robinson

endence Rock

A.H. Reel fight  x   x Elkhorn Creek fight

LARAMIE

Niobrara River

x
Lt. Robinson fight

Fort Laramie

ORY

MOUNTAINS

Fort Mitchell

Oregon Trail

Cheyenne

lorado

0    25    50
miles

Elizabeth Rosenberg

Northern Plains
ca. 1867–1890

# OPENING THE
# BOZEMAN TRAIL

CHAPTER

**1**

BY THE 1860s the ever-increasing settlement of the American West was escalating the conflict between the white settlers and those who had roamed the Plains for centuries, the American Indians. Conflict was not new to these indigenous peoples, as they had practiced intertribal warfare for as long as memories could recall. But this new invasion of the white man, searching for land and riches, was more than they could allow or understand.

Fort Fetterman was founded in 1867, but its story actually began five years earlier, during the height of the Civil War. In 1862 two prospectors, John White and William Eads, discovered gold on Grasshopper Creek in Montana Territory. When news of their strike spread, thousands of men, women, and children began a rush into Montana Territory nearly as great as the California rush of 1849. Both the governments fighting the Civil War needed new wealth for their treasuries and encouraged prospectors to secure gold for their war needs. Once the extent of the discoveries was known—$16 million in minerals shipped in the first year alone[1]—the floodgates were opened. Within two years, rich ore deposits were found in Alder Gulch and Last Chance Gulch. Communities sprouted up near the mines: Bannock, Virginia City, Helena, and Bozeman attracted an ever-growing number of prospectors, miners, and other profit-seekers.

Throughout the war thousands of miners journeyed to the Montana gold fields. Most traveled up the Missouri River to Fort Benton, then southwest through mountain passes to the mining district. A second route coursed through what became the state of Wyoming along the Platte River's Oregon Trail to Fort Hall, in what is now Idaho, and then doubled back into Montana. Both routes took time, and the region's riches would not wait for those who dawdled. A shorter route was needed to deliver this wealth to the east, but neither government could focus on this endeavor.

In 1864, as the Civil War neared its bloody end, the famous mountain man and government scout James Bridger left Fort Laramie, at the confluence of the Laramie and North Platte Rivers in Dakota Territory, searching the country to the north for a new trail to the Montana gold fields. Bridger knew of the Indians' determination to keep the white man out of Powder River country east of the Big Horn Mountains, so on the western side of the range he blazed a trail which parted north from the Oregon Trail near Fort Caspar and cut across the waterless prairie to the Bighorn River. Following the river for some distance, it wound northward into Montana. Bridger's trail was shorter than previous routes, but was hampered by areas of poor or no water.

During the same year, a former miner named John Bozeman explored another trail. Though Bozeman's route was shorter still, he plotted it with little regard to the Indians. This route left the North Platte River valley near LaPrele Creek about fifty miles east of Bridger's trail, and angled northwest along the eastern base of the Big Horn Mountains, ending at Virginia City. Bozeman's route soon drew traffic: it was more direct, had plenty of water, and was easier to travel than Bridger's. But Indian resistance would soon prove to be a serious problem.

At war's end, the newly reunited U.S. government turned its eyes westward, as did many of its citizens. Veterans newly released from service began to search for new homes and new beginnings. Many sought adventure or a chance to make a new life in the West where they could forget the years of conflict. Some sought quick riches in the mining districts. Those who failed to attain their fortunes soon pursued other livelihoods such as freighting, homesteading, or ranching in the vast wilderness.

By 1865 several parties of miners had traveled along what would be called the Montana Road or Bozeman Trail. That same year the federal government, still seeking a shorter route to the gold fields, authorized a survey beginning in Sioux City, Iowa. Colonel James A. Sawyer led the 250-wagon expedition of about one hundred men including engineers, miners, and two companies of "Galvanized Yankees": captured Confederate soldiers who had volunteered to serve the federal forces on the frontier instead of going to military prisons.

The Sawyer expedition met with intense Indian resistance but finally reached Virginia City, primarily by following Bozeman's road. The results of this survey received widespread publicity.[2] Soon, Indian conflicts escalated as larger numbers of miners trekked over the Montana Road. The government decided it was time for the military to halt the attacks.

General Patrick E. Connor led a military force into Powder River country in the summer of 1865 to punish the Indians who had attacked the miners. But Connor's expedition was largely a failure, as it sparked more determined Indian retaliations against the travelers and only succeeded in establishing another military post, Fort Connor (later called Fort Reno) at the forks of Powder River.

When military intervention failed to avert Indian hostilities, the government attempted a peaceful solution. In the fall of 1865 a peace treaty gained an uneasy armistice for the Northern Plains. The seven tribes of Teton Sioux and the Upper and Lower Yanktonai Sioux tribes agreed to "withdraw from the routes overland already established, or hereafter to be established through their country."[3] As with any mutual agreement, both parties had to comply with the terms. But both also felt that if one party broke a promise, the other could retaliate. There were other problems, too. Two key leaders were absent: Red Cloud and Old-Man-Afraid-of-His-Horses, whose people roamed Powder River country bisected by the Bozeman Trail. Further complicating matters, the chiefs who did sign the treaty did not always fully represent the smaller bands that made up their tribes, and they were unable to convince all their people to comply with the terms. Equally important, the tribal chiefs perhaps never fully understood what they had agreed to when signing the treaty.

Complicating matters still further was the belief of most Americans in "manifest destiny"—the perceived right of the United States to expand unimpeded across the North American continent. This impetus led to the inevitable conflict with the American Indian, even as it spawned the rapid settlement and development of the country west of the Mississippi River to the California coast. As the frontier moved westward, the eastern states were rapidly embracing the industrial revolution with all its technological advancements. By 1867, that technology was expanding across the West. Frontier mail service saw the rise of the short-lived Pony Express, soon replaced by the transcontinental telegraph and stagecoach lines. The stagecoach lines were, in turn, replaced by the rail network that proliferated after the transcontinental railroad linked the coasts in 1869. Thus this perception of the divine right of western expansion, coupled with greed on the part of some politicians and western settlers, undermined many treaties from the start and caused them to malfunction.

Acknowledging the weakness of the 1865 treaties, the peace commissioners attempted to get more chiefs to sign a new round of treaties during the spring of 1866. Some commissioners traveled the Missouri River country. Others met with tribes in the Fort Laramie vicinity, assembling an imposing representation of chiefs and sub-chiefs including the Sioux leaders who had decisively defeated General Connor's expeditions in 1865. Most notably in attendance were the Powder River chiefs Red Cloud and Old-Man-Afraid-of-His-Horses, who had refused to come to the previous conference. With so many chiefs present at the council, the commissioners, led by Indian Superintendent D.B. Taylor, viewed the treaty as promising.

But while peace was being sought at the council tables, the War Department was responding to public pressure to protect travelers on the Bozeman Trail. Major General John Pope issued orders on March 10, 1866, to revive Fort Connor as Fort Reno and establish two more military posts along the road. Pope also placed Colonel Henry B. Carrington in command of the Second and Third Battalions of the Eighteenth Infantry Regiment. The Third was ordered to garrison posts along the Oregon Trail as far as Utah, and the Second was to protect the Bozeman Trail. To draw attention away from the Bozeman Trail and the building of military forts along its route, the commissioners at the treaty conference focused their dialogue on the annuities to be paid to the Indians in the amount of $70,000 per year.

As Carrington's command approached Fort Laramie on June 16, the Indians who had assembled for the peace conference noted the large number of soldiers. When Chief Standing Elk learned of the command's mission he told Carrington, "The fighting men in that country have not come to Laramie, and you will have to fight them." Red Cloud was even more outspoken, telling Commissioner Taylor, "The Great Father sends us presents and wants us to sell him the road but the White Chief goes with soldiers to steal the road before Indians say Yes or No."[4]

Leaving the conference, the Powder River chiefs led their people northward. The remaining chiefs, who had nothing to lose, signed the treaty, ostensibly giving away the Bozeman Trail. Commissioner Taylor, even though he knew that the Powder River chiefs had not signed, telegraphed the commissioner of Indian Affairs, telling of his success in securing a lasting treaty.

On June 17 Carrington's command marched away from Fort Laramie, heading for Powder River country under the illusion created by the peace council that life would be easy along the Bozeman Trail. Combat seemed unlikely; they could deal with the Indians using patience and common sense. Carrington, who planned to dedicate all his resources to building the required military posts before winter, was not prepared for the onslaught. The Indians had no intention of relinquishing Powder River country, and conflict was inevitable.

One hundred and sixty-nine miles northwest of Fort Laramie, Carrington's command reached the forks of Powder River. Here were the ruins of Fort Connor, where eight companies stayed to re-establish the post as Fort Reno. The rest of the command marched northwest along the Bozeman Trail and encamped on July 13 at the three forks of Piney Creek. This site was selected for the second fort, dubbed Fort Phil Kearny.[5] Once construction was well underway, Captain Nathaniel C. Kinney, commanding two companies, was sent further up the trail to select a site for a third fort on the banks of the Bighorn River. This final Bozeman Trail garrison, Fort C. F. Smith,[6] was established ninety-one miles north of Fort Phil Kearny on August 12.

Initially, Carrington's men concentrated on building the forts, devoting little effort to protecting the travelers who immediately began to use the road. Less than one week after Carrington arrived on Piney Creek, Red Cloud commenced hostile action, attacking nearly every civilian and military wagon train that advanced northward on the trail. War parties began to raid the log trains at Fort Phil Kearny, and anyone who wandered away from the protection of the fort risked death at the hands of the Indians. While all three forts would be attacked, Fort Phil Kearny became the primary target. It remained almost constantly under siege for the next two years, until the Bozeman Trail posts were eventually abandoned in 1868.

On December 21, 1866, the conflict reached a new height when Carrington's command suffered a major military defeat, since known as the Fetterman Fight. The battle began when a large party of Sioux and Cheyenne Indians, led by Red Cloud and Crazy Horse, attacked a wood train hauling timber for construction near Fort Phil Kearny. The Indians' tactic was to use the attack on the wood train as a decoy to draw out a relief party from the fort. They succeeded. Back at the fort, claiming seniority, Captain William J. Fetterman demanded that Colonel Carrington place him in command of the relief column. Carrington explicitly ordered Fetterman to relieve the wood train but not to pursue the Indians beyond Lodge Trail Ridge, a precipitous slope that divided Big Piney and Peno Creeks three miles north of the fort. North of this ridge were deep ravines and broken terrain which two weeks earlier had been the scene of a similar attack—a near-disaster for the military.

Captain Fetterman's command consisted of forty-nine men from the Twenty-seventh Infantry armed with muzzle-loading muskets and twenty-seven men from the Second Cavalry bearing Spencer breech-loading carbines. Lieutenant George W. Grummond was placed in command of the cavalry under Fetterman. Captain James Powell and two civilians, James Wheatley and Isaac Fisher, both armed with Henry repeating rifles, volunteered as well. The total relief force numbered three officers, seventy-six soldiers, and two civilians.

What happened after the command disappeared from view of the fort will never be completely known. What is known is that Fetterman's command did proceed over Lodge Trail Ridge and became engaged with between 1500 and 2000 Sioux and Cheyenne warriors. A brief battle ensued, in which the entire command was killed.

At the sound of heavy gunfire, another relief column left the fort under the command of Captain Tenodor Ten Eyck, who witnessed the final destruction of Fetterman's men and the eventual Indian withdrawal northward from the summit of the ridge. After the Indians had left the battle scene Captain Ten Eyck and his men discovered the bodies of Fetterman and his command. Horribly mutilated and stripped of clothing and weapons, the bodies lay bleak and white upon the snowy battlefield.

Their numbers decimated, those left at Fort Phil Kearny now expected the Indians to sweep down on the depleted garrison. Colonel Carrington sent John "Portugee" Phillips on a legendary four-day ride through extreme cold and drifting snow to Fort Laramie with news of the disaster and a request for reinforcements. Phillips arrived there on Christmas Eve and immediately the news was telegraphed, reaching General Philip Cooke the day after Christmas.

Almost overnight the battle made newspaper headlines, and the public demanded that those responsible for this military debacle be held accountable. A scapegoat was immediately found in Carrington, who was relieved of his command by Colonel Henry W. Wessells. But General Grant was unwilling to solely blame Carrington, and he issued orders on January 9,

1867, to replace General Cooke as departmental commander with General Christopher Colon Augur.[7]

Augur decided to strengthen and consolidate what he had inherited: the primary defense system along the Platte River. During spring and early summer of 1867 he ordered the closure of Fort Mitchell, Nebraska, and Fort Caspar, in Dakota Territory. Simultaneously he directed that a new fort be built near the point where the Bozeman and Oregon Trails split, thus commanding the country at the southern extent of the Bozeman Trail.[8] The trail's fourth fort was to be designated Fort Fetterman, honoring the military's tradition of naming new forts for the officer most recently slain in the line of duty.

⁓ ⁓

Over the next fifteen years, the rise and fall of Fort Fetterman would create a microcosm of American frontier society. The area became central Wyoming's melting pot—or perhaps a pressure cooker—where eventually both Indians and Euro-Americans, soldiers and civilians, ranchers and entrepreneurs and outlaws would reside together. It remained up to these various nationalities and interests to meld a society of trust and understanding, or the complete opposite. Almost from the beginning, the inhabitants in and around Fort Fetterman would be embroiled in lawlessness and open hostility, with the military seeking to maintain a semblance of peace and security. Fort Fetterman was actively involved in some of the American West's most violent conflicts. The occupants of this garrison would observe both the prelude to the Treaty of 1868 and its aftermath, the ensuing Indian conflicts, and the resulting campaigns of 1876–1877, precipitated by the Black Hills gold-seekers.

They also witnessed the development of Wyoming's cattle industry and the swift settlement of the area. Indeed, like few other western posts, Fort Fetterman would be transformed into a town after it had outlived its military usefulness. Notorious as a wild cowtown and den of iniquity during the 1880s, the town of Fetterman later captured the imagination of Western novelist Owen Wister when he visited Wyoming in 1895. Later still, Wister fictionalized it as a town called "Drybone."[9] The name made sense. By that time, Fort Fetterman's heyday was past, and it would soon become a relic, its skeleton bleaching under the prairie sun. By the time Wyoming won its statehood in 1890, the railroad's western expansion had written the final chapter in Fort Fetterman's history.

# Building a Post
# 1867–1869

CHAPTER

2

On a bleak, sagebrush-covered plateau, Major William McEntire Dye, Fourth Infantry Regiment, surveyed the site for the fort that would secure the southern end of the Bozeman Trail. Below him flowed the Platte River, its banks sparse after the spring floods. Beyond the river valley, the country to the north supported a vast carpet of windswept grass and sagebrush. LaPrele Creek merged with the Platte less than a mile to the west; there, willows and cottonwood trees struggled to survive. East of the plateau, rugged hills extended deep ravines toward the valley. To the south rose the foothills of the Laramie Range with its highest point, Laramie Peak. Dye's soldiers called these the "black hills," blanketed as they were with dark forest.

Dye's orders had come from the commanding general of the Department of the Platte, who was at that time Lieutenant Colonel C.C. Augur. Responding to Special Order Number 84, issued on May 9, 1867, Dye had reported to the commanding officer at Fort Laramie. There he received instructions to lead Fourth Infantry Companies A, C, H, and I—probably about 150 men—in founding a new garrison near the confluence of LaPrele Creek and the North Platte River.[1] It would stand on the river's south bank near the junction of the Oregon and Bozeman Trails; its purpose was to protect travelers, settlers, and gold-seekers on those routes. With these orders in hand, Major Dye and his command departed Fort Laramie on July 16 and after a three-day march reached their destination eighty miles to the northwest.

Assistant Surgeons C. Mackin and F. Le Baron Monroe described the plateau as

> …almost 600 feet from and 130 feet above the stream. Latitude 42 8' 3" north, longitude 105 7' 4" west; elevation above Gulf of Mexico about 5,250 feet. The plateau rises from the river bottom by steep

almost precipitous bluffs, and then rising gradually, merges into the Black Hills, fourteen miles distant.[2]

By General Order Number 33, Headquarters Department of the Platte, issued on July 31, the post was named Fort Fetterman after (Brevet) Lieutenant Colonel William J. Fetterman, Captain Twenty-seventh Infantry, who had been killed in the Fetterman Fight at Fort Phil Kearny the previous winter.

For the next several weeks, Dye and his troops lived in tents on the plateau while they explored the area. Scouting parties searched for alternate sites, but by August 10, Major Dye concluded that the plateau was the most favorable. He wrote to Acting Assistant Adjutant General Colonel H. G. Litchfield, "we did not feel justified in fixing on this position so long as there was reasonable hope of the commanding general's arrival in time to select the site," but apparently that did not occur. So he described it in detail:

> The Post is situated on a plateau (containing nearly one square mile)— the first step (in the vicinity) above the valley of the Platte being neither so low as to be seriously affected by the rains and snow; nor so high and unprotected as to suffer from the (prevailing Westerly) winter winds. It is on the South side of the Platte and East of the LaPrele and is within five hundred yards of either water course. There are three fords of the Platte within the vicinity, which have hitherto been used by the Indians: one is about a half mile above and the other within three or four miles below. We have found another one (of rock and gravel bottom) immediately in our vicinity: it was first used on the 5th instant. Trains now cross and recross at pleasure. Two or three hundred yards below this ford a bridge can be built with little expense. At this point the river at its highest stage cannot be more than one hundred and ten yards wide and its bottom appears to be solid rock... Timber and stone being near, the bridge can be put up probably at a cost less then that which would run a ferry for two or three years.
>
> The road to [Fort] Laramie on this side of the river is quite as short if not shorter and better than that on the other side.
>
> We find plenty of acceptable (pine) timber from fifteen to eighteen miles of the Post.
>
> On the four streams, "Viz" La Prele, Deer Creek (20 miles), Box Alder (10 miles) and LaBonte (15 miles) can be cut at the proper season probably two or three hundred tons of good hay.

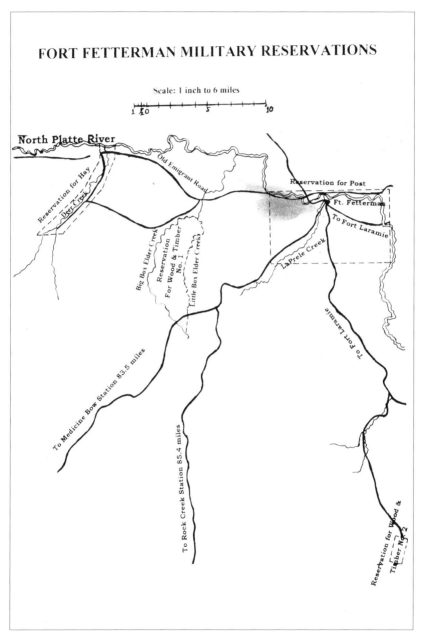

# FORT FETTERMAN MILITARY RESERVATIONS

Scale: 1 inch to 6 miles

*This map shows the Fort Fetterman military reservations and the wagon roads to the fort. Major Dye recommended the large reservation around the fort to prevent "whiskey squatters" from locating near the post.* (National Archives.)

A thousand cords and more of dry Cottonwood (fuel) within twelve miles, also ceder and pine in considerable quantities within the same distance.

We find a number of veins varying from three to ten inches in thickness of good lignite (and some coal) within two miles. It appears to burn well and no doubt is a cheaper fuel than wood...

No signs of Indian *war*[†] parties have been seen within this vicinity but Stealing parties or their tracts are seen every day or so.[3]

With the site established, enlisted men began construction. The new post's reservation was a sixty-square-mile rectangle, six miles north to south, ten east to west, with the fort centered one mile from its north boundary.[4] Stone markers indicated each corner. Such a large area was needed partly to secure adequate hay and timber for the reservation, but also, as Dye pointed out, to keep

> ...*whiskey squatters* from a too close proximity to it; and it crossing the Platte into what is understood to have been recommended by the Commissioner as part of the Indian's Reservation in order that we may, should it become necessary, establish and control a Ferry at high stage of water, to communicate with the Indians on the other side of the Platte.[5]

The fort also had a hay reserve encompassing the Deer Creek drainage, and a timber reserve fourteen miles south of the Platte, spanning the mountain lands between Box Elder and Little Box Elder Creeks. (A fourteen-square-mile timber reservation was later established there in 1872 by General Order Number 48, Headquarters Department of the Platte, and in 1877 another was established on LaBonte Creek about fifteen miles south of the fort.[6])

The sheer difficulty of building the post was not the only challenge facing Major Dye. Civilian temptations in the form of prostitution soon arrived and threatened the morale of the troops. As early as August 22, 1867, he wrote to Lieutenant Colonel Innis N. Palmer, who was commanding Fort Laramie:

> Today I send a disreputable character in route to Omaha for dealing in whiskey etc, etc, causing a great deal of trouble amongst the men.
>
> I have the honor to request that you will furnish her the necessary transportation and rations to the next post. She is rationed up to the last day of this month.[7]

[†] Words underlined in the original source material have been converted to italics throughout this book. Misspellings in the source documents have been retained.

With Fort Fetterman on the rise, there was little need to maintain Fort Caspar, about fifty miles up the Platte. Late in the summer the decision was made to abandoned that garrison, and steadily the men and supplies were removed. On October 1 Major Dye asked permission, since Caspar's telegraph operator was gone, to "take down at once seven miles of line beyond here to construct [a] branch into this Post."[8] His request granted, Dye directed his troops to erect a telegraph line to Fort Fetterman from the original transcontinental line at the old station on LaPrele Creek. The line was completed and operational on October 23. Within two more days, all of Fort Caspar's troops had been withdrawn and its building materials earmarked for use at Fort Fetterman. With winter fast approaching, shelter for men and supplies was of utmost concern. Major Dye's small command began to build permanent and temporary housing.

On October 1, Colonel Henry W. Wessells, leading six companies of the Eighteenth Infantry and the regimental band, had arrived at Fetterman to assume command. Wessells reported to Lieutenant Colonel Litchfield at department headquarters:

> Quarters for two companies may be completed during this month, one store house may also be finished. There is no Hospital. Contractor fails to fulfill certain specifications of contract on wood but I can make satisfactory compromise… The quality of hay and coal is insufficient and will soon be exhausted. Can get a small supply of the former at high price… The troops are very uncomfortable… I request authority to issue double allowances of fuel not hardwood. No fresh vegetables to be furnished this post.[9]

Private Herman S. Searle, too, told of slow progress in a letter to his parents on October 23: "they have no buildings finished yet, have four partly done. They are Commanding off. quarters, Comisary & two sets of baracks. There are 8 companies here at present, A, H, D, F of the eighteenth & the others are of the 4th."[10]

Matters only looked grimmer as winter approached. On November 5, Wessells wrote again to Litchfield:

> Subsistence Stores now due should be sent at once… No quarters have been commenced for it here. Hay is short and cannot be procured at this season unless sent in bales. Fuel is also short and the contract should be

extended. I telegraphed and reported deficiencies on my arrival. Four Companies are to be crowded into quarters for two, the fifth Company is hutting at the saw mill leaving Maj. Kelloggs still exposed. There is no hospital and public property is not yet properly sheltered. No quarters for Officers...[11]

The next day, Wessells filed an itemized report to Litchfield, despairing of the slow progress:

I.     *Garrison.* Having relieved the battalion of 4th U. S. Infantry the garrison was composed of Companies A, D, F, H, I & K the Head Quarters and band of the eighteenth U. S. Infantry, the first named Company being supposed to be under orders for Fort Reno.

II.     *Quarters.* All the troops, both Officers and men were found under canvas, exposed on a bleak plain to violent and almost constant gales and very uncomfortable, the whole being employed in labor, except a sufficient number for guard and escort service. Two adobe buildings were in course of construction without roofs or floors but are now progressing rapidly towards completion, by crowding the men into these two houses it is believed that four Companies (D, F, H & I) will be sheltered for the winter. Company "K" has been stationed at the Saw Mill, near timber, and is expected to hut itself for the winter. The remaining Company (A) as above stated is supposed to form part of command at Fort Reno. There are no quarters for the Non Com Staff and band but efforts are being made to procure material from Fort Caspar from which it is hoped that temporary shelter can be constructed, but the season is now very far advanced.

There is one adobe building designed for Officers but—as yet —without floor or roof, it will be completed probably during the month and for the winter must afford shelter for all the officers. They will be crowded and uncomfortable, but there seems to be no other resource.

An *adobe building* for *Laundresses* is also in course of construction, but as yet *without roof or floors.* The capacity of the Saw Mill is inadequate to the demands for lumber, it is about fifteen miles from the post and timber is hauled to it from a distance of seven miles, all this causes great delay in preparing for winter.

III.　*Hospital* There is no building for this purpose and the sick are still under canvas. A *log building* from material hauled from Fort Caspar has been commenced, but the time of its completion cannot be determined.

IV.　*Guard House* There is no *guard house*. The guard and prisoners being in tents, it is designed to construct one as soon as possible in the same manner as stated for hospital.

V.　*Storage* There is *no Store House* either for subsistence or other stores. An adobe building designed for the Q M [Quartermaster] Department is in course of construction, but as yet *without roof or floors*, when completed, it must afford shelter for public property of both departments, as far as its capacity will permit. Some of the property is under canvas, but a vast quantity is entirely exposed to the weather.

VI.　*Magazine* There is *no magazine* or storage for ordnance property and can only be sheltered in tents or under paulins.

VII.　*Forage* The supply of corn is large, but that of hay is entirely insufficient for the number of teams necessary to be employed in hauling material to and from the Saw Mill.

VIII.　*Fuel* The contract calls for 1200 cords of wood which has been delivered and should be very much increased.

IX.　*Quartermaster Store* The supply seems to be liberal, but I have not been able to give the subject sufficient attention to report with accuracy.

X.　*Subsistence Stores* There is a deficiency in some important articles, but as stated before I have had no time to make myself familiar with the subject. *Flour is wanted*, but I am informed it is en-route. *Fresh vegetables* for the troops are needed as a few *cases of Scurvy* have already appeared, the ordinary Anti-Scorbutics furnished by the Subsistence Department have no effect upon that disease as far as my experience extends.

XI.　*Offices* There are no offices at the post, either for Regt. Head Quarters or for those performing duty in the General's Staff. All are under canvas and subject to great inconvenience from cold and violent gales.

　　Every effort will be made to provide shelter for the approaching winter, but it must be in a very crowded condition and from the foregoing it will be seen that the prospect is far from encouraging. The season is now too far advanced to commence new buildings and the mill will only furnish material in sufficient quantities to complete such as are in progress, and that so slowly as to cause great and unavoidable delay.

I have repaired the *telegraph line* as far as *Horse-Shoe Station* and will keep it in order to that point, depending upon *Fort Laramie* for the rest. I will keep you advised from time to time of the condition of things as they progress. There is *no plan* of this Post on file in this office.[12]

Now Wessells began to question the post's location. He broached the concern to Litchfield on November 20:

I have the honor to request a plan of this Post, with such instructions as may have been given from Dept. Head Quarters in reference to its location, style of building and material to be used in Construction of Quarters, Store houses & etc. I can find no papers on file to serve as a guide.

I am not aware of the reasons which controlled the selection of this particular site, but if not imperative, the place seems to me to be objectionable for the reason that irrigation, so important to the health, comfort & productiveness of a prairie post is impracticable. The Post is established on an elevated plateau, dry and arid and exposed to storms and gales from every quarter, at the same time being very distant from water, whilst timber for building purposes is at least twenty (20) miles from the post and fuel not very convenient. Deer Creek about twenty (20) miles above seems to offer greater advantages.

Bottom land adjoining the Platte at this post affords ample room for the necessary buildings of the post and if the LaPrele is a running stream could be irrigated with little expense.

Taking this view of the case, and subject to approval at Dept. Hd Qr's I shall only proceed with such work as will afford shelter for the troops and Stores during the coming winter, that is, finish such buildings as are now in progress with other temporary structures as necessities arise hoping to be able to cease labor by the end of December.

If the expense and labor already applied to this Post are deemed too great to justify its removal, or it this particular locality is imperative, I would recommend that full arrangements be made for work to commence as early in the spring as the weather will permit. A Saw Mill of twenty four horse power to be set up near the post, and contract made during the winter for supplying it with round timber, — Whilst the troops are constantly employed as guards and escorts along the road but little progress can be made in building if dependant on the labor of Soldiers.[13]

Yet at the end of December the barracks and mess halls were still unfinished, and the quartermaster was directed to "push them into completion as fast as possible."[14]

That first winter must have been miserable, with many troops still living under canvas. In February Wessells still had not heard whether relocation was an option. Finally, word arrived that the post would not be moved. Fort Fetterman was destined to remain on this dreary plateau. Wessells was to continue construction when weather permitted.

Work resumed that spring of 1868. Slowly the post took shape, in the standard military design of the day, with barracks, offices, and officer quarters surrounding a rectangular parade ground. At Fetterman, these buildings were enclosed by a plank fence, rather than the stockade with parapets and guardwalks found in some other western forts. The fence was not intended to protect against attacks, but simply to discourage soldiers from leaving the post without authorization and to keep livestock from grazing around the quarters and parade ground.

By November 1868 a quartermaster corral had been built of adobe, to the east of the fort, to protect the wagon teams for the Post Quartermaster Department. To the west of the parade ground two barracks were built, each 100 by 25 feet, with fourteen-foot adobe walls, wooden roofs and floors, two doors, and ten windows. To the rear of these barracks were company kitchens and mess halls.[15] More quarters for officers were underway as well.

On March 1, 1869, acting post commander C.H. Carlton, who had replaced Wessells, listed the fort's buildings:

One Magazine
Two (2) Sets Company Quarters
Two (2) Sets Mess Rooms
Two (2) Sets Kitchens
Ten (10) Sets Laundress Quarters
One Corn House
Offices for QR. MR. and Commissary one Building
One building for Adjutants Office, School Room and Post Library
One Bake House

*Well-known artist/photographer William Henry Jackson made this drawing of Fort Fetterman in 1870 from a viewpoint to the southwest of the fort. Note the post and wire fence around the parade ground.* (Courtesy of the National Archives.)

> Quarters for five Officers
> Quarters and Mess Houses for Q. M. Employees
> Shops for Saddlers, wheelwright and Blacksmith
> Cells for Guard House
> Privies required at nearly all the Quarters
> Fencing for Quarters, etc.
> Nearly all the buildings now at the Post require more or less work
> to complete and repair, they were all built of Green Pine Lumber. The
> roof will all require reshingling this season and the Company Quarters,
> Guard House and Store Houses reflooring.[16]

If new construction was not enough to keep the soldiers busy, rebuilding and repairing structures damaged by weather and fire only added to the labor. [17] After the bakery burned on May 11, 1869, acting post commander Captain C. H. Carlton ordered 2,500 hard-fired and 2,000 soft bricks from Fort D.A. Russell to rebuild the ovens.[18] Then on July 16 a bad storm struck, damaging not only the roof of the southern barracks, but the new bakery as well.[19]

In May of that year, the post surgeon wrote that, despite a "Commissary well stocked and provision of good quality," the "quarters of the men are in poor repair, the barracks-rooms dirty and ill kept in every respect."[20] A third barrack was ordered on October 25, 1869, to be built of log with the same dimensions as the others. The post quartermaster placed four civilian carpenters in charge, with soldiers providing the bulk of the labor.[21] The kitchens for all three barracks were constructed from salvaged log buildings hauled from Fort Caspar a year earlier.[22]

As the third winter arrived in 1869, the garrison at Fort Fetterman had become as comfortable as possible considering the location, isolation, and the incessant westerly wind. Eventually, more substantial buildings began to replace the makeshift ones. As the years progressed the dreary military post began to take on the appearance of civilization, an island in a desolate land.

# Transportation
# and Communications

**CHAPTER 3** | Two major technological developments increased the American military's efficiency during the latter half of the nineteenth century. The first was the invention of the telegraph and its subsequent traversing of the western territories. The second was the building of the transcontinental railroad.

Communications on the trans-Mississippi frontier were exceptionally slow, by modern standards, before the arrival of the Western Union Telegraph Company's transcontinental line, which by 1861 had crossed Wyoming. Before the telegraph, discourse with the eastern states could take months as wagon trains carried mail to and from frontier communities and military posts. The short-lived Pony Express system offered faster delivery, but at a cost the average citizen couldn't afford. With the telegraph, messages were relayed nearly instantaneously. Fort Fetterman was fortunate in having this mode of communication from its inception.

Prior to 1867, military operations and all transportation west of the Mississippi River were tied to centuries-old modes of travel: foot, horseback, and wagons drawn by mules or oxen. These animals consumed from ten to twelve pounds of grain a day, which meant the wagon train had to carry large amounts of feed, reducing its freight capacity. This constraint limited the army wagons' efficiency in the vast expanses of the West.

During the two decades before the Civil War, railroads in the eastern United States evolved from a curiosity to a highly developed and essential component of the nation's industrial and commercial economy. Expanding the rail system westward was already seen as a matter of vital national interest, and the Civil War proved the railroad's value to the supply and movement of troops. After the war's end, the labor and money required to build a transcontinental railroad became available.

∽  ∾

In late 1865 the Central Pacific Railroad began laying track eastward

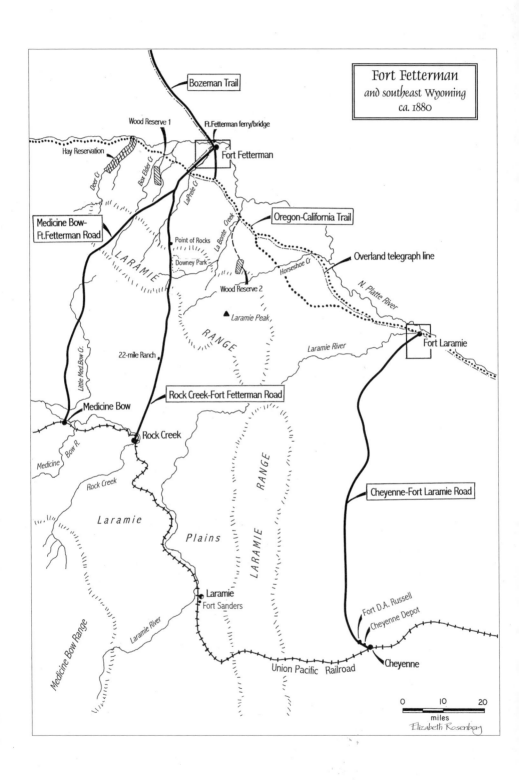

Bozeman Trail

Fort Fetterman
and southeast Wyoming
ca. 1880

Wood Reserve 1

Ft. Fetterman ferry/bridge

Hay Reservation

Fort Fetterman

Deer Cr.

Box Elder Cr.

LaPrele Cr.

Medicine Bow–
Ft. Fetterman Road

Oregon-California Trail

LARAMIE

Point of Rocks

La Bonte Creek

Overland telegraph line

Downey Park

Horseshoe Cr.

N. Platte River

Wood Reserve 2

Laramie Peak

RANGE

Laramie River

Fort Laramie

22-mile Ranch

Little Med Bow Cr.

Rock Creek-Fort Fetterman Road

Medicine Bow

Rock Creek

Medicine Bow R.

Rock Creek

LARAMIE

Laramie

Plains

RANGE

Cheyenne-Fort Laramie Road

Laramie River

Medicine Bow Range

Laramie
Fort Sanders

Fort D.A. Russell
Cheyenne Depot

Union Pacific Railroad

Cheyenne

0        10        20

miles

Elizabeth Rosenberg

through the rugged mountains of California and Nevada, while Union Pacific graders, followed by rail-laying crews, rapidly progressed westward over the plains. Over the next three years, four military posts—Forts Russell, Sanders, Steele, and Bridger—were built or reassigned to protect the crews in what would become Wyoming Territory. After the tracks were completed, these new posts served the military along the rail line and supplied the army posts and campaigns that radiated from it.

The Union Pacific track-laying crews reached eastern Wyoming in the summer of 1867, and on July 19 surveying crews staked off the townsite of Cheyenne. Not long afterward, Fort D. A. Russell was built on Crow Creek about three miles northwest of town, with a major supply depot nearby, known as Cheyenne Depot or Camp Carlin. Further west, Fort John Buford had already been established, on July 4, 1866, to guard the grading crews; it would later be renamed Fort Sanders. (Within two years, the community of Laramie emerged a few miles to the north.) About eighty miles west of Fort Sanders, on the North Platte River, the army founded Fort Fred Steele on June 20, 1868, and charged it, too, with guarding the rail-layers. The fourth post along the Wyoming tracks was Fort Bridger, which dated from 1857. Its original purpose was to guard traffic along the Oregon Trail, but when the Union Pacific passed within ten miles of the fort in 1868, it assumed a new role as protector of the railroad crews.

Wyoming Territory was established in July 1868 and five counties were organized: Albany, Carbon, Laramie, Sweetwater, and Uinta. Several forts fell within Albany County at the time, including Fetterman. Between then and 1882, Fort Fetterman and later Fort McKinney were Albany county's only population centers *not* located on the Union Pacific.

Increasingly, the rails, rather than the overland trails, were dictating the placement of the U.S. military's forts in Wyoming Territory. Fort Fetterman was among the last posts specifically charged with protecting those traveling by foot, horse, and wagon. While the railroad's progress across southern Wyoming was making newspaper headlines in 1867 and 1868, Fort Fetterman was rising sixty-five miles north of the UP tracks on the soon-to-be-abandoned Bozeman Trail.

ᔐ ᔑ

The long-established Oregon Trail was the major route for supplies, mail, and personnel for Fort Fetterman. But the birth of Fort Fetterman coincided with the railroad revolution, and the army soon began using the emerging railroad for its supply and communication needs. Fort Fetterman would need a road linking it with the tracks. Members of Company H, Eighteenth Infantry pioneered this road on their way to the brand-new fort in the fall of 1867. Private H.S. Searle described the journey from Fort Sanders:

> We left Sanders on the 13th of Oct. As there was no direct road here we tryed the new cut-of arangement from Sanders due north two days march till we found a road going to Fort larmey (on the larmey river). The wagons took this road. The Col. with fifty of us & four pack mules kept on across the country going due north to *larmey peak*. On the mules we carried two blankets a piece, beside tow camp kettles, three skillets, three tent flys, 60 lbs of bacon & sugar & coffe for four days.
>
> We went five days march before we arived here. After we left the wagons we had three guides—the larmey peak—compas & map. This post being so new that it is not down on the map.[1]

The following spring, post commander Wessells was instructed to "open a good road to the nearest point on the U.P.R.R. probably in the vicinity of the mouth of Rock Creek."[2] In May, soldiers of the Eighteenth Infantry, commanded by Major James Stewart and guided by the famous mountain man Jim Bridger, began building such a road. It led sixty-five miles due south to the railroad town of Rock Creek. For the next twenty years this town served as a supply distribution point for the military posts north of the Union Pacific.

Beginning at the fort, the Rock Creek–Fetterman road paralleled the west side of LaPrele Creek until it reached Spring Creek, then extended up that creek to Spring Canyon. It then took a southerly route, crossing Red Canyon and upper LaPrele Creek and going past the landmark known as Point of Rocks. Next it skirted the edge of Downey Park, crossed two branches of upper LaBonte Creek, traversed the Laramie Plains, and finally terminated at the town of Rock Creek.

The road saw heavy use, but nine years later, in 1877, post commander Coates scouted a slightly different route:

> The result of my observation is that a far better road in almost every respect especially in wood, water and grass can be made to Rock Creek Station than the one now used. Going down I was unable to get correct

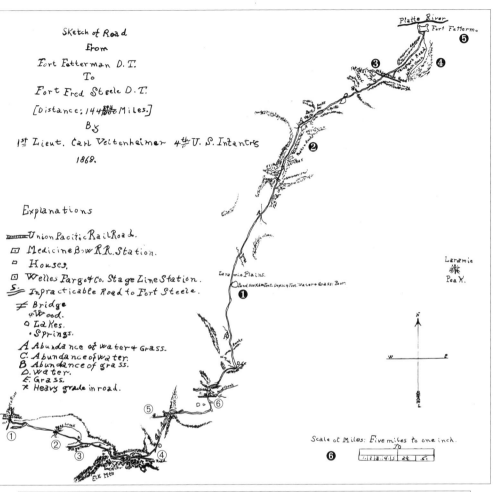

① Ft. F.E. Steele. Platte River
② Pass Creek.
③ Stage Road.
④ Ft. Halleck. Stage Road
⑤ S. (Impractical road to Ft. Steele). (UPRR crosses road here.)
⑥ ☐ (Medicine Bow RR Station). Rock Creek. Medicine Bow (River).

❶ Pond 500x600 Feet. Depth 4 Feet. Water & Grass Poor
❷ Peaks & Rocks
❸ Old Emigrant Road
❹ Telegraph Road (to left). LaPrele Creek (to right).
❺ Fort Fetterman
❻ (Scale of original 16 inch by 16 inch map. Map and scale are reduced here.)

*This early map shows the wagon road from Fort Fred Steele to Fort Fetterman. Traffic to Fort Fetterman often started at the Medicine Bow Station on the Union Pacific. (Map recreated from the historic map drawn by First Lieutenant Carl Veitenheimer, Fourth U.S. Infantry, 1868. Numerals in circles have been added to assist in legibility.)*

measurements of the distance but the reading of the odometer returning, show that we traveled a trifle over 64 miles. Our trail for nearly 20
miles from the Post is up LaPrele Creek, it gradually ascends over a high
grassy mesa until the canyon is reached which was the only point when
any work was done and less than two hours with axes and spades passed
our wagons through[.] the canon is less than two miles, and the country
from that point to Rock Creek is similar to that on this side of the
canyon...[3]

Lieutenant Joseph Keeffe of the Fourth Infantry was charged with
building the new road. He got to work and reported on July 29 that the
road through the canyon was complete and that within ten days it would
be complete on either side of the canyon.[4] But apparently it stayed unfinished until the next summer, when some repairs were completed on July
25, 1878. Coates telegraphed Department of the Platte Headquarters:
"...I consider road finished, Freighters who have been over it report it far
better than old road."[5]

Wishful thinking on Coates's part, perhaps. Local pioneer and rancher
John Hunton did not like the new road. After traveling it—albeit before
the repairs were complete—he wrote in his diary on May 16, 1878, that he

> ...started to Rock Creek over the new road... Went from George Har-
> ris' up La Prelle (sp) on east side, passed the mountains until I struck
> Rock Creek road... Party of troops from Fetterman to haul poles for
> bridges. Pass through canon (sp) and found it rough but short. Road
> impracticable for freighting unless much work is done on it . . .[6]

Lieutenant Colonel John S. Mason, who became the post commander
on March 8, 1879, did not share his predecessor's enthusiasm, either:

> I wish to inform you that, I consider the "Rock Creek Road" for the
> purposes of transportation an utter failure. It has been blocked by snow
> for two weeks, and is now, besides the La Prele is now impassable at this
> point. If the road must be kept open, number of bridges will have to be
> repaired or rebuilt each year. While this route has been blockaded, the
> other one by Fort Laramie kept open, and trains made regular trips.[7]

An earlier road improvement project, too, had been disappointing. Built
in hopes of easier passage in winter and spring, a new road branched off the
old one by 1872. It led to the railroad town of Medicine Bow, about twenty

miles west of Rock Creek. The two roads parted on upper LaPrele Creek north of Spring Canyon. The new branch then followed the old Oregon Trail to Big Box Elder Creek, then led southwesterly to its headwaters. It then continued south to Little Medicine Creek on the Laramie Plains. First it followed this stream, then the Medicine Bow River, to the town of Medicine Bow. However, Wyoming's severe climate took its toll on this road as well, and it too proved impassable during the winter months.

Indeed, moving mail and supplies over such rugged, exposed terrain was always a challenge. Three routes were used to Fort Fetterman, none of them trouble-free. Postal service was provided by War Department personnel as a joint effort of the garrisons at Fetterman and Fort Laramie until 1875, when private mail contracts were issued. The earliest and most dependable mail route was by weekly quartermaster stage from Fort D. A. Russell, near Cheyenne, to Fort Laramie—a two-day trip in good weather—and thence to Fetterman. The Fetterman detachment met the Fort Laramie party halfway at Horseshoe Creek, on the old overland stage road, and exchanged outgoing for incoming mail, for a total round trip of about a day and a half.

The second mail route proved the shortest but, due to mountain passes, tougher in winter: this was the original Rock Creek-Fetterman road. Starting July 1, 1875, the Postal Department provided a weekly mail carrier service on this route. In good weather mail arrived in a light spring wagon, in winter on a sled; in foul weather or flood conditions it might not arrive at all. Little baggage could be forwarded due to the rough road.[8]

The third route was over the Medicine Bow road, which, too, was unreliable in winter. Nevertheless, this was the route ultimately used by a contract mail carrier, who generally arrived at Fetterman on Tuesday nights.

Post journals recorded the pitfalls of the Medicine Bow route in January 1874:

> Mail left Post. The mail had difficulty to get through on the last trip so the wagon was left at a ranche on Box Elder about thirty-five miles from the post and which was built this winter by the Post Guide Joe Merivale. The mail was carried on pack animals from this ranche to the first crossing of the Little Medicine Bow a distance of about 12 miles. The road is difficult here on account of snow drifts, in some places nearly ten feet deep. There is much sage bush which catches the snow.

The fall of snow thus far have been very light—unusually so.

The mail has been run by the post guide by agreement with the Qr. Mr. for $166 per month.

The Post Office was for some time kept at the Trader's but as the salary was only some $12 per year and the trouble considerable, it has for about six weeks been kept at the Adjutant's Office. It can't be made a money order office & without regular P. M. [Postmaster] appointed letters can't be Registered.[9]

Joe Merival (sometimes spelled Merivale) was the agent for his brother Frank who held the mail contract with the War Department.[10] By December 1874, post trader Ephraim Tillotson had the mail contract and was allowed to buy rifle cartridges from the post ordnance stores to protect himself while on the Medicine Bow road.[11]

On July 1, 1875, an official post office opened in the post trader's store. The first postmaster was Mr. A. C. Jordan, assisted by R.V. Halpole. This ended the War Department's responsibility for transporting the mail, as Congress made the Medicine Bow road the official mail route. Under the new agreement, the carrier arrived at the post on Wednesday and departed on Thursday each week.[12] Fetterman authorities tried to get deliveries three times a week, but their efforts failed.

No solution seemed permanent. By 1878, mail was routed to Rock Creek Station instead of Medicine Bow. Fisher Stage Company had the contract to deliver the mail to Forts Fetterman, McKinney, and Custer but was negligent in its duties. The War Department lodged a complaint on December 13, 1878, because some civilians had found mail lying by the road; they returned the mail to the fort. Later, in 1879, the mailbags containing the muster rolls for April and March were lost while the carrier was crossing LaPrele Creek, and duplicates had to be mailed to the post.[13]

～ ～

Crossing the North Platte River could be dangerous in late spring and early summer. During these seasons, the Platte could, and often did, flood well over its banks. After the floods, the river became a shallow stream, easily crossed on foot or horseback. To assist military personnel and civilians, several ferries had already been built before Fort Fetterman's establishment. Jim Bridger had built a ferry as an immigrant crossing over the Platte near present-day Orin Junction. The military had also constructed a ferry at

Fort Laramie, so Fort Fetterman's had a local precedent. (Bridges would eventually replace the ferries at both forts because in fast-running water even a ferry was less than safe.)

Fort Fetterman's ferry was established on the wide bend of the Platte River, north of the quartermaster and commissary storehouses, in 1868. Between two posts on each riverbank a stout, four-inch rope was stretched several feet above the water. Two boats of different sizes were built; these were attached to the rope and dragged from one shore to the other.[14] In June 1868, Major Dye issued the following circular:

> The *Ferry* across the Platte at this Post is under the exclusive management of the Quartermaster who will make such further expenses based on the following, as he may find necessary to secure the object of the Ferry.
>
> All orders for Ferrying whether for Citizens or persons connected with the Military Service, will be obtained from the Quartermaster, who will state on each order (for the guidance of the Ferrymen) the number of teams & c. [etc.] and whether the person holding it is entitled to free passage.
>
> The order when complied with will be endorsed by the Ferryman in charge and returned at once to the Quartermaster, for file.
>
> All persons, and their baggage, in the employ of the Government are entitled to free passage… The following rates will govern for those who are not entitled to free passage, I. e., Citizens not in the employ of government, (including Contractors) Viz
>
> | | |
> |---|---|
> | Man, Horse or Mule | $0.25 |
> | Wagon | 1.00 |
> | Wagon Load | 1.00 |
> | Wagon with Load | 1.50 |
> | Six mule or horse team with empty wagon load of government stores | 2.00 |
> | Six mule or horse team with wagon loaded with stores not government | 2.50 |
>
> No trip of Boat will be made for less than one dollar $1.00. Boat not to carry at any trip more than thirty-five (35) men including boatman.
>
> Eight (8) Mules or Horses
>
> One (1) Wagon and load
>
> One (1) Wagon and six mules or Six thousand (6000) pounds.

Persons crossing the Ferry do so at their own risk. The money aris-
ing as above will be collected by the Quartermaster and expended in
paying the Ferrymen and keeping the Ferry in good repair; and all
money thus accumulating (over and above what it will require for these
objects) will be transferred to the Post Treasurer to be expended for the
exclusive benefit of the Post as provided by the regulations.[15]

The three soldiers serving as boatmen, and the corporal supervising
them, earned additional monthly salary, the corporal fifteen dollars and the
boatmen ten dollars. [16] In 1877, a civilian was employed to direct the ferry
operations instead of enlisted men; he was paid eighty dollars per month.[17]
Charges for crossing civilian contract freight teams were discontinued in
1878, but other civilians were still charged.[18]

Later, constant troubles with the ferry rope during the Centennial Campaigns of 1876 prompted the post commander to order a metal cable. In
January 1877, troops installed a new wire cable about one inch in diameter
across the river.

Two years later the ferry was abandoned when a new bridge made it
obsolete. Under the watchful eye of post commander J. S. Mason, bridge
construction began on July 30, 1879, after the lumber and timbers had
been delivered.[19] Completed by November 22, the span was painted with
oil as a preservative.[20] Mason described it in his annual inspection report:

A bridge has been recently constructed across the Platte River at this
post. Including approaches it is 440 feet long with nine (9) spans. It is
the ordinary brace and straining beam plan, with spans of forty (40)
feet. The piers and abutments are of framed crib work filled with stone
and planked. The structure is a good and lasting one.[21]

Post Quartermaster Keeffe stated, "it is a substantial structure, which I
have no doubt will last many years, and will add very much to northern
travel."[22] Indeed, this bridge became property of the future Converse
County, and was used until around 1920, when it was rebuilt.

∿  ∿

The Western Union Telegraph Company had established its Overland
Telegraph Line through present-day Wyoming in 1861, along the path of
the Oregon Trail and Overland Stage. This route included Fort Laramie to
Fort Caspar, but it passed seven miles away from the site of the future Fort

Fetterman. Due to Indian hostilities, in 1865 Western Union moved this line to span southern Wyoming along what became the route of the Union Pacific Railroad. The original line along the Oregon Trail was the abandoned except from Fort Laramie to Fort Caspar. A line from the new southern route branched off to Fort Laramie, allowing Forts Laramie and Caspar contact with the outside world.

In October 1867, as Dye and his men camped on that windswept plateau at Fort Fetterman, a branch line was erected from the old Fort Laramie–Fort Caspar line, starting at LaPrele Creek and running seven miles north to the new Fort Fetterman.[23] Fetterman was thus linked with Fort Laramie to the east, and, at least briefly, with Fort Caspar to the west.

Although the lines and equipment were still Western Union property, the troops had to maintain them. To the east, Fort Fetterman was responsible for the line between its post and Horseshoe Creek; Fort Laramie soldiers maintained it from there to Fort Laramie. Repairs were needed often: Indians, outlaws, animals, and weather hampered the lines constantly. As early as spring 1868, post commander Wessells reported: "Ten miles of telegraph line was removed. There is no material to replace it. Much of the line is down far beyond. It will require time and labor to put it in order."[24] All summer long, details sent from the post toiled on the lines.

Fort Caspar was abandoned in 1868, and so was the line west of Fort Fetterman.

For over a decade, entries in the Post Journal told of the near-weekly struggle to keep the remaining wires alive. Early in 1873, for example: "Tuesday, February 25, Lt. Yestman and 11 men left to repair telegraph and return on Feb. 28th." On March 14: "Two privates deserted on stolen horses and cut telegraph line. On Saturday, March 15, Lt. Yestman & 7 enlisted men went to repair the line. Began working same day. Party returned March 17."[25] Despite constant effort, year after year, the line was nonoperational more often than not.

Apparently many unauthorized soldiers and civilians were trying to access the telegraph; a post circular was issued October 9, 1874, telling who could and would use it:

### Circular #32

I.   The Telegraph Office at this Post will be under the exclusive control of the Post Adjutant who will be Office Manager and responsible

*This early map from military records shows Fort Fetterman in 1882 at the time it was abandoned. (National Archives)*

FORT FETTERMAN, WYO.

North Platte River

To Ferry

Scale: 100 feet to 1 inch

To Fort McKinney 163 miles

Telegraph Line to Fort McKinney

Telegraph Line to Fort Laramie

Hay Corral

| No. | USE | MATERIAL |
|---|---|---|
| 1 | Comdg. Officer's Quarters | Frame |
| 2 | Officer's Quarters | Adobe |
| 3 | Officer's | Adobe |
| 4 | | Frame |
| 5 | | Frame |
| 6 | | Logs |
| 7 | | Logs |
| 8 | Barracks & Mess Halls | Frame |
| 9 | Barracks & Mess Hall | Frame |
| 10 | Laundress Quarters | Frame & Adobe |
| 11 | Quarters | Adobe |
| 12 | Quarters | Logs |
| 13 | Hospital | Logs |
| 14 | Quarters | Frame |
| 15 | Guard House | Frame |
| 16 | Officers | Frame |
| 17 | Quartermaster Storehouse | Frame |
| 18 | | Frame |
| 19 | | Adobe |
| 20 | Ordnance | Adobe |
| 21 | Commissary | Frame |
| 22 | Theater | Frame |
| 23 | Bakery | Frame |
| 24 | Butcher Shop | Frame |
| 25 | Blacksmith Shop | Frame |
| 26 | Carpenter Shop | Frame |
| 27 | Cavalry Stables | Logs |
| 28 | Quartermaster Corral | Adobe |
| 29 | Saw Mill | Frame |
| 30 | Reservoir | Stone |
| 31 | Pump House | Stone |
| 32 | Lumber House | Frame |

that the Office be properly conducted and will see that the reports and remittances are made according to the regulation to the District Superintendent's Office.

II.   The Telegraph Operator will report to the Adjutant, and receive orders only from the Commanding Officer or him, so far as his duties as Operator are concerned.

III.   No one but the Operator will send or receive any message over the line, nor will any person interfere or meddle with the instruments or books of the Office.

IV.   The Telegraph Office will not be used as a place for loitering; persons having business will transact it and leave.

V.   When other duties require the Operator to leave his Office he will lock it.

VI.   All messages sent or received will be subject to the same rules of secrecy that govern other Offices.[26]

Later, in 1876, the year of the Centennial Campaigns, post commander Captain Edwin Coates reported that rotted telegraph poles had hampered communications throughout an already busy summer of action against Indians. He wrote: "Had it not been for the entire absence of rain since the 1st of Aug. the line could have scarcely worked a single day, it being on the ground in many places."[27] Repairs were made to the line. Two summers later five hundred new poles were installed on the line connecting Cheyenne to Fort Laramie to Fort Fetterman.[28] Yet the new poles were strung with the old wire, which had become brittle over the years.

During the summer of 1877, near the ruins of old Fort Reno on Powder River, Cantonment Reno was established as a supply depot for General George Crook's continuing campaign against the Cheyenne Indians. Fort Fetterman soldiers provided the labor to construct a telegraph line from their post as far as Antelope Springs, fifty-four miles to the north. Twenty poles a day were to be set by the Fort Fetterman detail.[29] The line was completed by mid-December 1877.[30] Fort Fetterman was now telegraphically linked—on a good day—with Cantonment Reno. A year later, now renamed Fort McKinney, Reno was moved sixty miles to the northwest along the Clear Fork of Powder River, flowing less than two miles east of the Big Horn Mountains. The telegraph line was re-routed to maintain contact between the two forts.

In July 1880 post commander William Powell requested that the wire along the Fort Fetterman–Fort Laramie–Cheyenne route be replaced, as the slightest pressure caused it to break.[31] Earlier that year, he had reported other problems:

> ...A repairing party on the telegraph line between this post and Fort Laramie has just returned, and report that four telegraph poles were found cut down within two or three feet of the ground between Fort Fetterman and LaBonte river—insulators and everything carried away—this in addition to those already reported in my general report. It is impossible to ascertain the perpetrators of this vandalism. The line is in such condition both north and south of this post that it would take a whole company about a month to cut, haul and replace poles, and put the line in proper repair. The non-commissioned officer in charge of the party also reports that a number of poles have been rubbed against so much by the cattle that they will probably fall as soon as the frost is out of the ground.[32]

Additionally, the ninety-four miles of telegraph line from Horseshoe Creek north to Antelope Creek were in "deplorable condition." The seven repair parties who worked on the lines between April 9 and May 7 of that year confirmed that indeed some poles had been "chopped off by freighters, or other parties for fire-wood; that the wire is badly blistered, has been broken and repaired so often, and when repaired, snaps like a pipe-stem, owing to its crystallization."[33]

Maintaining the telegraph lines proved troublesome throughout Fort Fetterman's existence. No one could depend on telegraph messages being dispatched or received with any consistency. However, when operational, the telegraph provided a vast improvement in communication.

# The Peace Treaty of 1868 and Its Aftermath

**CHAPTER 4** | On Wyoming's northern plains in 1865, the Indians considered hostile by whites largely consisted of the Oglala, Hunkpapa, and Minneconjou Sioux, the Northern Cheyenne, and the Arapaho, while the Teton, Yanktonai, and Santee Sioux also claimed some representation in the area. Conversely the Shoshoni and Crow tribes remained predominantly peaceful toward the whites, and often served as allies against the warring tribes. Several treaties between whites and Indians preceded the Fort Laramie Treaty of 1868, but both sides violated them. Settlers continued to encroach on Indian lands, and Indians continued to raid white settlements, ranches, and emigrants in Montana, Nebraska, and Wyoming. Protecting the frontier placed a huge burden on the military in maintaining troops and posts. Congress wanted a less expensive solution to the "Indian problem" and in 1867 authorized another approach.

While Fort Fetterman was being established that summer, peace advocates in Washington convinced Congress to provide a commission to meet with the Indians and effect another peace treaty with the warring tribes of the northern plains. A peace commission was formed by an act of Congress dated July 20, 1867.[1] From that date the military confined its operations to defense and was "now principally engaged in garrisoning the most important posts."[2] Hedging its bet, Congress at the same time authorized recruiting an additional four thousand men if peace was not obtained. That fall, commissioners secured a treaty at Medicine Lodge Creek in Kansas with tribes in that area. But when the commissioners arrived at Fort Laramie in November to negotiate with the northern Plains Indians, few tribal leaders appeared. Red Cloud sent word that until the Bozeman Trail forts were abandoned no peace could be effected; however, his people would cease hostilities and come to Fort Laramie in the spring. The commissioners left for Washington, returning to Fort Laramie in April to meet with the Indians.

Negotiations for the Peace Treaty of 1868 were held through April and May. At Fetterman, one indication that the Indians were converging nearby for the peace council was recorded on May 3 when Sorrel Horse and twenty Arapahos passed through the post. On June 4, Major Dye asked if Fort Laramie's Indian agent had made arrangements with the military authorities to ration "the Indians who are constantly passing to and fro?"[3]

By the end of May terms had been reached, but Red Cloud still refused to sign the treaty until the troops had abandoned the Bozeman Trail forts. Although General U.S. Grant had ordered those posts vacated on March 2, 1868, it was August by the time the stores and material were hauled away, due to winter-damaged roads. Red Cloud signed the treaty in October after the forts were emptied. However, Fort Fetterman, on the south side of the Platte, was not included in the closures.

The Treaty of 1868 gave the Sioux all of what is now South Dakota west of the Missouri River as a reservation. It also granted them control and hunting rights in the large territory north of the North Platte River and east of the Big Horn Mountain range as unceded Indian lands. Finally, it provided for agencies to be built on the Missouri River near Fort Randall; the Indians were to trade there instead of at Fort Laramie. Many Indians objected to this as it deviated from a long-established custom and so in 1870, temporary agency buildings were constructed thirty miles east of Fort Laramie on the Platte River.[4] Meanwhile, to the south, the Medicine Lodge treaties provided for two large reservations in Indian Territory (present-day Oklahoma): one for the Cheyenne and Arapaho, and the other for the Kiowa, Comanche, and Kiowa-Apache.

The peace commissioners knew that the Bozeman Trail was becoming obsolete: the nearly-completed Union Pacific Railroad would soon offer new options for miners going to Montana. Still, relinquishing the trail up Powder River seemed unwise to many military minds. General of the Army William T. Sherman was not pleased with the terms of the 1868 Treaty. Over a year earlier, already anticipating where the peace commission's policy would lead, he wrote on July 1, 1867: "to abandon this road now, under pressure would invite the whole Sioux nation down to the main Platte Road, and would in my judgement, increase our troubles."[5] Referring to the Fetterman Fight, Sherman went on:

> ... the destruction of Colonel Fetterman's party ... was surely one result
> of the occupation of that road, as stated by the commissioner; but

instead of talking with the Indians who did the deed, I would have preferred to have followed the savages to their own country, and to have avenged the massacre in such a way that it would not have invited repetition; but Congress, in its wisdom, with a full knowledge of all the facts, and all its connecting circumstances, has preferred to send out civil peace commissioners to confer with the perpetrators, and during such conference the military would not have been justified in adopting extreme measures. All that we have done or could do to strengthen that line so as to form a base from which, in due season, we may avenge the death of Colonel Fetterman and his command when it becomes necessary; but the Sioux have not confined their efforts to resist the opening of that single road. They have carried war down several hundreds of miles south, have killed our people and stolen our horses at Brady's Island, at Ash Hollow, and even to the south of the South Platte...

Sherman agreed to enforce the peace policy, although he found it untenable:

But to show the honorable Secretary of War that we, the military, are not disposed to precipitate matters, I refer to my circular herewith, requiring all officers acting under me to respect all treaties and rights of civil agents entrusted with their execution, except when their hostility is undoubted... So long as the two distinct races of people, with such diverse interest as subsist between the roving Indians of the plains and our own white settlers, remain together, so long will actual war exist; and if there be an earnest desire on the part of the law-making power of the government to save the weaker party from absolute annihilation, some provision must be made for separating these conflicting races... These roving tribes have no real chiefs, but they are a pure democracy; each man does as he pleases regardless of his so-called chief, as at this very moment, what we term their war parties are made up of every tribe, Sioux, Cheyenne, Comanches, and Kiowas, all fighting together in large or small bands... To deal therefore with these professedly friendly chiefs is but a mockery. The time is now opportune for declaring all treaties abrogated by reason of their hostile acts, and to prescribe by law terms binding on all alike, but just, liberal, and fair in character, and then we, the military, will know exactly what to do and enforce. As the case now stands we are put to fearful expense in maintaining troops and post where the Indians are professedly peaceful, but who may at any moment break out in open war. Congress alone can do this, and it is grievous wrong to force our soldiers into the unnatural attitude in which they now stand, when the people of the frontier universally declare the Indians to be at war and the Indian commissioners and agents pronounce them at peace, leaving us in a gap to be abused by both parties.[6]

Indeed, the Sioux, Cheyenne, and Arapaho had been launching hostile actions in the area for over a year. The first recorded Indian attack on an unprotected supply train in the vicinity, in the spring of 1867, was retold by Robert David in his book *Finn Burnett, Frontiersman*:

Crossing the Platte at Bridger's crossing, the train continued up the river on the north bank for a days drive. There the soldiers who had been scouting in advance, came back with the report that an ox-train was being attacked by Indians a few miles ahead of their column.

Wood corralled the trains while Finn and his teamsters accompanied the soldiers to look over the ground. There was a great area of open grassy land at that point, with high hills to the east. It was the spot where the town of Douglas, Wyoming, was later established.

An outfit of seventy-five teams was corralled close to the river, with men prone beneath the wagon-boxes firing between the spokes of the wheels at the encircling redskins. A large contingent of Sioux were massing at the moment in a draw to the north of the corral, and, as Finn's group looked over a hill, these Indians were slipping quietly down upon their victims. They were so intent on reaching their objective that the approach of assistance for the white men was unnoticed.

It seemed but a matter of seconds before Finn and his outfit reached the edge of the draw where they delivered a devastating fire into the surprised Sioux. Several of the warriors fell dead or wounded at the first volley, and the rest turned and sped eastward toward the hills, yipping with chagrin, and pursued by the vengeful whites...[7]

On November 18, 1867, Indians attacked another contract mule train about six miles east of LaBonte Creek, near the new Fort Fetterman. The freighters won the engagement and defended their train of supplies.[8] But this attack had a profound, sobering effect on both contract freighters and the military. Three days later, post commander Colonel Henry W. Wessells wrote that "Supply trains arrive at this post without guard—it is unsafe, and compels me to furnish escorts both ways."[9] With this decision, travel on the Platte River road once again became safe for supply trains and travelers, at least for a few months. But while the attacks on the guarded wagon trains diminished that fall, they increased in other areas. On November 30 the abandoned Fort Caspar received a visit by Indians who set fire to the bridge and three small buildings.[10]

On February 18, 1868, Indians stole a herd of cattle belonging to an unidentified settler southeast of Fort Fetterman. Wessells could not assist, as he had no mounted troops, so he wrote to the commanding officer at Fort Laramie, requesting that he send a troop of cavalry to pursue the marauders.[11] Again on March 2 and March 18 the Indians struck in small stock-stealing raids.[12] On March 12 Wessells reported:

A mule team has been captured by Indians between this post and the saw mill and driven north. I have sent in pursuit, but having no organized mounted force have little hopes of recovering them. It seems evident that hostilities have been actively resumed. Red Cloud has lately come down to Powder River below [Fort] Reno. Sioux stole animals from Cheyennes near Reno but brought them back. Supposed them to belong to the Post. Please communicate substance of this to Dept. Head Quarters and Indian Agent.[13]

This attack was only the beginning of a continual, though sporadic, assault on the fort's sawmill and loggers in the foothills around Laramie Peak. Six days later, while loading logs, the company working the sawmill was attacked by a large Indian party. Private Thomas Bourke was killed and the mule teams were driven off in a running fight of about three miles.[14] Bourke was the first soldier to lose his life to hostile Indian action while stationed at Fort Fetterman. He would not be the last.

Later, to protect his men and the government's property, Wessells directed the "… party in the woods to build a stockade on a prominent point: Also instruct them that one man during the day should keep constant watch that the party be not surprised. Their stockade should be so built that they cannot be cut off from it by Indians."[15]

On March 10, a mail party from Fort Reno under command of Lieutenant Dougherty of the Eighteenth Infantry had been fired on by Indians, though no casualties were reported.[16] Almost daily, reports of Indian raids continued through the month of March. But the attacks were not solely in the Fetterman vicinity. All along the Bozeman Trail the raiding intensified, even as treaty negotiations were underway at Fort Laramie. By July Indian attacks were reported along the Union Pacific Railroad.

On July 4, 1868, post adjutant Lieutenant Rufus Brown, Fourth Infantry, wrote to Samuel Harper, father of a Fort Fetterman soldier:

> In reply to your com'tn. of May 14, 1868, inquiring about your son Abraham Harper, I am directed by the Comd'g Officer of the Post Bvt. Col. Wm. McE Dye, Major 4th Infantry to state that inquiries have been made and it has been learned from an eye witness that your son was killed at Twin Spring Ranche (which was on the road to Fort Laramie and about forty miles from this Post) about the 21 of last Month by a party of about sixty Indians. He was buried a few days after by Captain G. B. Dewees 2 Cavalry near the Platte River in that vicinity.
>
> The witness mentioned above is Mr. M. A. Mousseau, who is now on business at this Post. He says he wrote to Mr. Joseph Harper, Aylinor, Ontario giving all particulars. I believe it is Mr. Mousseau's intentions to write to you. He will no doubt if you ask him. Mr. Mousseau states that he was in partnership with your son at the time of his death. That the accounts were being settled preparatory to Harpers going to Sweet Water Mines, that your son owed him some eight hundred dollars and a clerk who is also at this Post, (a citizen teamster in the Quartermasters Dept.) about two hundred dollars. The clerk makes the same statement. The accounts are all in the hands of Mr. Mousseau if further information is desired. It is stated by both these men that the property your son owned was destroyed by the Indians, which is no doubt questioned and all his stock run off.[17]

Hostilities by the Sioux, Cheyenne, and Arapaho tribes continued throughout that summer. After a band of Indians drove off a herd of mules near the railroad on July 20, General C.C. Augur ordered Lieutenant Thomas J. Greggs, commanding Company D, Second Cavalry, to pursue them. Greggs departed Fetterman on July 22 with Company D, a detachment of Company A, Second Cavalry, and a mountain howitzer for additional firepower. Greggs' command returned to Fetterman a week later. They had found the Indian trail where it crossed the Platte near

Deer Creek and headed into the Powder River area where the camp of Old-Man-Afraid-of-His-Horses was known to be located.[18] But apparently they did not engage with the Indian band.

In August, another "stealing party" of Indians passed near Fetterman; their trail indicated they were heading for the Union Pacific Railroad.[19] Greggs' cavalry was already in the field, camped near the Indians' usual crossing at Deer Creek; this forced the raiders to cross the Platte near Fetterman. The Indians did not raid the Union Pacific this time but stole over a hundred head of government-owned horses and mules from Camp Carlin, near Cheyenne, on August 28. Greggs again was sent out to intercept the Indians before they reached the Platte River, but failed to make contact.[20] Several times the Indians attacked the hay-cutting detachments near Deer Creek during August and September; on September 19 they raided a supply train en route to the Deer Creek hay camp, but no casualties were reported.[21] No more Indian raids were recorded that year, probably because of the approaching winter.

In December General Sherman sent a letter to General Augur at Fort Fetterman which limited trade with the Indians except at selected agency offices:

> Your letter of December 1st and enclosures received. I reiterate my orders that there must be no trade with the Sioux outside of Harney's Reservation. All these Indians had plenty of time to go there. If any are likely to suffer for tobacco or flour, you may authorize the commanding officers to issue out of their public stores, if on hand, and to take the furs and skins to be sold at Omaha for their benefit, viz: to reimburse the Commissary, and the balance to go to the Indians, provided no Trader gets a cent of profit. I know that they have prepared for this very contingency which is of their own making. If those Sioux make the least trouble by spring we will give them our attention. Sheridan has knocked the Cheyennes, Arapahos and Kiowas all to pieces, and they are all running for Hazen's Reservation. I think the same process will have to be applied to those Powder River Sioux, and by early spring we will have the troops available.[22]

Sherman's reference to having "knocked" the Cheyenne, Arapaho, and Kiowa alluded to Custer's expedition against those tribes and the battle of the Washita.

Despite orders from the General of the Army, the Indians still frequented Fort Fetterman attempting to trade. Post commander C. H. Carlton refused this trade within the confines of his orders. On January 19, 1869, he wrote to General George D. Ruggles, at Department of the Platte Headquarters, telling how the Sioux responded to the ban, and to their orders to remove to Fort Randall, on the Missouri River:

> I have the honor to inform you that Grass with forty young Sioux were here on the 17th of January. Grass wished me to inform you that he would never go to Fort Randall to trade or for any other purpose: that this was his country and he intended to remain in it. That he accompanied Red Cloud when he signed the treaty at Fort Laramie in October last. That Red Cloud informed the Com'dg. Officer there that he (Red Cloud) had come in without invitation to sign the treaty, that he wanted it understood that he and his people (the Sioux) were to be treated as white men, to be allowed to go where they pleased and to trade where they pleased, that there was but one thing that he objected to and that was Fort Fetterman.
>
> That as Red Cloud was permitted to sign the treaty afterward it was considered by all of the Sioux that his wishes were to be complied with and that Red Cloud, Red Leaf, Man-Afraid-of-His-Horses and himself would never go to the Missouri, also that the Commissioners at Laramie last Spring informed them that if they signed the treaty Laramie would be the only Post left in their country north of the Rail Road and that would be a trading post. That he would be here again in thirty days to receive your reply. Grass's language intimated that he considered the refusal to trade as an hostile declaration and was, I think restrained from openly saying so by not knowing the view of Red Cloud and the principal Sioux Chiefs.[23]

In addition to their off-reservation raids, the Sioux and Cheyenne often peaceably visited Fort Fetterman itself for about three years after the Treaty of 1868 was signed. Perhaps the most vivid accounts of these visits are found in the diary of Ada Vodges, wife of Lieutenant Anthony Wayne Vodges, who was stationed at Fort Fetterman from 1869 to 1871.

She recorded that on January 5 and 6, 1870, the post was "filled with Indians and have had my house full for the last two days" and that she was

*Red Cloud, shown here in a photo thought to have been taken about 1870, informed the commanding officer at Fort Laramie that "there was but one thing he objected to [in the Treaty of 1868] and that was Fort Fetterman."* (Courtesy Wyoming State Archives)

"bothered to death with Indians."[24] Whatever her feelings, she took care to describe the visitors. When the Northern Cheyenne and Sioux Indians arrived at Fetterman in late March, to hold another peace council and receive gifts, she wrote:

> There are about thirty Cheyenne Indians in, northern Cheyennes from the Powder River Country. Fierce, and painted looking. They are the most horrid looking creatures of all the Indians that I have seen... looking in all respects like perfect fiends. These northern Cheyennes

are a finer, and hardier race than the southern. They had their faces painted in the peculiar manner. One of the big chiefs whom I met, had a painted chicken foot over each eye, done in blue paint, then under each eyelid, a red streak, then on each cheek bone, a mark looking like two cropped dumb bells, and horses shoes all around the face, and then the chin was painted in long blue lines, from the lower lip down under the chin. This completed his face toilet. Then his head was dressed off with feather, and…hair was painted a deep vermilion color. It made me shudder, and tremble with fear to look at them out side the window. They all left last night for "Pumpkin Buttes" where they have their lodges.[25]

Considering the Indian point of view, Ada continued that if the "Whites felt so friendly towards them, why did they not give them up this Post! Good logic on the part of the Indians." [26]

Red Cloud, Old-Man-Afraid-of-His-Horses, Brave Bear, and several other Sioux leaders arrived at Fetterman on April 24 and camped with about 250 followers on the north bank of the Platte.[27] Two days later they held a council with the post commander, Colonel Alexander Chambers. Ada Vodges reported:

> The Indians came over this A.M., to hold a council. We had them cross over in the ferry boat, as the river is now so high. They came up the hill singing at the top of their voices arranged in four battalions. Red Cloud (Mauck pea a tuter) his Indian name heading the band, with his men, then "Grass" with his men, then The-man-Afraid-of-his-horses, and his son with his men last, it had a war like appearance, but they are all peaceably disposed so they say. Although our mail party was attacked last Wednesday, at midnight.[28]

The next day Red Cloud had lunch with Lieutenant and Mrs. Vodges, who wrote:

> Red Cloud came up this morning and I had a lunch prepared for him, he ate rather a large dish of preserves, drank two cups of tea, bread, and other things in preparation, and when he finished, asked me to put up the rest for him to take to his "papooses," five in number. He had dropped all the fine clothes which he appeared in yesterday at the Council, and today he came only in the ones provided by nature, with the

*Ada Vodges reported that Young-Man-Afraid of-His-Horses accompanied his father, Old-Man-Afraid-of-His-Horses, into Fort Fetterman for a council on April 26, 1870. The son is shown here, photographed on another occasion.* (Courtesy Wyoming State Archives)

exception of a buffalo robe, and mocassons. I thought as I sat at the table with him, how strange it would seem to an Eastern person coming in suddenly to see me sit with this naked man, but it does not seem strange to me at all now. I am not shocked if I see them with no clothes on.[29]

"Red Cloud had not changed in the least, since I saw him at Laramie, one year, and a half ago," she went on. About the leader called Red Dog, she added:

"Red Dog" had nothing on but the skin in which he was born, only ornamented, a buffalo robe thrown around his waist, and I never saw such shoulders, arms, and legs, and hands, his arms were as round as a beautiful womans and tapered down beautifully to his waist, his legs were equally as fine looking, and he said, "he was proud of his form, that he lived well up in the Powder River country, was the cause of it. He wore large ear rings, in the shape of cart wheels, around his neck a black something I could not tell what, with a large piece of mother-of pearl attached. I suppose he had heard lockets were fashionable and the robe thrown around his horse part of his body, and mocassons were his full, and only dress. He was painted a delicate buff all over, and it gave him such a smooth clean look. He was quite fat for an Indian.[30]

The purpose of their visit with Chambers was to discuss traveling to Washington D.C. to meet President Grant. They also wanted to obtain a pardon for Joe Richard, cousin of John Richard, Jr., who was a mixed-blood interpreter for the military at Fort Laramie.[31] It appeared that Joe Richard had shot and killed a white man named Toussaint near the military lime kiln south of Fort Fetterman. Eluding capture, he had joined the Sioux living in Powder River country. Richard had a camp on Box Elder Creek where many acts of violence occurred throughout the fort's history.[32]

Chambers granted the pardon, and the talks about a trip to Washington, too, proved fruitful. But in the meantime, another incident at Fort Fetterman briefly strained Indian relations once again. On May 4 the post ferryboat swamped and sank. The accident occurred at about seven in the evening, "while a detail of seven soldiers was ferrying over the Indians, the boat filled and precipitated all into the river," wrote assistant post surgeon F. Le Baron Monroe. Two soldiers and three young Indian boys drowned. "Medicine Man says he saved twelve squaws—Dull Knife pulled out

*This photo shows Red Dog—years after Ada Vodges wrote admiringly that Red Dog's "shoulders, arms, and legs, and hands, his arms were as round as a beautiful womans and tapered beautifully to his waist, his legs were equally fine looking."* (Courtesy Nebraska State Historical Society)

three—most of them came out on this side—one was admitted to the Hospital for the night—a rather feeble old woman."[33] Ada Vodges wrote a similar account:

> Last night the ferryboat, across the Platte River, swamped, and nearly all on board liked to have been lost. Several Indians were drowned, besides two soldiers, and several papooses were lost, and the squaws followed after their little drowned babies down the river, making a most melancholy and mournful noise. The medicine man of the Cheyennes, was quite angry, at first thinking it was done intentionally.[34]

Six days later the ferryboat was dragged ashore.[35]

Red Cloud and his chiefs did make the trip to Washington and visited the president. Afterward, on July 8, they passed through Fort Fetterman and again camped on the north bank of the Platte River. In an all-day conference with Chambers, Red Cloud reported that their trip was satisfying, and expressed his desire to keep the peace.[36] While at Fort Fetterman the chiefs again were invited to lunch at the Vodges quarters, as Ada Vodges noted:

> A large number of Sioux came in yesterday, amongst them, some of the big Chiefs that have just returned from Washington. I had them to lunch to A.M., amongst the number, was Red Cloud, Red Dog, Red Shirt, Grass, and Brave Bear. They had just come from Mrs. C's [Chambers's] where one would think they had all they could eat, but no they came here, and the way they did eat doughnuts, preserves, and drink tea, was funny. I told the interpreter to tell Red Cloud that my father tried to see him while in N.Y. and the crowd was so great he could not. "Yes!" says R. C., "the people were as thick as the fingers on his two hands," holding them close together as he spoke.

Mrs. Vodges continued that Red Dog:

> ...was gotten up in the most exquisite style for a red man. He had on a full suit of buff linen, with an emmacuately white pleated bosom shirt, with the gazed kind of neck tie, and a palm leaf fan that he made incessant use of all the time. I said to him "Red Dog you have a real N.Y. look", which pleased him very much.[37]

She noticed that they had picked up several "Eastern tricks" while in New York; "one was when they wanted more coffee, they knocked their spoon on the side of their cup to show they wanted more." [38]

But if the Sioux were in good homecoming spirits, it was short-lived. On their journey to Powder River, anguish swept through Red Cloud's camp at the news that the chief's brother had been dragged and kicked to death by his mule in a battle with the Crow, in which the Sioux were soundly defeated.[39]

Peace with the Euro-Americans seemed to be Red Cloud's highest priority and the military authorities at Fetterman were likewise determined to uphold the 1868 Treaty. The post surgeon wrote in his daily record that on

August 31, large herds of cattle had passed Fetterman on their way to Utah Territory and that the Sioux had demanded trespass payment of ten head of cattle and two horses, which they received. They further demanded that no herds cross their territory in the future.[40] For now, the treaty was working for the benefit of all.

On September 8 Ada Vodges recorded that "the Post is full of Cheyenne Indians, come in to make big peace, hundreds of them."[41] Five weeks later Red Cloud returned to the post and brought with him nearly a thousand Sioux to trade and receive gifts.[42]

Further indications that Red Cloud was endeavoring to keep the peace came in December when Colonel Chambers telegraphed Headquarters, Department of the Platte:

> Sioux, Cheyenne & Arapahos are now daily besieging me to know when their agents and traders are to be appointed. They say they have plenty of robes and are in need of Traders… I have telegraphed the impoverished condition of the Arapahos to [Wyoming Territorial ] Gov. Campbell and hope he will aid them. My opinion is that now is the time to make a lasting and durable peace. Red Cloud when going to war with Snakes said that any depredations committed against the whites would be punished with death, showing a determination to keep the peace. The camp of Sioux & Arapahos is on Deer Creek and I expect Medicine Man of Arapahos in a short time, please telegraph me any news of appointment of Traders & agents as it will be of much use in keeping young men in camp.[43]

But in January 1871, the Indians still were without agents or traders, and the tribes needed food. The Sioux were to be supplied at Fort Laramie and the Arapaho and Cheyenne at Fort Fetterman during January and February 1871.[44] Red Cloud was taking five hundred lodges to the Nine-Mile Ranch near Fort Laramie and wanted them provisioned. He told Chambers that 250 more lodges were coming in for rations in two months.[45] But in March, First Lieutenant John M. Tobey, the post adjutant, issued a circular which indicated that no agents or traders had yet been assigned. Tobey advised diplomacy:

> In view of the fact that a considerable number of Indians are expected to visit the post to-morrow, and as it is now the policy of the Government

to conciliate them by every proper means in order that the horrors of Indian warfare may be, if possible, averted, and the Indians themselves brought under the influence of civilization, all officers are enjoined to warn the men of their respective commands that the Indians are proud and sensitive; resentful of insult and revengeful under injury, and that any hasty or harsh act toward them may have consequences of far reaching and deplorable significance. In their deportment towards the Indians, both officers and men are enjoined to bear patiently the annoyance of their presence at this post; and the curiosity which prompts them to look into windows and come about the quarters. If it is necessary to warn them away, it should be done by motions rather than by speech, and in a manner which while calculated to be distinctly understood, is not likely to be construed by them as offensive.[46]

The Cheyenne had already returned to Fetterman in mid-February to trade and confer with the post commander. Indeed, tolerance was required of everyone. Ada Vodges wrote of her encounters with the Cheyenne women:

> ...a poor squaw sitting all alone, with a young baby upon her back, was putting up a most pitiful tone, I stooped down, and asked her what was the matter, she tried to tell me, and while I was trying to understand, one of the ladies came up and said the guide had told her that she was crying for a son she had lost a year ago, and when she looked amongst the soldiers of the camp she missed him so, and was bewailing his vacant place, while I was looking at her she blew her nose, and wiped her hands on my dog. I turned away in disgust, and all my sympathy departed in this performance... The next thing that struck me, was the squaws while waiting for the presents to be given out, were vigorously at work exterminating the bugs in their childrens heads, and now, oh ye that are weak of stomach, if you can bear what I have to relate follow on, as they succeeded in their hunting each one was eaten with a relish, I rushed to the ambulance and got inside, and wished that they could have been exterminated in the twinkle of an eye for they seemed too disgusting to be left to live another day, and I felt mad with the Gov. that it should feed, cloth, and strengthen such creatures to carry on...[47]

Despite her dismay, Mrs. Vodges kept her eye on the Indians and their customs:

When these people move, these old men are carried in baskets or cages I may say for they look more like the latter, tied on the lodge poles, which drag on the ground, behind the horses, the children in like manner are carried... I saw at a distance a cunning little tepe too small I knew for anyone to live in, so I had the curiosity to examine, and find to my great surprise it contained young *puppies*, that looked as cosey, and comfortable as anybody could. A tepe for puppies was a novel idea to me, and we all had a good laugh at these little fat creatures. I suppose they had them fattening, as we do chickens for a feast.[48]

Throughout the summer of 1871, Fetterman served as the treaty distribution point for the Cheyenne and Arapaho tribes. This changed when departmental headquarters ordered that as of August 29 these tribes, as well as the Sioux, were to receive their allotments and rationing at Fort Laramie.[49] Thereafter, Indian visitors to Fort Fetterman were much less frequent.

While the Indian and Euro-American cultures often seemed irreconcilable, there were those who belonged, in some sense, to both. One was John Richard, Jr., the mixed-blood cousin of the aforementioned Joe Richard who was wanted by the military. Indeed, several Richard men (the name was pronounced and sometimes spelled Reshaw or Rechaw) attracted the attention of the authorities.

John Richard, Sr., had a run-in with Indians as reported in the Ada Vodges diary:

Old Rechaw [Richard] came in saying his camp was surrounded, and he feared everything would be captured. Lieut. Broglin(sp) went out with sixty men in pursuit of them. They came upon them four miles from the Post where they were comfortably quartered in their tepees. The Interpreter went up to them to find out if they were the Indians who came in here this morning. They said they were "peaceable Indians", and Lieut. Breolin(sp) took their word for it, coming home not having fired a shot. The Commanding Officer, Capt. Patterson was furious with him, as he was sent out to *kill* them and not to have a *pow-wow*. They were all painted up, and had on their war dress, and this was sufficient cause to have fired into them.[50]

The younger John was born around 1844 to John Richard, Sr., who had traded with the Indians in the Fort Laramie and Platte Bridge regions in earlier years, and his Sioux wife. Young Richard became well known as an Indian trader and civilian contractor for the military at such forts as C.F. Smith, Laramie, and Fetterman during the late 1860s and 1870s. A popular young man, Richard enjoyed considerable fame in the area, but he had two major flaws: a fondness for hard liquor and a weakness for women. He also tended to get into trouble with both civilian and military authorities, either by his own design or the schemes of others. Moreover, Richard had voiced friendship with the Crow and purportedly declared himself an enemy of the whites during the 1868 peace treaty negotiations, where he served as an interpreter. He was further accused of urging the Crow to ally with other tribes so as to force the whites from their lands. To this charge peace commissioner General John B. Sanford responded:

> The charge that he endeavored to incite the Indians to war, otherwise than to join our troops against the Sioux, is absurd and preposterous. The messengers were all charged to do their utmost to prevent such a result. No other one did so much to prevent this as John Richard, Jr. He visited the Crows and induced them to come all the way to [Fort] Laramie, where they had not been since 1851, to meet the commission. When he had accomplished this, he went to the Sioux camp of Man Afraid of his Horse and Red Cloud, with his life in his hand, where he came very near to laying it down, and held a council with both of these chiefs, and brought to the Commission their sayings and conclusions, viz., that they would not make peace until the military posts were removed from the Powder River Road...
>
> I therefore feel confident that the Crow chiefs never made the statements ascribed to them, and that the charges had their origin in the interested and fertile brain of some interpreter who appreciates filthy lies above the truth, and therefore request that they shall not be construed as creating a stain upon Richard in the department.[51]

As a result of his role as interpreter for the treaty talks, Richard obtained a license from the Commissioner of Indian Affairs to trade with the Powder River Sioux in February 1869, but it was revoked within two months. Richard then went to Fort Fetterman as a civilian wood contractor. But his troubles continued. That fall he worked as a subcontractor under Wilson & Cobb, a freighting firm with interests in cattle, serving as the post trader at Forts Fetterman and Laramie. On September 9, Richard, apparently without provocation, shot Corporal Francis Conrad of Company E, Fourth Infantry, near the post trader's store. Two civilians witnessed the murder. Conrad, who had been unarmed, died the following day. Meanwhile, Richard left the post with his Indian wife for the encampments of the Powder River Sioux. The military impounded his belongings and sent the following physical description: "He is about twenty-five years of age, five feet eight or ten inches high, a dark mustache, slight figure, of good appearance and address, speaks English well." [52]

Ada Vodges wrote in her diary:

> This P.M., we had a quite another excitement. One of the half breeds (John Reshaw) shot one of our best Sergeants, in a drunken fit, and the whole garrison was in arms against him. To night the sentinels, are posted in all direction to catch him in case he should try to get in to night after his things. As Wayne is Officer of the Day, and has to visit the guard, and sentinels, every two hours, I feel quite anxious about him, as he said he would be in again. The orderly sleeps here to night, in case he should be wanted. [53]

Mrs. Vodges incorrectly called Conrad a sergeant, but two days later she noted "the corporal" was buried in the afternoon.

According to Baptiste Pourier, who was employed by Richard, John had been at the house of a "loose woman" some time earlier when Conrad had entered and directed him to leave. Unarmed at the time, Richard complied, telling the corporal that he would get even with him. [54] This incident, coupled with the Richard's belief that soldiers had been sent to protect Conrad's camp, set the stage for the murder.

The murder was also recorded in the *Secretary of War Reports*:

> An affair has recently occurred at Fort Fetterman which may prove to be of considerable importance. John Richards, a half-breed Sioux, well known throughout this country as a smart active business man, possessed of a good deal of property, and recently a sub-contractor for wood and hay at Fort Fetterman, has recently abandoned everything and joined the Indians, with the avowed intention of endeavoring to procure a concert of action among all northern bands to make war upon the whites. On the 9th of September, before leaving Fetterman, he deliberately and without the slightest provocation killed a soldier,

and before he could be arrested mounted his horse and with his squaw left to join the Indians.[55]

Many feared that Richard's action would incite the Indians to attack white settlements in the Sweetwater mining district at the south end of the Wind River Range. On October 21 Ada Vodges recorded: "An order out this evening, as to what is to be done in case of an attack. I am to frightened, that I would give all I ever expect to possess, to be in the States far away from such constant excitement as we are now having."[56]

John Richard, Jr. became an outlaw and was considered a dangerous man. He devoted himself to revenge on the whites by trying to incite the Crow, Sioux, and Cheyenne into war against them. Richard then sought a pardon, which was granted in June 1870. He returned to doing business at Forts Fetterman and Laramie. But shortly thereafter, June 17, he was killed by Indians after he murdered his former brother-in-law Chief Yellow Bear in a dispute over one of Yellow Bear's sisters.[57]

# Fort Fetterman and the
# Centennial Campaigns

CHAPTER

# 5

DURING THE YEARS after the Fort Laramie treaty was signed, Red Cloud tried to preserve the peace by assisting the U.S. military and dissuading his young warriors from raiding white enterprises. Fort Fetterman military records clearly show his good intentions; his men returned stolen animals and served as army scouts tracking deserters and bringing in white renegades for trial. The military also showed good faith by feeding hungry Indians and keeping white settlers from encroaching on Indian lands north of the Platte. Ranchers who contracted with the government to supply beef to Fort Fetterman were warned to keep their animals south of the North Platte River "… in order that the Indians in the neighborhood will not be subject to unjust suspicion should any of your animals stray away." [1]

But despite these good intentions, conflict was coming that leaders on neither side could prevent. The Cheyenne and Arapaho made little or no effort to preserve the peace, and even Red Cloud struggled to keep his Sioux warriors in check. In February 1869, Sioux war parties were reported as far away as the Sweetwater mining district at the south end of the Wind River Range, attesting to the limits of Red Cloud's control.

The raids and skirmishes around Fetterman were constant. That spring, on March 23 and 24 and on April 3, Sergeant Robert Rae led several Fourth Infantry detachments out to repair the telegraph lines, returning each time without incident. Their luck ran out on April 6, when Rae left the post again, this time with a corporal named Sanders, six privates, a six-mule army wagon and two horses, to continue the job. Sanders later reported that the party was attacked near LaBonte Creek, on LaBonte Hill, and that Sergeant Rae and Private Russell B. Emery were killed. Privates Babcock and Sullivan were missing, but they returned to Fort Fetterman three days later after traveling at night and hiding by day. Emery's body was recovered and returned to the post, but Rae's was not found. [2] The Indian raiders were identified as

Arapaho. Cavalry units from both Fort Laramie and Fetterman were ordered to locate and kill the party, but no contact was made.[3]

Throughout 1869, Indian war parties south of the North Platte River were reported with weekly regularity. They disrupted telegraphic communications, stole stock, raided the Union Pacific Railroad and the Sweetwater mines. In every case these war parties were defying the efforts of Red Cloud and Old-Man-Afraid-of-His-Horses to curb such attacks.

In October a Sioux war party attacked ranches near Medicine Bow and stole most of their stock. Cavalry from Fetterman and Laramie pursued them for several weeks, but the stock was not recovered.[4] On October 28 three soldiers of Company K, Second Cavalry, who were hunting about twelve miles from Fetterman, camped near the entrance of LaPrele Canyon. During the night the Indians fired on the camp, killing privates John A. McCallister and George McKenna immediately. Another private named Wentworth survived, but his long walk back to the post severely lacerated his bare feet. When soldiers reached the site of the engagement they found that the two dead men had not been mutilated, scalped, or robbed.[5]

The final Indian depredation of 1869 occurred on December 2. Fetterman's mail detachment, under command of Sergeant Conrad Bahr, Company E, Fourth Infantry, arrived at Horseshoe Creek to meet the Fort Laramie mail party, which had not yet appeared. Sergeant Bahr went on towards Fort Laramie expecting that the other party had met with Indians, which indeed it had. About eight miles east of Horseshoe Creek, a force of sixty to a hundred Indians attacked the Fetterman party, killing Private Johnson. Bahr returned his command to Horseshoe Creek, then proceeded to Fort Laramie the next day. The Indians had also torn down the telegraph line east of Horseshoe Creek.[6]

The new decade opened on a dark note when an Arapaho runner brought word on January 1 that a large Sioux war party was headed southwest to Fort Steele or the Sweetwater country.[7] Any edginess at Fort Fetterman would have been understandable by now, and Ada Vodges was relieved to record a false alarm ten days later:

Last Thursday night we had a scare in the night for the first time since we came. Shots were fired by all the sentinels and we felt sure for a moment that Indians it must be. Wayne was out in a moment, and it proved to be a soldier out of the garrison, after mid-night who had been at one of the Laundress quarters, and when he was challenged *three* times did not answer, the sentinel at the hay stack fired at him, which caused so much excitement in the hours of mid night.[8]

On April 12 post interpreter Joe Merival was tending his beaver traps on LaPrele Creek about two miles south of the fort when a large party of Minneconjou Sioux tried to ambush him. Only a snort from Merival's horse saved his life. He "mounted amidst a shower of balls" and reached his camp unhurt, though his dog was killed. Later that day two Indians thought to be part of this band tried to cut the ferry rope at Fetterman but were fired upon by the sentry with the water wagon. The Indians returned fire but there were no casualties on either side. Merival crossed the Platte River in pursuit and fired ten shots at long range. The Indians rode off to the northeast.[9] Again in April Fetterman's mail party was fired upon while encamped on LaBonte Creek. The party retaliated and the firefight lasted all night, but the only casualties were three wounded mules.[10]

Hostilities continued on June 28, when about sixty Cheyenne Indians attacked the contract woodcutters on LaPrele Creek. Post guide employee Vivian Chaves, known as "Picaqune," who "was driving an empty wagon and four mules to the hills, and is said to have been entirely unarmed," was shot with seventeen arrows and scalped. He was buried in the post cemetery the next day.[11]

Sporadic action with Indians continued through the summer and fall but tapered off during the winter of 1870–71. Most of 1871 was unusually quiet for Fort Fetterman, with no major raids recorded. But trouble erupted again that December, when a Sioux band drove off all the horses and mules belonging to "Mexican Joe," the post guide, and forty-three horses belonging to Joe Merival.[12] In February 1872, Indian hostilities had so escalated that the post commander felt compelled to request a troop of cavalry be stationed at Fort Fetterman. But his request fell on deaf ears, for the moment.

On May 1, 1872, Sergeant James A. Mularkey, of Company E, Fourteenth Infantry, fell victim to the Indians while escorting the mail. Mularkey's six-man party had nearly reached LaBonte Creek when he went ahead of the detail to select a campsite. For some unknown reason he ventured forward without his rifle and met two Cheyenne Indians from Chief Old Bear's camp.

While he shook hands with one, the other Indian shot and killed him, steal-ing his cartridge belt and mule.[13] A few days later the stolen mule was surren-dered to post authorities by members of Old Bear's band.[14]

On October 29 acting post commander David Krause sent a telegram to Department Headquarters: "Indians have killed work cattle in sight of post. Can't we have a company of Cavalry at once?"[15] Headquarters issued orders that same day to call in all small parties and to consider all Indians south of the North Platte River hostile and to "treat them as such."[16] On Christmas Day in 1872, Fort Fetterman received its first permanent cav-alry detachment. Company C, Third Cavalry, under the command of Captain Van Vliet,[17] would now take over escort duties and provide for rapid pursuit of marauding Indians.

Hostilities erupted again on February 28, when a party of forty to fifty Sioux and Cheyenne warriors attacked a man named Speed nine miles south of the fort on LaPrele Creek, stealing eight ponies. Fetterman's new cavalry pursued them but failed to recover the animals.[18]

The rest of 1873 saw relatively few raids. Then on February 9, 1874, Lieutenant Levi H. Robinson, of the Fourteenth Infantry at Fort Laramie, met his fate while leading a woodcutting detail, a mixed command of sol-diers from the Fourteenth Infantry and Second Cavalry, back to their post. He, Corporal Coleman, and a private had wandered away from the main train when they were ambushed by Indians about ten miles east of the sawmill near Laramie Peak. When his horse ran off, the private was able to hide from his pursuers. But Robinson and Coleman, still mounted, were killed. Neither man was scalped nor mutilated, probably due to the other soldiers arriving upon the scene. After this incident, the troops were ordered to "spare no Indians south of the Platte."[19] Later, when a new mili-tary post was established near the Red Cloud Agency in Nebraska, it was named after Lieutenant Levi Robinson.

Hostilities continued on March 22, when nineteen head of cattle were run off near Fort Fetterman. The following day the civilian owners, led by mixed-blood guides, pursued the hostile Indians and surprised them. Ten Sioux were killed in the resulting skirmish, and one was wounded.[20] Six days later the sentinel near the commissary storehouse saw ten Indians across the Platte River and fired a warning shot to turn out the guard. The Indians left the vicinity but returned to the area in late April, firing shots into the Indian scout camp on LaPrele Creek.[21]

That summer, on July 2, Indians attacked the wood camp about fifteen miles south of the post on Box Elder Creek at a place known as the "Blacksmith's Shop." The logging crew included Nathan Williams, Jesse Hampton, and two men named McMillen and Robinson. At noon three of the men had just returned to their camp when they were fired on several times by the Indians. No one was injured. But Jesse Hampton, still in the timber cutting logs, was not as fortunate. He was wounded badly, taking a shot in the chest. Williams was the first man to reach Hampton after the shooting and reported that Hampton told him

> ... that he recognized the son of "Cut Nose" and a son of "Sioux Jim". There were also two more grown Indians and two small boys—an Arrapahoe boy, aged about twenty was also present. The two boys first named rode up behind him, and shot him, and after he fell, they fired two more deliberate shots at him. He pointed to his head and begged them to kill him. Several shots had been previously fired at him from the top of the hill.[22]

Six cavalrymen escorted McMillen and Robinson back to the wood camp to retrieve Hampton. The next day, at the post hospital, a musket ball was found lodged against his spine, which paralyzed his bladder and lower limbs. He had taken four pistol shots. Hampton died of his wounds a week later. [23]

On July 16, an Arapaho band attacked the hay contractors near the mouth of Deer Creek. The raid came at three o'clock in the morning, and the corporal in charge of six soldiers guarding the site repulsed the Indians after exchanging thirty to fifty rounds. Neither side acknowledged any casualties.[24] In response, Captain Van Vliet of the Third Cavalry was directed to patrol the Deer Creek area and punish any Indians south of the Platte; he was authorized to pursue any Indians seen crossing the river. But the command returned with no sightings.[25] Another attack occurred on July 2, when seven Indians killed and scalped civilian woodcutter Michael "Pat" McDonald on Big Box Elder Creek. McDonald was under the employ of Malcolm Campbell who had a contract to burn charcoal for use at the post.[26] Second Lieutenant James Allen and twenty men of Company C, Third Cavalry, left Fetterman the following day to recover the body.[27]

The last reported encounter with hostile Indians for 1874 was noted on December 10, when a man named Smith, the servant of Colonel

*General Crook's tent camp on the north side of the North Platte River in 1876. Fort Fetterman is on the bluff above the river.* (From sketches by officers in the field, the Sioux Campaign. Harper's Weekly, July 22, 1876)

Chambers, was fired upon about three miles from the post. A cavalry detail investigated, but without success.[28]

Not every encounter was hostile, however. That winter, post commander Lieutenant Colonel John S. Mason allowed three lodges of "poor" Northern Cheyenne Indians to camp on the north side of the Platte until spring because they had no horses to move their camps. During their stay, Mason authorized supplying them with livestock heads and feet from the post butcher shop, located on LaPrele Creek, for food. On February 24 they obtained some whiskey and two of the men fought; one was killed and the other wounded.[29]

The cold winter months kept hostilities to a minimum, but in spring 1875 the depredations resumed. In June a dispatch warned that a party of Indians had run off a hundred head of horses belonging to area ranchers, among them George Harper in the Rock Creek Valley. The raiders had headed north toward Powder River. First Lieutenant George A. Drew led Company C, Third Cavalry in pursuit, but they failed to recover the horse herd.[30] In September, Indians threatened the hay cutters at Bridger's Ferry, and a stronger guard was sent out from Fetterman. On October 3, a freight train was attacked and a man traveling alone to Fort Fetterman was killed.[31]

〰 〰

All these incidents were but a prelude to more aggressive campaigning, however, when the Black Hills were at stake. The Black Hills of South Dakota and northeastern Wyoming were so named because they appear dark, from a distance, as they rise majestically from the rolling prairie. These mountains were claimed by the Sioux during their acquisition of the northern Plains in the late eighteenth century after they migrated there. Considered sacred by the Sioux, the Hills were rich with wild game. Until 1874, only rumors suggested to the white man that this area was also rich with valuable gold deposits. The Black Hills were first explored by the military in 1857 when Lieutenant G.K. Warren traversed the area near Inyan Kara Mountain before he was turned back by hostile Indians. In 1859 Captain W. F. Raynolds skirted the Black Hills with Jim Bridger as a guide. During both of these expeditions, gold had been discovered. But the news that leaked to the nation in 1859 did not create a "rush" to the Hills—not yet. That would only occur sixteen years later.[32]

The most famous exploration of the Black Hills was commanded by Lieutenant Colonel George A. Custer in 1874. His men marched from Fort Abraham Lincoln, on the Missouri River, and spent the entire summer in the Hills. Custer had been charged with selecting a site for a military post from which more efficient control of marauding Indians might be gained. By 1874 this was increasingly important, due to the number of depredations outside the area reserved for the Indians by the 1868 Treaty. N.H. Winchell, the geologist in his party, was to determine if there were large deposits of gold in the Black Hills. Winchell's report stated that he never saw paying quantities of gold during the expedition. Yet as in earlier explorations, some gold was indeed found, and news would spread soon enough.

The Sioux bitterly resented the Custer expedition, as they felt it was an encroachment on the lands allotted to them by the Treaty of 1868. Yet Article II of that document specified that "officers, agents, and employees of the government" had the right to enter the reservation in the "discharge of duties enjoined by law." Later that year the military sent a second expedition of the Black Hills. Reverend Samuel Hinman of the Indian Service (later known as the Bureau of Indian Affairs), accompanied Captain Charles Meinhold for the purpose of settling upon a location for a new Sioux agency. But Hinman reported that the area was a barren and unproductive wilderness, unfit for human occupation.[33]

*Troops encamped north of Fort Fetterman during Crook's summer campaigns of 1876. The quartermaster's corral is on the left bluff. The pump house for the water system is on the right center edge of the drawing.* (Indian Story Land, Author's collection)

Although Custer's expedition only reported small amounts of gold, that was enough to launch a stream of miners into the Black Hills, each party hoping for one of the earliest and richest claims. The crisis that developed was to change the life of the Indian forever and rapidly alter the settlement of the western frontier.

By presidential decree, the army began to expel miners from the Black Hills at once. Throughout the spring and summer of 1875, soldiers from forts on the Missouri River, as well as Forts Laramie, Robinson, and eventually Fetterman, effected this service to the best of their ability. Nevertheless over eight hundred miners worked the streams of the Hills throughout the summer of 1875.[34] Keeping the miners out of the region soon became a lost cause for the army, which indeed at times seemed to side with the miners rather than the Indians.

In the meantime, with miners invading the Black Hills and the army ostensibly trying to expel them, another scientific and military expedition entered the Hills in 1875. Its goal was to determine the true extent and value of the gold in the area. Newton Warren and Walter P. Jenney led the group, escorted by over four hundred soldiers under the command of Lieutenant Colonel R.I. Dodge. It was this expedition and the pursuant publicity that accelerated the stream of miners into the gold rush of 1875.

Fetterman's Company C, Third Cavalry, had been directed on March 29 of that year to establish a base camp at the mouth of Deer Creek and "patrol up and down the Platte River to stop any parties of miners" heading for the Black Hills. If they captured any parties, they were to escort them to Fetterman.[35] Continuous patrolling during the summer resulted in no miners being turned back, although on June 21, a party of six miners camped near Fetterman was stopped and questioned. They were let go when they professed they were simply prospecting the vicinity around the post. Two days later a detachment of Fetterman's cavalry was sent toward Bridger's Ferry to find this party, but without success.[36]

Realizing that they could not keep the miners out, the government attempted to purchase or lease the Black Hills from the Sioux during the summer of 1875. But these negotiations failed. On November 3, President Grant met at the White House with Secretary of War William W. Belknap, Secretary of the Interior Zachariah Chandler, Commissioner of Indian Affairs Edward P. Smith, and Generals Sheridan and Crook. The men hammered out two decisions. The first was to withdraw the military from the Black Hills and allow the unimpeded flow of miners. The second was to force all Indian bands onto their reservations, thus curtailing their continual hunting and raiding parties.[37]

With their "invasion," the miners violated the Treaty of 1868 as they searched the Black Hills for gold. When significant amounts were discovered, word spread, and the rush was on. The War Department found itself in a tenuous position: if they tried to honor the treaty by keeping miners out of unceded Indian lands, they flew in the face of public sentiment. At the same time, the Sioux considered these hills sacred and were determined to fight to protect their property, while a faltering Congress tried to gain their permission to allow the miners to extract the gold for the federal treasury. The army was caught in the middle; its orders were to expel the miners and keep the Sioux on their reservation until an agreement could be reached.

By 1876, the United States government had appropriated more than $6 million over and above the amount stipulated by the treaty to keep the Sioux nation from starvation. At this price the government felt it would be cheaper to buy the Black Hills from the Indians than to try to keep the miners out. In 1875, presidential commissioner George Manypenny had begun negotiating—with only ten percent of the Sioux chiefs—for the

*Crook's camp below Fort Fetterman during the 1876 campaigns against the Sioux.
The buildings on the edge of the bluff are the Quartermaster and Commissary
Storehouses.* (Courtesy National Archives)

surrender of the Black Hills, which was achieved in 1876. By this agreement, the Sioux were to be provided with subsistence rations as long as
needed for survival. In return, the Sioux relinquished all rights to the
Black Hills and their rights to hunt on unceded lands. But with so few
Sioux signatures, this new pact violated the Treaty of 1868, which
required that seventy-five percent of the male population had to approve
any such transaction. The resulting controversy continues to this day.

In December 1875, acting on the instructions of the Commissioner of
Indian Affairs, General Phil Sheridan had ordered all Indians to return to
their reservations by spring or be considered hostile and subject to military force. Even if they had wanted to, the Indians could not have complied because of severe winter weather. Thus the stage was set for the military conflicts of 1876 and 1877.

☙ ❧

With the Indians ordered onto their reservations, the troops at Fort
Fetterman ceased patrolling for miners. That spring of 1876 the garrison
began preparing for military maneuvers that became known as the Centennial Campaigns against the northern Plains Indians. Three avenues of
attack were planned against the Sioux and Cheyenne, to force them onto
their designated lands. The first column, composed mostly of infantry

under General John Gibbon, began operations from western Montana. The second, led by General George Crook, advanced north from Fort Fetterman, and the third, under General Alfred Terry, was launched from Fort Yankton. This column included the ill-fated Seventh Cavalry under Colonel Custer's command, which was stationed at Fort Abraham Lincoln. The army felt that any one of these commands was strong enough to overpower any straying hostile groups; the intention of the triple-pronged strike was to trap the hostile Sioux and Cheyenne between the three forces and compel combat.

General Crook, commander of the Department of the Platte, began his campaign against the Indians in March 1876, using Fort Fetterman as his primary supply depot and assembly point. General Joseph J. Reynolds commanded the first expedition, leading six companies of the Third Cavalry north into Powder River country. On March 17 he surprised a village under Crazy Horse on Powder River, destroying their lodges. More important, the cavalry captured about eight hundred horses. But it failed to keep possession of the herd when the Indians rallied and counterattacked. Reynolds' command was forced to retreat, and the Indians escaped. The loss of the prized horse herd was fateful: General Crook stripped Reynolds of his command and eventually pressed charges, reasoning that Reynolds should have shot the horses rather than allow the Indians to retake them. Crook took charge of the expedition, but lacking supplies and needing to care for the wounded, he returned to Fetterman and immediately began to refit and plan a summer campaign.

General Crook began organizing his Big Horn and Yellowstone Expedition by directing forces from all over the West to assemble at Fort Fetterman in May. Spring weather and heavy snow runoff hampered travel, especially for those units crossing the mountains from Medicine Bow on the Union Pacific Railroad. Five companies of infantry—C, H, and G of the Ninth Infantry, and D and F of the Fourth Infantry—were placed under the command of Colonel Alexander Chambers of the Fourth Infantry, with approximately forty-five men in each company. Companies A, B, C, D, E, F, G, I, L, and M of the Third Cavalry, and Companies A, B, E, I, and G, Second Cavalry, were under the overall command of Colonel William B. Royall of the Third Cavalry. Captain Nickerson and Lieutenant Bourke were designated aides-de-camp, while Captain George M. Randall of the Twenty-third Infantry was assigned as chief of scouts. Captain William Stanton became chief engineer officer and Captain John V. Furey was appointed chief quartermaster in charge of 103 six-mule army wagons and teams, as well as over two hundred pack mules. First Lieutenant John W. Bubb was named commissary of subsistence officer, and assistant surgeon Albert Hartsuff was named medical director. The civilian guides were Frank Grouard, Louis Richard, and Baptiste Pourier, known as Big Bat. General Crook placed himself in command on May 28, immediately before leaving Fort Fetterman on the long journey north in search of the hostile Sioux and Cheyenne.[38]

On May 29, Crook's imposing column began moving from its camps along the Platte toward the abandoned Fort Reno where Crook was to meet the Crow and Shoshoni scouts. Crook telegraphed to General Sheridan that Captain James Egan

> ...encountered about six hundred warriors going north from Red Cloud Agency. He has information of all young warriors going north from the Agency, leaving families to be protected, can't you do something to stop this, either warriors return or families join them? Indications are that we shall have the whole Sioux Nation to contend with. Command marches to-day. I shall wait till toward evening and join camp sixteen miles out. Hostiles are said to be concentrating at mouth of Powder River.[39]

On June 1, the command neared the Big Horn Mountains in a snowstorm. General Crook's courier arrived at Fetterman five days later and dispatched the news to Department of the Platte Headquarters: Yellow Robe had returned from the hostile camp to the Sioux Agency six days earlier, and over eighteen hundred lodges were now camped on Rosebud Creek. Crook's forces were about to leave for Powder River, below where Reynolds had fought Crazy Horse, and the "Indians say they will fight and have about three thousand Warriors."[40] And indeed they did put up a fight.

There on Rosebud Creek, Crook's first battle with the Indians, on June 17, lasted nearly a full day with the Indians showing great leadership and overwhelming numerical superiority. While his command remained in control of the battlefield, Crook failed to attain his goal of capturing and destroying the encampment. Had he accomplished this, the Indians would have been sent reeling back to their reservation. Instead Crook was forced to retreat the following day. Eight days later the Indians, emboldened by their victory, would engulf and nearly destroy Colonel Custer's command.

*Officers of the Fourth U.S. Infantry in front of the south side porch of the commanding officers' quarters, 1876. Left to right: First Lieutenant Henry Seton, First Lieutenant George O. Webster, Second Lieutenant Henry E. Robinson, Captain Edwin M. Coates, Captain Gerhard L. Luhn and Captain William H. Andrews, Third Cavalry.* (Courtesy of Dr. John Langellier)

After the battle on the Rosebud, Crook realized that he faced a formidable force, too large to attack again without reinforcements and more ammunition. He thus retraced his line of march to Goose Creek and Camp Cloud Peak. From there he sent another courier to Fetterman to report on the fight on the Rosebud and request reinforcements and supplies.

The courier arrived at the fort on June 20.[41] The wounded began to arrive on June 24, under command of Colonel Alexander Chambers, Fourth Infantry. The escort carried seventeen casualties of the Rosebud battle, including Captain Guy V. Henry who was severely wounded in the face.[42] As luck would have it, the ferry rope had recently broken, but a stout new replacement rope had been ordered, four inches in diameter and 625 feet long.[43] Just in time, the rope was replaced on June 24, but broke again the next day under the weight of more wounded men. On that day, while soldiers at Fetterman were trying to save the lives of the men on the raft, Custer's command was overwhelmed in the Seventh Cavalry's epic battle on the Little Bighorn River.

On June 30, reinforcements from Medicine Bow arrived at Fetterman, en route to General Crook's camp on Goose Creek. These four companies

*Lithograph of the commanding officers' quarters at Fort Fetterman when it was being used as General Crook's headquarters in 1876.* (Harper's Weekly, December 16, 1876)

of the Fourteenth Infantry and Company G, Fourth Infantry, were commanded by Captain William H. Powell, Fourth Infantry, another veteran Indian fighter.[44] Further reinforcements arrived weekly at Fetterman, including one company Second Cavalry, two companies Third Cavalry, six companies Fourth Cavalry, two companies Fifth Cavalry, four companies Fourth Artillery (serving as Infantry), six companies Ninth Infantry, two companies Fourteenth Infantry, three companies Twenty-third Infantry, and parties of Pawnee and Sioux Indians as scouts. These arrivals raised Crook's total military strength to approximately two thousand fighting men. The wagon train now numbered nearly 160 six-mule wagons, which were placed under the command of Major Furey, with orders to withdraw to Forts Fetterman and Laramie by easy marches. Later in the campaign, while Crook's men were freezing and starving north of the Black Hills, Furey's wagon train was camped on the Belle Fourche River about seventy-five miles south.

An angry General Sheridan directed Crook to avenge Custer's losses by continuing to pursue the warring Indians. But the Indians broke their large village into smaller ones and virtually disappeared into the vast plains wilderness of Wyoming, Montana, and Dakota Territories. On September 8, after an exhausting summer and surviving on sparse rations, ultimately horse and mule meat, General Crook's command headed for Deadwood, Dakota Territory, to obtain provisions. Colonel Anson Mills, in command of the advance guard, came upon the village of American Horse camped on Rabbit Creek near Slim Buttes. Even though Mills's force was greatly outnumbered, he ordered an attack. The soldiers charged and, after a brief skirmish, captured the village, managing to hold it until the main column arrived. Shortly after Crook's arrival Crazy Horse and his braves, camped not far away, joined into the fight, but they had arrived too late. American Horse and several of his warriors were trapped in a cave and refused to yield. The surrender came only when American Horse was mortally wounded. Casualties were few on either side of the conflict. Nevertheless, the U.S. army's victory at this engagement, known as the Battle of Slim Buttes, was small consolation after a disastrous summer's work.

Determined to resolve the Indian problem and accomplish his assigned task, Crook ordered yet a third campaign. This one was a winter march. The Powder River Expedition was launched from Fort Fetterman on November 14, 1876. Crook's command was impressive: six companies of the Fourth, two of the Fifth, two of the Third, and one of Second Cavalry; along with six companies of the Ninth, two of the Fourteenth, and three of the Twenty-third Infantry, and four companies of the Fourth Artillery (serving as infantry) plus guides and Indian scouts. When Dull Knife's band of Cheyenne were discovered on Crazy Woman's Fork near the foothills of the Big Horn Mountains, Crook dispatched Colonel Ranald Mackenzie with the cavalry and scouts to strike the village.

After a cold night's march Mackenzie's command attacked the Cheyenne in the early morning light of November 25, routing the occupants and burning the village of 205 lodges full of the tribe's winter provisions, blankets, robes, clothing, weapons, and ammunition. They captured a herd of 705 ponies; many more were killed or wounded during the battle and ensuing night. That night was bitter cold, creating extreme hardship for the homeless Cheyenne as they struggled to survive without food or shelter. Total Indian losses are unknown, but thirty bodies remained on the battlefield. The army lost one officer, Lieutenant John A. McKinney of the Fourth Cavalry, and six enlisted men. Twenty-five men were wounded, sixteen severely enough to require immediate evacuation to Fort Fetterman, where they arrived on December 6.[45]

During December the members of the Powder River Expedition returned to the friendly confines of Fort Fetterman. Those stationed elsewhere soon returned to their duty stations for the remainder of the winter. With this last campaign successfully over, the Indian wars in the vicinity of Fort Fetterman diminished.

While these troops were on the campaign, Fort Fetterman's garrison had been stripped to a skeleton force and Indian raiding parties had harassed travelers, freighters, and ranches throughout the area. Perhaps the most dramatic raid, which became known as the Indian Fight on the Elkhorn (also called the Heck Reel Fight), occurred on August 1, 1876. The story was told by Sylvester Sherman, a member of a wagon train owned by George Powell, whose freighting company supplied military forts in central Wyoming. Heck Reel was the wagon master. Sherman's story starts in Cheyenne:

> On the 5th day of July 1876, we commenced to hire men and load up with government freight for Fort Fetterman. We had to hire all kinds of men from good bull-whackers and Mexicans down to a few long haired Missourians.
>
> We broke camp at the lake above Cheyenne the morning of the 7th of July 1876 and traveled the old road Cheyenne to the Black Hills until we got to Bordeaux, and from there we traveled the cut-off by the way of the Billy Bacon ranch on the Laramie River, and by the old Tobe Miller ranch on Cottonwood Creek, and by the St. Dennis ranch on Horseshoe, and we struck the old Fetterman road, from Fort Laramie to Fort Fetterman.
>
> At Elkhorn [Creek], we were to camp for the night. The hill at Elkhorn was a long hard hill, and both Throstle and I stayed back until the last wagon was up it. Each wagon had one trail wagon and some had two. After we had got up the hill, we rode out ahead of the teams to look over the road. When we were about three hundred yards from the lead team (we were traveling along a divide, Elkhorn on the left and some deep draws to our right) when it seemed that a hundred Indians jumped out of a draw shooting at us.
>
> Three bullets struck Throstle while only one struck me. He was next to and just a little ahead of me. He threw up both hands and said "Oh! My God," and fell.

*Crook's third campaign into Powder River country and the Big Horn Mountains was launched from Fort Fetterman on November 14, 1876. This illustration by a* Harper's Weekly *artist shows the columns crossing the Platte as they headed north from Fort Fetterman.* (Harper's Weekly, December 16, 1876)

Every Indian yelled and made a dash to cut me off from the wagon train. It was a close race as Throstle's horse made a wild rush for the train, and the Indians whipping, shooting and yelling caused both horses to circle instead of running straight. I had no time to shoot as I used both feet and both hands to whip with.

As they came closer to the train they pulled away a little but kept up a constant fire at the men running up and down the teams, until they shot Irish Pete through the leg, and he yelled out cussing as loud as he could, "Corral the wagons, Ves, or they will kill every one of us."

Sylvester Sherman took his words seriously:

Then I came to myself and called to the lead man to corral, and all of the good men were driving the lead teams and knew what to do and in a short time we were corralled. In the mean time the men were each shooting at them with a six shooter, as they came up closer…

They seemed to have good guns and plenty of ammunition, and while they did not kill any of us, they were doing lots of damage to the work cattle and the few saddle horses we had. A Mexican was driving next to the last wagon and a long haired Missourian the last team. The Missourian saw that there was no show to get his team in so left it and came on up to the Mexican…and whacked in on it.

It looked for a while as if the Indians would get him but he shot with one hand and whacked the bulls with the other. After we got in a few good rounds with our guns they fell back and would only come up in sight. We laid there all day, and as night came on they came up to the wagon which was left on the outside, at about three hundred yards distance, that was loaded with ten thousand pounds of bacon, and forty kegs of beer, and threw off the beer rolled it down a long hill and set the bacon on fire.

The blaze seemed to reach two hundred feet high and we could have seen to have picked up a pin in the corral. We knew that if they could get on a hill and look down on us they could see the situation, and charge us after dark, but they seemed to be afraid of us, and never even shot into the camp.

It was probably a sleepless night for the freighters, with the blaze illuminating the wreckage:

> …The next morning we unyoked our oxen and drove then back to Elkhorn to water, while others went to hunt for the teams that were hitched to the [burned] wagon. The wheel oxen were burned to death, and the next team was burned some, but they had pulled the front wheels out from the wagon, and five teams were grazing around still hitched together.
>
> We broke camp about eleven o'clock, drove the lead wagon up to where Throstle had fallen, and found that they had taken his clothes, scalped him and cut out his heart. We laid him on a tarpaulin, on top of the groceries and covered him…
>
> We camped at La Bonte that night, and on to Fort Fetterman the next day. While we gave poor Throstle a good decent burial, there was no ceremony.[46]

The authorities at Fetterman were notified of the attack on August 2. A dispatch the next day stated that thirty Indians were involved; the wagon master was killed and another man was wounded.[47] As for the cargo, eighty-two sacks of bacon, sixty-four sacks of flour, and twenty water kegs were destroyed.[48]

The same Indians who attacked Heck Reel's train struck again four days later at Bridger's Ferry, threatening Fetterman's hay contractor, but without casualties.[49] They raided another crew there on October 7. John Ottens, one of George Powell's hay crew, was seriously wounded in the shoulder but his comrades drove the raiders off, killing two of twenty-three. Ottens died of his wounds eleven days later.[50] Another supply train was attacked on October 16, en route from the Cheyenne military depot to Fetterman. This train was involved in three separate actions, one on Horseshoe and twice on Elkhorn Creek, where the wagon master was wounded.[51]

Indian attacks in the Fetterman vicinity ceased after the October 16, 1876, encounter. Peace finally had arrived along the Platte River as winter approached. With the cessation of fighting to the north in 1877, Fort Fetterman had fulfilled its main mission as a military post. But the War Department waited until peace with the Indians was certain before issuing orders to abandon the post five years later.

# Garrison Life
## at Fort Fetterman

CHAPTER

# 6

FORT FETTERMAN CAN perhaps be seen as a microcosm of American frontier society during its fifteen years as a military post. It was at the center of a far-flung community of sorts, where frontiersmen and women mingled with soldiers and Indians. Within the fort's confines lived officers, enlisted men, and civilian government employees such as blacksmiths, laundresses, carpenters, and other tradesmen and artificers. Gathered around it were those who provided other essential services and products—firewood, hay, dairy products, and fresh meats—to the garrison or anyone else who needed them. Most of these entrepreneurs were under contract with the U.S. government. Indians occasionally camped on the LaPrele Creek floodplain below the bluff occupied by the fort, temporarily adding to the local population. Numbers at the fort itself fluctuated, too, perhaps averaging about two hundred officers, enlisted men, and civilians at any one time. Soldiers, some with wives and families, came and then went when they were transferred, or resigned. Some even deserted. Government employees, too, came and went. The fort's population was an ever-changing melting pot on a harsh frontier.

On April 30, 1869, Major Dye—whose troops had been first at the post—was reassigned to Fetterman, replacing Colonel Henry W. Wessells as post commander. With him came a young first lieutenant, Anthony Wayne Vodges, and his wife Ada, whose diaries described their Indian visitors. On their arrival the Vodges shared quarters with Captain Caleb H. Carlton, but later they moved into quarters with Dye, of whom Mrs. Vodges said, "but for his kindness, I should have given up life."[1] She also wrote her first impression of the post:

> I am agreeably disappointed in Fetterman, at the looks of everything, after the dreadful stories that I have heard all winter. This day has been a splendid one, after two terrible ones we had, when we first started, &

*This illustration of Fort Fetterman, drawn around 1876, is by an unknown artist. (Courtesy Nebraska State Historical Society)* the looks of the post far surpassed anything, that I could have imagined for an extreme outpost as it now is.[2]

On August 17 Major Dye and his family left Fort Fetterman on a twenty-day leave of absence with permission to apply for a three-month extension.[3] Captain C.H. Carlton replaced him as post commander. Ada Vodges lamented their departure:

> Truly has some one said, "there is nothing half so sad *as life*." This separation of friends, this breaking up of ties, & old associations is almost too much for our frail bodies, with its tender and sensitive organizations, such have I found life in the parting from Mrs. Dye this morning, with whom I have lived for ten months, in the most delightful and agreeable manner. With her absence will go the only amusement which we could indulge in here, namely, that of croquet. For ten months we have played this game, through sunshine, & cloudy weather, mud & snow, nothing in nature seeming too severe, to bring us together. Truly has some one said "There is no union here of hearts, which finds not here, and the house, every time I turn my eyes in that direction, has so forlorn an appearance, that my heart comes up into my mouth, & my eyes fill with tears to overflow." Mrs. Dye's absence is but another bead added to my long string of regrets.[4]

On October 11, barely two months later, Captain Eugene Wells, Fourth Infantry, assumed command of the post.[5] By November 14, Mrs. Vodges noted, new recruits had arrived at the fort which "created quite an excitement at these ends of the earth."[6]

Most often the highest-ranking officer of the regiment assigned to a military post was designated post commander. When that officer was on leave, reassigned, or on duty elsewhere, the next most senior officer temporarily assumed command. In some instances a succession of junior officers took on the role until the post commander returned or was replaced. This constant changing of leadership often resulted in confusion for the post's occupants.

Over the next year and a half, Mrs. Vodges wrote tellingly of daily life at the garrison, which had plenty of grim moments. On December 22, a bizarre tragedy occurred in the quarters of Company H, Fourth Infantry. At about eleven o'clock that morning a Private Smith, relieved of guard duty, entered his barracks and sat down by the stove. He placed his rifle across his knees and, while drawing the hammer of the weapon, it slipped and discharged. That one bullet wounded three men nearby. Private John W. Keller was the first hit when the bullet passed through his upper thigh. It then severed one of Private McGuiness's fingers and lodged in the right knee of Private White. The bullet was removed successfully from White's knee, but Keller died of his wound several days later. He was buried on December 31.

Post records explained why the rifle was loaded:

> On the previous evening he [Smith] missed his gun from the Guard House arms rack and after careful search among the arms there in could not find it. He then informed the Sergeant of the Guard who on counting found an Extra Gun which he told Swift to take until his own was returned the next morning.[7]

Ordinarily the noncommissioned officers of the guard inspected all weapons to ensure the ammunition had been removed, but this safety action had not been carried out on that particular morning.

Ada Vodges recounted it tersely: "One of the soldiers who had just come off guard, was fussing with his gun in the quarters & he knew not that it was loaded, went off, wounding three men, one is thought will die. *Did die.*"[8]

Despite this sobering accident, Christmas night was festive: the post trader, Robert Wilson, gave a party for the officers and their families. Ada Vodges recorded: "… we had a nice time even though there were only two ladies present."[9]

On January 16, 1870, Mrs. Vodges wrote that the post had "The coldest weather we have had the whole winter. Water barrel frozen solid in the kitchen, and difficult to keep warm." She also maintained: "I have never felt such weather, the doors crack with cold, and the fires burn cold, and the outside world is obliterated with the heavy white frosty landscapes on the window panes. Until to day the weather has been all that one could wish for."[10]

The post journal of the same date likewise mentioned the cold weather:

> The water service was so hard that all the transportation at Post, nearly, was employed at it daily, and simultaneously. No other work except the care of the animals in the corral, and the usual guard duty, which latter

was so arranged as to obviate the exposure for more than one hour at a time of any sentenal to the extreme… Cold spell (-44) since Jan. 1 below zero—so cold only work done was getting wood supply for quarters and water for cooking.[11]

On the heels of the cold snap came an ever-so-common windstorm. Ada Vodges wrote on January 19: "A most terrific sand storm blowing, obscuring everything with its solution of dust. Not a clean spot in the house and the dust pouring in from every point of the compass. By degrees I am slowly, and surely being buried alive should it last long enough."[12] Ada's diary and the post records indicate that the entire winter and spring of 1870 was plagued by high winds and constant snow. There were a few respites; she wrote that March 9 was a "beautiful day overhead, and under foot, but very windy" and by March 30, Ada was playing croquet; in fact "the whole garrison" was playing the game. But such pleasures were few. By April 30, she wrote, "Arrived here one year ago today and long has the year seemed to me."[13]

Ada Vodges seemed to be a dog lover, but even that small pleasure was denied her that winter, when acting commander Captain Eugene Wells imposed General Order # 5 on January 17, 1870:

A tax of five dollars per head is hereby imposed on all dogs at this Post.

Those dogs for which this tax shall not have been paid by 12 M, noon, to-morrow will be killed.

The Post Treasurer is designated to receive this tax.

All bitches in heat running at large after the above named hour will be killed whether tax on them has been paid or not.

The Officer of the Day will carry out the provisions of this order, relating to the killing of dogs & bitches and will learn from the Post Treasurer the names of persons who have paid the specified tax.[14]

Distressed, Ada Vodges wrote in her diary:

This morning the 18th, Jan, 1870 an order was issued by the commanding officer to have all the dogs in the garrison shot, or their owners to pay a tax of five dollars, which the soldiers willingly did, and the proceeds amounted to a *hundred* dollars. Seven only had to suffer the penalty of the tyrannical order. I miss, greatly miss, their little faces, and the garrison already has a forlorn and deserted appearance. It was true happiness to watch them, after nights separation to see how glad they were to see each other, and how touchingly they expressed themselves in their little dog language. I have been mad all day about such an order being published, for if there is any thing that I do *love*, it is the kanine tribe.[15]

The following January saw some unusually balmy weather and the inhabitants of the post left their dwellings for fresh air. Ada Vodges wrote:

Like June all day. Went skating this A.M. leaving my house all in confusion because Dr. came for me, and said never would we have such another day for skating, so I went leaving a new man, to attend to the house. Discharged Sullivan this morning, as he went off on a spree, and was only too glad of any excuse to rid myself of such a horrid creature.[16]

Sullivan was an enlisted man serving as "striker" for Lieutenant Vodges.[17]

Lieutenant Vodges received a transfer on March 7, 1871, and he and his wife left Fort Fetterman and the West. Ada wrote: "The joyful news arrived this P.M. that we were to be ordered to Louisville, Ky, and I feel too happy ... never did I expect to hear such news."[18]

↶ ↷

The daily routine at a military post was strictly regimented. Throughout the day, soldiers and officers alike were summoned to work and drill by drum or bugle calls. In garrisons where many branches of service were stationed together, such as infantry, cavalry, and artillery, their duties varied. For example, the cavalry had stable call to groom their horses twice daily, generally in the morning and afternoon, while the infantry was called to a drill such as "school of the soldier" or perhaps summoned to longer hours of work details. The post commander set this schedule through a Post General Order and could adjust it at will.

A typical day began with reveille at daybreak, followed immediately by police call, which gave the men half an hour to dress, groom, and clean their quarters. Then breakfast (or mess) call was sounded and the men were allowed about one hour to eat. When sick (or surgeon) call sounded, soldiers who were ill could report to the medical officer, who would determine if they were fit for duty.

Then fatigue call mustered all soldiers not on other assignments to begin work required at the fort, such as policing the grounds, constructing and repairing buildings, and hauling water and rubbish. Meanwhile, others might be on detached service such as mail duty or logging in the mountains.

Generally about mid-morning the guard mount ceremony was called, beginning a twenty-four-hour vigil for the members of the new guard and ending a long day for the old guard.

The soldiers not called to fatigue were then summoned to drill: marching or the manual of arms. Those on fatigue either joined them or kept working, at the commander's discretion. Those still laboring were recalled at noon, when another mess call gave them about one hour to eat before returning to the schedule.

At one o'clock the men returned to fatigue duty. Then around two o'clock another drill call summoned some of the soldiers, while those remaining on fatigue were recalled at about four-thirty. With the five o'clock mess call, the men took their evening meal, then enjoyed some free time before reporting for the retreat roll call generally at or before sunset. This ceremony could include a full-dress parade and inspection, or simply a roll call to ensure that all were present or accounted for at some other duty. Then the soldiers had more time for themselves until tattoo summoned them to their barracks. Generally a half-hour later, the final scheduled call for the night was taps (extinguish lights) when all lights in the enlisted men's quarters were doused.

ﾝ　ﾍ

From the early 1860s until the turn of the century, the daily fixed ration for a U.S. soldier consisted of either twelve ounces of pork or bacon, or one pound four ounces of salt or fresh beef. To this was added either one pound six ounces of soft bread or flour, or one pound of hard bread (the infamous hardtack), or one pound four ounces of cornmeal. Finally, according to the Revised Army Regulations of 1863, for every one hundred rations issued, the following supplemented the soldiers' diet:

> Fifteen pounds of beans or peas, and ten pounds of rice or hominy.
> Ten pounds of green coffee, or eight pounds of roasted (or roasted and ground) coffee, or one pound and eight ounces of tea.
> Fifteen pounds of sugar.
> Four quarts of vinegar.
> One pound and four ounces of adamantine or star candles.
> Four pounds of soap.

Three pounds and twelve ounces of salt.

Four ounces of pepper.

Thirty pounds of potatoes (when available).

One quart of molasses.

Later, in the late 1880s, the U.S. Army's commissary would vary the ration with canned tomatoes, beans, and dried vegetables. During Fort Fetterman's existence, however, these were not offered to common soldiers. If they wanted such non-issue foodstuffs, they had to produce or buy their own. As a result many companies sold back to the commissary a portion of their daily ration, investing this money into a "company fund." Supplements such as dairy products, fresh eggs, and vegetables could then be purchased from the commissary, civilians at the post, or the post trader. Ada Vodges recalled on September 4, 1869, a truck farmer brought fresh produce from Cheyenne that had recently arrived from California. The produce included fresh fruits, potatoes, onions, and cabbages.[19] Surely it was a treat: fresh produce, especially fruit, was a rarity at more isolated military posts such as Fort Fetterman. Some officers required their troops to grow company gardens, but this was met with at best occasional success at posts of the northern plains due to drought and insects.[20] Fort Fetterman would experience both.

As a foundation of the soldier's diet, the army was expected to provide good-quality bread. At isolated frontier posts like Fort Fetterman, this was not a simple task. There were no civilian bakeries; bread had to be made at the post by the soldiers. The individual company mess kitchen ovens were too small; bake houses were needed to supply the entire garrison. Two departments shared in this task: the quartermaster department was charged with the construction and repairs to the bake houses, while the commissary was responsible for providing the baked goods or their ingredients.

At this time the army had no official positions of bakers and cooks. At Fetterman, enlisted men were assigned to the bakery for ten days on extra duty; these post bakers and their assistants produced the entire garrison's bread. Most were untrained privates who loathed the duty, but occasionally an enlisted man with prior civilian experience as a baker was found. The quality of the bread ration thus depended on the attitude and skill of the baker. When a competent baker was found, the extra duty rotation was often ignored and this man could keep his job for some time.[21]

To vary the soldiers' diet, gardening was attempted at various times, with varying degrees of success. The first documented experiment at Fort Fetterman was reported in 1869 in the post journal: "April 28 — Began work on Post Garden. Cool day," and on May 18, "Planting of gardens completed."[22] Those gardens' success is unknown, but the next post commander, Colonel Alexander Chambers, felt that gardens could be productive with proper irrigation.[23] For the 1870 growing season, he directed that the post gardens be located west of the fort, with irrigation ditches watered by LaPrele Creek. Crops were planted and placed under the charge of enlisted men. The post surgeon experimented with "hot-beds" and was delighted to report "The first *Lettuce* of the season" was eaten in the hospital on May 28,[24] while Ada Vodges planted flowers around her quarters.[25] By December of the next year, a small adobe shed at the gardens housed supplies and tools.

But it was not until March 1872 that a large-scale agricultural plan was launched; it took two years to bear fruit. A dam was built on LaPrele Creek and the irrigation ditches were improved. Huge piles of manure for fertilizer were hauled from the quartermaster corral's manure dumps.[26] Seeds and a plow were delivered from Cheyenne in March 1874, so that planting could commence with the arrival of spring.[27] Finally, during the last days of May, the soil was prepared and planting was completed.

As predicted, the gardens flourished, yielding small quantities of peas, onions, beans, and cabbage throughout the summer.[28] But this success was short-lived. Grasshoppers ravaged the next year's crops for two days in August and destroyed the entire garden.[29]

After this disappointment, efforts diminished. The extensive irrigation system was allowed to deteriorate to the point where even small gardens could barely survive. In 1879, post commander Captain Coates wrote, "onions can not be grown and potatoes only in small quantities, not sufficient to supply the garrison due to poor irrigation."[30] J.S. Mason made the last reference to agriculture in an inspection report on September 5, 1879: "Post Gardens are very successful here when Grasshoppers do not get away with them. They require irrigation."[31]

While gardening, hunting, and trout fishing occupied the troops during the growing season, winter was a time to prepare for the spring and summer activities and needs. Ice was needed to cool meat lockers and ice chests during the summer months. On December 26, 1870, the Platte

River had iced over to the depth of twelve to fourteen inches and the soldiers began cutting ice for the ice houses. Ice cutting was completed by January 19.[32]

৶  ৵

As early as 1802, Congress recognized the need for laundresses at military posts to serve officers and their families as well as enlisted men. Many laundresses were married to soldiers, and their authorization to receive rations and quarters greatly augmented the family salary. Most of these women have been characterized as of Irish descent; industrious, red-armed women ever ready for a fight. Captain Charles King, who wrote a series of novels about military life, described a washerwoman he knew as: "A little, old Irish camp-woman... She had much true Irish wit, and her small, withered face was full of fun. A thick, close-fitting white muslin cap with a deep ruffle hanging from it added to her comical expression."[33] At times she might withhold her services; at Camp Hallack, Wyoming, the post laundress refused to do wash for officers' wives. Sometimes such stubbornness earned a washerwoman her discharge. Such a case was described in an 1877 letter sent by the post adjutant to the commanding officer of Company F, Fourth Infantry, via Cantonment Reno:

> ...laundress Kelly of your Company having been drawing the regular allowances as laundress up to the present time, at this post, (Fetterman) being unemployed and reported fit for duty by the Post Surgeon, being directed to act as laundress for Major C. H. Carlton Third Cavalry, and Lt. Bubb of your Company declined to perform either of the duties ordered, and was therefore deprived of her rations as laundress and ordered to leave the reservation. This woman was rationed to include the 10th of May.[34]

Regulations required that enlisted men pay the laundress on every pay muster. Captain King acknowledges this: "one of the unwritten laws of the rank and file in the good old days [was] to square with the laundress if you didn't square with anybody else."[35]

Between 1878 and 1883, Congress phased out army laundresses. They no longer were placed on company rolls entitling them to quarters and rations, although a soldier's laundress-wife could remain on the roster until her husband finished his enlistment. This new congressional act was issued as General Order Number 37, Headquarters of the Army on June 19, 1878, and apparently was a bit ambiguous. Captain E. M. Coates, commander of Fort Fetterman, wondered whether it meant "only to prohibit Laundresses from being furnished with transportation when troops change station or is it the intention of the law to abolish Laundresses altogether, except the wives of Enlisted men now in the Service, and they only until the close of their husband's present term of Service... Will the issue of ration to a Laundress of a Company in Garrison be allowed hereafter, even though she be not the wife of a soldier?"[36] In reality, these hardy women were generally recognized as "acceptable adjuncts to a garrison in post, and [were] of no little service outside the strict letter of the law."[37] Laundresses, dubbed "Hay Bags" by some soldiers, remained an essential part of the army during the nineteenth century, despite the efforts of the leadership in the military.

Aside from the laundresses, Fort Fetterman also employed a few women at the fort hospital. On May 31, 1870, hospital matron Ellen Ryan, a mere child of fifteen, was married to Sergeant Dague of Company A, Fourth Infantry. The service was performed by Reverend McFoley, a Catholic priest from Cheyenne who had traveled with the paymaster to Fetterman to officiate at the wedding.[38]

⌒  ⌒

Other than Indians, precious few visitors came Fetterman's way. But August 15, 1870, saw the arrival of a Smithsonian Institute-sponsored scientific and exploration party led by Dr. F. V. Hayden, en route to the Great Salt Lake via the Sweetwater River drainage. The expedition camped on LaPrele Creek for five days. This party included the following prominent men:

| | |
|---|---|
| F. V. Hayden, Chief | James Stevenson, Superintendent |
| Cyrus Thomas, Entomologist | Henry Elliot, Artist |
| R. Gifford, Painter | S. A. Bartlett, Commissary |
| W. H. Jackson, Photographer | I. W. Beaman, Topographer |
| C. P. Carrington, Ichthyologist | A. S. Ford, Mineralogist |
| C. T. Tumbull, Anatomist | H. Schmidt, Ornithologist[39] |

Evidently William H. Jackson, the famous photographer and artist who was traveling with Dr. Hayden's party, had arrived early to document Fort Fetterman and vicinity. On June 18, he traveled to "natural bridge and other places." This rock formation in LaPrele Canyon, carved by the creek through the limestone, was a favorite picnic site for the garrison.[40]

Jackson both photographed and drew views of the fort, as seen here and at the end of Chapter Two. The Hayden party surveyed the surrounding area for several days; Ada Vodges's diary acknowledged their visit on August 18.

༄     ༅

With few visitors, little female company, and frequent tedium and discomfort, it is little wonder that some men turned to alcohol. Alcohol has always plagued the military, especially in isolated posts such as Fetterman. Officers tried to limit the amount of beer or whiskey served to soldiers at a given time, but disreputable local businessmen regularly seemed to circumvent the rules or ignore them entirely. Such was the case at Fort Fetterman in its first year, 1867, when the post adjutant wrote to post traders Robert Wilson and Charles Cobb:

> I am directed by the Commanding Officer to inform you that the order with regard to the sale of whiskey to the Enlisted men at this Post is suspended until further orders and hereafter no Enlisted man will be allowed to purchase a drink of liquor unless he has an order for the same from his Company Commander and the Post Sutler will be sure and satisfy himself that all orders presented are genuine.[41]

By the next summer, liquor restrictions had been relaxed; Wilson and Cobb were told, "instead of two (2), the Sutler is permitted to sell three (3) glasses of Beer with the interval prescribed in the communication from these Headquarters to Mr. F. D. Yates in charge of the Bar and Billiard Saloon..."[42]

But it seems that Mr. Yates, the post traders' saloonkeeper, ignored this new regulation. On July 9, post commander Dye issued another letter via the adjutant, Lieutenant Rufus Brown:

> I am directed by the Post Commander to say that Major Gordon informed him this morning that some of his men were drunk and that they had a bucket of beer in their camp Yesterday.
>
> Mr. Yates sold some weeks ago a bucket full to a soldier after it had been ordered that beer be sold only by the drink.
>
> He was told then very clearly not to do the like again. There is no place to get beer I believe excepting from Mr. Yates or the brewery. The Commanding Officer wishes you to learn if possible where this beer came from.
>
> The Brewery of course should sell none under any circumstances.[43]

*This photograph of Fort Fetterman was taken by William Henry Jackson in 1870. The view is from "cemetery hill," southeast of the fort. The North Platte River can be seen below the bluff in the right center of the photo.* (Courtesy National Archives)

This second warning, too, failed, forcing Dye on August 24 to order the traders to "shut up your establishment. You will dispose of no more beer or ale at or in the vicinity of this Post to Soldiers or Citizens. Moreover you will inform the person, who persists to violate the orders, that he must leave the Post at once."[44] By September 28, the matter had been straightened out, and beer again was being served by the glass to the enlisted men.[45]

Earlier that summer a civilian beef contractor named Dickinson had been found drunk and refused to supply meat to the garrison. He was arrested for intoxication in a military establishment and sent to Fetterman's guardhouse. On July 1, Dickinson was granted his freedom and escorted from the post, ordered by Major Dye never to return.[46]

On June 7 of the following year the post commander sent a letter to Wilson and Cobb restricting liquor sales to certain enlisted men who tended to get drunk immediately after the paymaster had paid the troops.[47] Several of the men belonged to Companies E and A, Fourth Infantry, including privates John Taylor, James Nolan, Patrick Leary, and John Smith. These men left the post and found a "friendly Indian camp" where they assaulted the Indians and knocked down their lodge, making them flee for their lives. The soldiers were arrested and sentenced to forfeit their pay and spend fifteen days at hard labor under command of the guard.[48]

In October the post commander, still seeking the right balance on the alcohol issue, notified Wilson and Cobb that although they could serve the enlisted ranks whiskey by the drink and beer by the drink or the gallon, "every precaution must be taken to prevent drunkenness, which breach of discipline will not go unpunished."[49] The problem continued under the new post trader, Ephraim Tillotson. On April 20, 1871, the post commander scolded him for letting a quartermaster employee get drunk and "riotous in your store." A day earlier Private Horse of the Fourteenth Infantry had been arrested for drunkenness and the post commander had admonished Tillotson, "similar occurrences during the past few weeks indicated that the letter, as well as the spirit of existing instructions regulating sales of liquor to enlisted men and civilian employees have been violated by persons in your employ."[50]

Soldiers also visited the Indian camps near the post for recreation. In January 1874, the post surgeon noted that

> A party of soldiers with some citizens and negroes returned from a night excursion to an Indian camp whooping and yelling and firing their pistols. One of their number, an officer's servant, on this occasion shot himself in the foot and was admitted to the hospital.[51]

This drunken spree was not isolated to this group; the acting sergeant major was arrested for getting drunk and firing at another soldier.[52] In March the post surgeon described one payday as a "battle" whose casualties included three stabbings, two lacerated wounds to the scalp and face, several black eyes, and uncounted minor injuries.[53] Again the post commander chastised the post trader and threatened to close the bar if the drunkenness continued.[54] At least once a year between 1874 and 1877, the post trader was warned about problems with selling alcohol to soldiers and civilians. But with the assignment of a new post trader, E. K. Nichols, in August 1880, alcohol abuse seems to have tapered off, official correspondence making no note of the problem thereafter.

✍ ❧

Excessive drinking and associated adventures did not represent the majority of the post's population. Most officers and enlisted men sought more subdued forms of recreation: hunting, baseball, gymnastic exercises, picnics, exploring parties, and theatrical plays. Excursions to the "natural bridge" mentioned by William Henry Jackson were a frequent attraction.

Hunting seemed to be a favorite pastime of officers and enlisted men, and also provided meat to supplement the military rations. Hunting parties went out weekly from the post searching for game and fowl. One of the West's last recorded buffalo hunts occurred in July 1869 near Fort Fetterman, led by Major Dye.[55] The following winter Captain Almond B. Wells, Lieutenant Patrick H. Breslin, the post guide, and twenty enlisted men went on a hunt, bagging eighty-three elk and nine deer in a week.[56]

Holidays, too, were welcome diversions. Independence Day offered a break from all but the necessary duties. On this day in 1870, there was no ceremonial observance but the soldiers played baseball and enjoyed the "first performance of the Dramatic Corps" in the evening. The surprising feature was the lack of intoxication by the garrison.[57] The 1871 July Fourth celebration was more official. It began with the firing of a twenty-one gun salute at 4:15 A.M. At six that morning the troops "paraded and marched to a previously prepared locality about two miles up the Creek [LaPrele] on the left bank where the day was passed in various sports, and prize games, races, shooting at targets and etc. The 'declaration' was read by Sergt. Stewart, Co. F, 14th [Infantry]. The Officers and their wives participated—the troops returned to the Post about retreat. In the evening a display of fire-works closed the day, which was happily concluded without an accident or a single unpleasant feature."[58]

The 1875 celebration was not so lucky. A national salute of thirty-seven guns was fired by using two artillery pieces, and Private Ferguson, Company I, Fourth Infantry was wounded when the cannon he was manning prematurely discharged. The cartridge and ramrod were forced through his hands causing severe "but not dangerous" lacerated wounds to his right hand and slighter injuries to his left.[59]

Christmas was also an eagerly awaited time of rejoicing and social gathering. On December 15, 1880, a special wagon train was ordered to leave Fetterman the following Friday, to obtain "any supplies which the officers or families may need at the post for the Christmas holiday."[60] A post Christmas tree with "presents for all the children at the post" was lighted at six on Christmas Eve. "All men, women and children at the post are invited to attend."[61]

Through the years baseball gained popularity within the military, as a sport building *esprit de corps*. However, in 1869, while the parade ground was being grassed, no games of any kind were allowed in front of the barracks. They had to be played outside the plank fence surrounding the post or behind the mess halls.[62] On several occasions during the 1870s Fetterman's companies played against each other. Over at Fort Laramie, Lieutenant Emmet Crawford of the Third Cavalry established a "Base Ball Club" and in August 1872, two games were played with the "Fetterman Club." Fetterman's team lost both games.[63] Adding insult to injury, orders were issued the next month that "all games of ball must hereafter be played outside the garrison enclosure" due to too many broken windows.[64]

Winter's cold discouraged outdoor sports, but ice skating and sleigh rides were popular. So were theatrical performances. Occasional plays by professional touring troupes and amateur plays acted by the soldiers and their wives were the vogue, even inspiring the soldiers to construct a theater building. On January 15, 1874, the first performance—a minstrel show—was given in the new theater. The post clerk deemed it "good" with "quite good" scenery. There was an encore performance near the end of the month.[65] The soldiers produced several more plays and minstrel shows that year and in May of 1875 the Pardeys, professional actors, gave three shows at Fetterman.[66]

Dances, known as balls or hops, were presented by officers, enlisted men, and civilians. Local ranchers and their families were frequent guests at these dances. They often spent the night at an officer's home and returned to their isolated ranches the following day. Dances given by officers were generally restricted to officers and their families and friends, but the enlisted men traditionally invited the post commander and their company officers. One such dance in 1875 spawned a scuffle which landed Private Thomas J. Mason in the guardhouse. The post commander wrote:

Company "C" was authorized to give a ball the night before Christmas. All officers and ladies of the garrison were there, for a short time in the early part of the evening. Everything was properly conducted and orderly. Private Mason was a member of the Post Guard and was permitted to visit the ball for an hour whilst not on post. Upon his appearance in the room he became boisterous, and was requested by Private Martin, one of the floor managers, to be quiet, and upon his refusal, an attempt was made to eject him; he resisting, Private Martin struck him a blow. Private Mason immediately went to the quarters of his company, broke open a chest of one of the Sergeants and took there-from a loaded revolver, returned to the Theatre building, called Martin — who happened to be outside of the building — and upon receiving an answer, remarked "Your time to die has come," and thereupon fired inflicting a wound as reported by the Surgeon.[67]

Unfortunately the records do not reveal the nature of Private Martin's wound, except that it was serious enough to discharge him from the service. The post commander requested that the severest charges be brought against Private Mason.[68]

᷒   ᷒

Death — by disease, accident, or crime — was never far from daily life at Fort Fetterman.

At least two deaths occurred before the freak rifle accident that Ada Vodges noted in 1869. On June 22, 1868, Major Dye wrote to the commanding officer of the Eighteenth Infantry, stationed at Fort D. A. Russell, that Private Joseph Jordon of Company K was found floating in the Platte River on June 6, an evident drowning victim, and Private Joseph Hoffman of Company D died of inflammation of the bowels on June 19. Both men were members of the Eighteenth Infantry Regiment.[69]

Other diseases, too, took lives at Fetterman. Rafael Gallegos was admitted to the post hospital on February 24, 1871, and died of gastric fever two days later. He left a Sioux wife and four children.[70] The next month the post surgeon reported that an influenza epidemic had taken the life of a civilian associated with the post. Private Cornelius Cameron, Company F, Fourth Infantry, was admitted into the hospital on February 2, 1875, suffering from mental "unsoundness." The post surgeon kept him under observation until April when he was sent to the insane asylum in Washington, D.C.[71]

Accidental death claimed other garrison members. Another drowning occurred on June 10, 1871, when Private Sullivan of Company C, Fourteenth Infantry fell victim to the Platte River. He drowned while bathing after retreat call; his body was found the next day on a sand bar two miles below the post.[72] Private John Davis Company C, Third Cavalry drowned two years later while fishing on the Platte, and like Private

Sullivan, his body was recovered on a sand bar three miles below the post the following day.[73]

Ordnance Sergeant McGaughlin and Hospital Steward Walsh incurred injuries in the dispensary on September 26, 1872, when the chemicals they were working with exploded. Walsh's left hand was seriously maimed and he lost two fingers.[74] Private John O. Ward, Company C, Fourth Infantry severely wounded himself while on extra duty as post butcher in December 1874.[75] The post journal reported that a Miss Ella Harrington committed suicide by shooting herself through the head on October 14, 1876. No explanation was given, nor was there any information concerning her affiliation with the post.[76] Quartermaster teamster James Daley committed suicide on July 23, 1877, but left no clue as to why he took his own life, nor any other personal information.[77] In September 1877, Benjamin Wilson, a cowboy from northern Texas, accidentally and fatally shot himself with his own revolver while intoxicated. At the time of his death Wilson was working south of the post at the Six Mile Ranch owned by cattle dealer George Hadley of Big Springs, Nebraska.[78]

Some deaths, of course, were calculated. The Fetterman area had its share of outlaws and criminals, and the military heard demands for justice from both civilians and those subject to military authority. At least three murders occurred at or near Fort Fetterman, all involving civilians. The earliest known case was in 1867, when post commander Wessells reported that he was detaining a murderer named Morrissey; his victim was a civilian. Major Wessells sent the accused to Fort Laramie where he was turned over to civil authorities.[79] Eight years later, in August 1874, a fight broke out between civilians Bob Yeager and James H. Payne while they were working for Malcolm Campbell at his wood camp eight miles from the post on LaPrele Creek. Payne fired at Yeager and missed; then the two fired simultaneously, which resulted in Payne's death. Yeager surrendered himself to Campbell and was taken to the post and interned in the guardhouse. On August 24, Yeager was sent to Laramie City and turned over to Sheriff Thomas Dayton.[80]

In November 1875, an attempted murder was recorded when a man named Cully shot at another civilian named Roe, wounding him. Roe was admitted to the post hospital to recover and Cully was placed in the guardhouse to be later tried by a civilian court.[81]

⌁ ⌁

After the Indian Wars of 1876, the area surrounding Fort Fetterman began to attract settlers. Not all of them were scrupulous. The population was diverse, with Indians, ranchers, entrepreneurs, and outlaws often working at cross-purposes. Many settlers engaged in ranching or businesses such as the so-called hog ranches, which sold liquor and offered prostitutes to soldiers and civilians alike. Many of the latter establishments were operated by holdup men or rustlers, far from the reach of civil law. One such gang operated in the hills six miles south of the post, stealing government and Indian stock. All the military's efforts to arrest them failed as "they received warning from their friends among the Ranchmen."[82]

In September 1878, the post commander received a telegram that a "band of thieves" had stolen fifteen horses from the Nobles ranch north of Green River City and were driving them east past Independence Rock, about 120 miles west of the fort. They had also robbed the mail and had $25,000 in gold brick and gold dust. The civilian authorities guessed they were headed toward Fort McKinney and asked if Fetterman troops could intercept and arrest them. General Crook authorized the post commander to act immediately. It was discovered that the outlaws were headed toward Pumpkin Buttes where they had a hidden camp, but they eluded capture this time. This gang generally operated between Deadwood and Fort McKinney, stealing stock from one fort and reselling it in the other. Then, on September 27, the gang robbed the mail between Fort Fetterman and Fort McKinney. The robbery gained them no money, but they did take the arms and horses of the two Fifth Cavalrymen escorting the mail. On May 16, 1879, the army caught two of the desperados after a brief skirmish and turned them over to U.S. Deputy Marshal Snider.[83]

Fetterman soldiers were also alerted to watch for the outlaw group of Bill Davis, Jim Mann, Big Nose George, Tom Reed, Jack Campbell, Frank James (alias McKinney Sandy), Sam Kelley, and Cully Gime. These men were wanted for the robbery and murder of Sheriff Deputies Robert Widdowfield and H. H. Vinson, whom they had ambushed and killed near Elk Mountain on August 19, 1878. Stealing the deputies' horses and saddles, the outlaws had headed into Powder River country on the Dry Fork of the Cheyenne River and holed up on the John Erwin ranch.[84] Big Nose George Parrott (whose real name was George Francis Warden) was caught and, after he tried to escape, he was lynched outside Rawlins, Wyoming.[85]

The notorious Wyoming outlaw William Chambers, alias "Persimmon Bill," also operated in the Fetterman area. Known as a holdup man, he ventured into any criminal activities he found profitable. In early March 1876, Chambers and a man named Brown stole four ponies from the Indian camp of Arapaho Chief Black Coal. Sergeant Patrick Sullivan of Fetterman's Company F, Fourth Infantry, was ordered to help the Indians retrieve their stock. Sullivan and the Indians overtook the outlaws and retrieved two of the horses without violence.

But as Sullivan was returning to the post, he was murdered by Chambers. Chambers then stole Sullivan's horse and rifle and escaped to the hills to the south. Civilian James McGrew witnessed the murder and apparently reported it to the post commander. For his trouble, McGrew was incarcerated in the guardhouse for protection as a witness.

The following night more horses were taken from the Arapaho, who retaliated by stealing six horses from an unsuspecting civilian. The military was unable to pursue the outlaws, and they made their escape.

On March 8 Chambers's partner, Brown, was captured with one of the stolen horses and confined at Fetterman until the U. S. marshal took him away for trial. In the meantime, Chambers took the remainder of the horses and left the area. On March 26, he was reported in the vicinity of the Spotted Tail Agency. He eluded all of the military's pursuits, but eventually, Persimmon Bill Chambers was captured and hanged.[86]

Horse rustling was commonplace; the garrison also helped federal and territorial peace officers arrest horse thieves operating in the Fetterman vicinity during the later 1870s. One thief presented himself as a U.S. deputy marshal, traded a government mule to a civilian living near the post, then traveled toward Fort Laramie. The duped civilian reported the exchange to the post commander, describing the thief as "about five feet eight inches, Dark, Sandy beard, weight one hundred and sixty pounds— Has a dark bay horse and light bay pony, left hind foot white, branded V left shoulder."[87]

Some crimes seemed to lack any rationale. On March 4, 1880, Frank Peacock, who owned a ranch one mile north of the post, was shot and killed by Robert Wilson for an unknown reason. Peacock was buried in the post cemetery.[88] In August 1881 James Bridger (not to be confused with the famous mountain man and scout) was killed by William McFarland. This senseless death occurred over an argument about "mashed potatoes" at a boarding house at Fort Fetterman run by a Mrs. John Ward. Bridger pulled his gun on McFarland but the latter was quicker and shot Bridger while he sat at the table.[89]

〜 〜

Criminal activity was not confined to civilians, however. Soldiers also disobeyed the law. One infraction stood out in particular—nationwide. In the thirty-two-year period between 1866 and 1898, nearly one-third of all frontier army soldiers deserted their military posts. The Secretary of War noted in his annual report of 1877: "The life of the private soldier is a life of dull and monotonous routine, of which it is natural, if not inevitable, that men of spirit and ambition should weary."[90]

Fort Fetterman was no exception. Captain Van Vliet, commander of Company C, Third Cavalry, was stationed there between 1872 and 1874. In an 1874 letter he asked General George Ruggles to reassign his troop, due to the high rate of desertion. He told why the common soldier might want to leave Fort Fetterman:

> …No opportunity offers for procuring fresh vegetables and gardens are a failure. There is no *female society* for enlisted men, and the duty upon a single company of Cavalry has been more severe than anywhere in this Department. The enlisted men of the company are becoming very much dissatisfied, as they look upon being kept so long at this post (the worst in the Dept.) As an unmerited punishment upon a company which has done more severe duty than any other company of the same regiment.
>
> Whenever men get to the R. R. There are some desertions caused by dread of returning to this post. We cannot change human nature, and being deprived from intercourse with women is, in my opinion, one of the greatest causes of desertion…[91]

Catching deserters proved quite difficult in an era before identification documents and rapid communication. Generally the fort dispatched a patrol to apprehend an escapee, especially if he had stolen government property. It would seem the property was considered more important than the deserter! Further efforts were restricted to telegraphing a description to surrounding military posts. Very seldom was either tactic successful. Mr. Clay, the telegraph operator at Medicine Bow Station, reported that he had no instructions to arrest deserters and that soldiers were permitted to ride on the railroad trains by simply paying their fare, without showing orders or furlough authorizations.[92] Desertion was frustrated to some degree by Fetterman's remoteness; even the Union Pacific railroad was sixty-five miles away. But sometimes unsavory civilians assisted an escapee, who might then join their ranks to prey on the military and civil population.

Punishment for desertion varied, depending on the circumstances and if the man was a "good soldier." Imprisonment in a federal penitentiary was the harshest, while most men were sentenced to hard labor under guard and incarcerated in the post guardhouse.

Fetterman's first desertion was recorded on August 14, 1867, just a month after Dye and his men arrived on the plateau: two cavalrymen assigned from Fort Reno disappeared after they reached the post.[93] The next year, would-be deserter Private Williams of Company A, Fourth Infantry, was suffering his own hell back at the fort by wearing a ball and chain. On May 30, 1868, the post adjutant directed the officer of the day, Captain G. H. Dost, to have the restriction moved from one leg to the other because "The one is now lame and it is necessary that he wear the Irons to prevent his escape, he has deserted twice already."[94] Private Charles H. Smith, another escapee, suffered a worse fate than Williams: he was "to be indelibly marked on his left hip and his head shaved preparatory to being drummed out of the service" at nine o'clock on the morning of October 12, 1868.[95]

In 1871, Private John Callaghan, Company A, Fourth Infantry, disappeared from Fetterman and was captured. While he cooled his heels in the guardhouse it was learned that two years earlier he had also absconded from the Marine Corps at Brooklyn Barracks in New York. Callaghan requested to be remanded to Marine service.[96]

Indeed, many soldiers seemed eager to leave Fetterman in 1871. A mass desertion occurred on July 24, when eighteen men walked away from the post during the night. By August 15 the commanding officer reported that twenty-three captured escapees were awaiting trial.[97] Five deserters already confined in the guardhouse made their escape on December 11 by disarming the sentry, but were recaptured within two days.[98] The trend continued, to a lesser extent, in later years. Two soldiers decamped on August 17, 1872, with the aid of civilians assumed to be outlaws.[99] Two years later, seven men out of twenty-three took off while on mail detail to Fort Laramie. Privates Frederick Sparks and Frank Gould were the post's last recorded deserters on June 2, 1880. Dressed in civilian clothes and armed with stolen Colt revolvers, they were last seen on the Medicine Bow Road. As was the case with so many others across the West, they made good their escape from the military.[100]

〜 〜

Also found around the fort were a variety of other civilians. Like all military posts of the day, Fort Fetterman employed and housed skilled civilian artisans such as blacksmiths, teamsters, mechanics, and telegraphers. Sometimes their families joined them. Besides these officially recognized employees, others worked in the area under government contract to provide hay, wood, charcoal, or other supplies. A number of undesirables gained their living by prostitution, gambling, and illegal alcohol sales. Military authorities tried to keep them away to ensure harmony and discipline among the enlisted men. Civilians were thus no rarity around Fetterman. Later, when Indian hostilities had ebbed, ranchers also began to settle the productive bottom lands outside the military reservations.

Among the civilians Fort Fetterman counted on was post guide and interpreter Joe Merival. It was Merival whose horse's snort had saved his life during a close call with the Sioux in 1870. He lived on LaPrele Creek about two and a half miles south of the post. In 1875, Merival transferred as guide to Colonel Richard Irving Dodge and did not return to Fetterman.[101]

John Hunton was a civilian contractor and rancher who also lived near Fort Fetterman. In July 1874, Hunton established a "milk ranch" on LaPrele Creek two and a half miles south of the fort, near where Joe Merival resided until 1875. There he ran dairy cattle to supply milk and butter to the post.[102] Hunton closed his milk ranch in early December 1878 and sold his buildings to Robert Fryer who built a blacksmith shop on the site.[103] The next year Hunton won the government contract for haying on Deer Creek. That summer he encountered Major Frank Wolcott, later of Johnson County War notoriety, who was ranging his cows on the Deer Creek reserve, destroying the government's hay. Hunton reported this to the commanding officer on July 27, but Hunton said that Lieutenant Colonel J.S. Mason refused to confront Wolcott.[104] In August 1878, a Lieutenant Fisher was ordered to procure fenceposts a "full 16 feet long and 8 inches thick" and bring them to the fort. Then on October 23 Mason wrote a letter to Wolcott directing him to

> …proceed at once to fence the two meadows designated by him, in accordance with your agreement with Department Headquarters. When

*John Hunton arrived in Fort Laramie in 1867 and in 1870 took a contract to supply the fort with firewood. Between 1870 and 1880 he held government contracts to supply wood, hay, beef, charcoal, and lime to Forts Laramie and Fetterman and Camp McKinney. He held freight contracts from Medicine Bow Station to Fort Fetterman and other military post. In 1875, he started keeping daily diaries, which he faithfully kept up for the next fifty years. Six of the diaries have been published. He was the last post trader at Fort Laramie.* (Courtesy Wyoming State Archives)

these meadows are fenced the Commanding Officer will designate such other meadows for fencing as may require it under the processions of said agreement.[105]

Apparently Wolcott already had a contract to fence the reserve, but instead was grazing his cattle and cutting hay for personal use.[106] However, as the hay reserve was not being used by Hunton, who cut his hay for the government from his meadows near Chugwater, Department Headquarters decided not to pursue the matter.

Ranching became more established north of the Platte River in 1879. When H. A. Benjamin requested permission to establish temporary branding corrals and stables on the Fetterman reservation, it was granted provided he did not "support any kind of liquor business or store" which would compete with the post trader.[107]

# Expanding the Fort
# 1870–1881

CHAPTER

**7**

MOST MILITARY POSTS on the western frontier were built on a similar plan. While the building designs and specifications changed over time, the basic layout remained constant. The focal point was the parade ground, with barracks, officers' quarters, and offices flanking it. Outside this square were scattered the various buildings essential to operations. At Fetterman the guardhouse, magazine, post trader's store and dwelling, and ordnance storehouse stood to the south. To the east were the post headquarters, stables, corral, hospital, and laundress quarters. North of the post proper stood the quartermaster and commissary storehouses, granary, and, in the later years, the water reservoir.

Soldier crews provided the muscle power for most of the construction, often led by skilled civilian mechanics and craftsmen who were hired to teach them. Over the fort's fifteen-year history, construction and maintenance never ceased. Frame buildings gradually replaced hastily-built log ones; new residences and offices were needed to house a growing garrison, and weather-beaten structures cried out for repair. Meanwhile, the fort's sawmill fed it lumber nonstop. An ambitious water system was built in 1875—perhaps the jewel in Fort Fetterman's rough crown. By that time, most of the new construction was complete. A tour of the grounds tells the story of Fort Fetterman's growth.

**Parade Ground.**     The central quadrangle, used for formal inspection parades, company musters, guard mounting, and other company or regimental assemblies, measured about 250 feet east to west and 325 feet north to south, typical for a fort of the day. When the parade ground was laid out in 1868, it was delineated by posts and wires to remind the occupants that grass was to grow there; no one was to cross it without official permission. The fence remained until 1871, when it was removed presumably because

*Fort Fetterman from the southwest in 1874. The artist is unknown. (Courtesy Wyoming State Archives)* the grass had grown sufficiently or not at all.[1] A sundial was ordered in February 1869;[2] by March it was in place. But the only enlisted men allowed to use it were first sergeants, the quartermaster and commissary sergeants, hospital steward, sergeant major, and musician of the guard.[3] Gravel walks were laid around the quadrangle during the fall of 1870.

Originally the flagstaff stood on the south side of the post near the original guardhouse. But by 1870 it had been positioned, and would remain, on the parade ground in front of the middle barracks. About a hundred feet tall, it resembled a ship's mast with a "crow's nest" about halfway up. At least twice the wooden flagpole was replaced due to weathering and rot. Allowing for no gap, the new staff was erected near the old one, which was cut off at ground level; the wood remaining underground was allowed to rot. During the summer of 1873, a severe thunderstorm rolled in just before evening retreat, and soon lightning "struck the flag-staff and shivered the top mast." The top mast was not replaced until April 15, 1874.[4]

**Company Barracks.** Generally, each company of soldiers was housed together. Each barrack was furnished with bunks, arms racks, drinking water barrels, footlockers, benches, and other furniture that the army considered basic comforts. They also served as drill halls, social centers, and even at times as indoor target practice ranges. Some barracks had a library or reading room. Dining rooms and kitchens might be attached, or might be under a separate roof to the rear. The men also used these mess halls for bathing and grooming.

The high plank fence that originally enclosed the barracks and officers' quarters gradually fell into disrepair and in the late 1870s was removed partially. Ultimately the entire wall was deemed unnecessary and was torn down.

The barracks were heated by government standard wood-burning stoves. Apparently the stovepipes saw some wear; in 1874 post commander J. S. Mason reported an acute fire danger at the post due to "want of suitable chimnies."[5] On October 31 the post surgeon reported: "The command were chiefly employed during the month in cutting lumber and erecting new buildings, and in building new chimneys on the different sets of Barracks to take the place of the old and well used stove pipes."[6] By the next month, two adobe-brick chimneys had been added to each barrack.[7]

Whitewashed and roofed with pine shingles, the barracks had east and west windows and wide front porches. Two front rooms, 10 by 15 feet, served as the barracks office and quarters for the orderly sergeant. Inside,

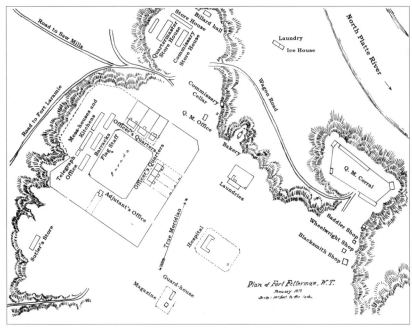

*These plans of the Fort Fetterman grounds and buildings in 1871 were approved by the Office of the Quartermaster General. Note the arrow indicating the "true meridian" near the map's center.* (United States Army Building, National Archives)

the barracks had plastered walls and painted canvas ceilings. The plank floors had been built of green sawn lumber and, with age, large cracks developed "through which the water used in scrubbing, the sweepings, and etc." found their way into the space underneath, which was not ventilated.[8]

In 1875, a new barracks was built on the southwest corner of the parade ground. A U-shaped structure, it had its mess hall and kitchen in one wing, and workshops, library, barber shop, and storage in the other. Company C, Third Cavalry, were the first occupants; thus it became known as the cavalry barracks.[9] Built of planking and lined with adobe, it measured 100 by 24 feet, and 14 feet high to the eaves. Like the others, it had a porch across the front with a sergeant's room and office at either end, plastered walls, a painted canvas ceiling, rough wooden floors, and stoves for heat.[10] That same year, the two adobe barracks and the log barracks west of the parade ground received a new finish; they were lathed, plastered, and painted, while the men lived in tents. The work was completed on September 29 and the soldiers returned to their refurbished quarters.[11]

The log kitchens for these barracks had been transported to Fetterman from Fort Caspar when it closed in 1868. Authorization to replace them

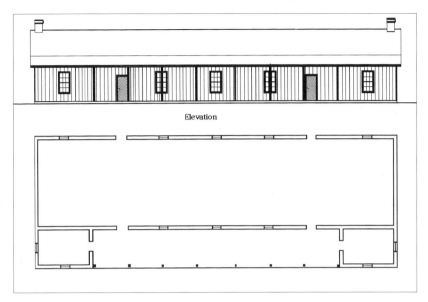

Elevation

*Plans for one company barracks. Three of these buildings stood on the west side of the parade ground.* (From the original drawings approved by the Office of the Quartermaster General. United States Army Building, National Archives)

with new, split-log kitchens was received in 1874 but lack of civilian carpenters and soldier labor delayed construction for two years. In 1876 the northwest barrack kitchen was completed, the others not until January 1878; all stood to the rear of the dwellings.[12]

On December 7, 1881, the unoccupied Cavalry Barracks was burned to the ground by an arsonist. The fire broke out in what had once been the barbershop. No longer a residence, the building had recently been used as a chapel and schoolroom. [13]

**Officers' Quarters.**　Officers' housing was assigned by rank and availability. No officer was allowed extra space except by order of the commanding officer when such room was available. Any officer could select quarters occupied by a junior officer, and force him to move. This often resulted in a flurry of activity along Officers' Row, which the enlisted men dubbed "the falling of the dominoes." Sometimes the most junior officer lived in a tent or hallway until proper quarters could be provided.

The 1863 Revised Army Regulations allowed all officers a private kitchen, and living space commensurate with rank. Lieutenants were

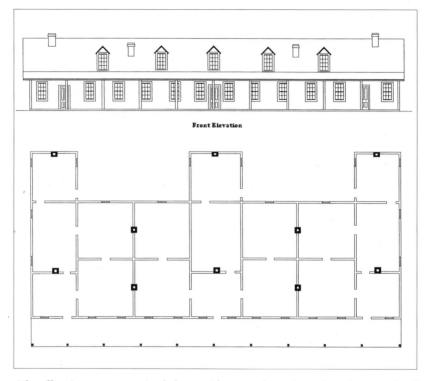

Front Elevation

*The officers' quarters contained three residences and was located on the east side of the parade ground. This building became the Fetterman Hotel. (From the original drawings approved by the Office of the Quartermaster General. United States Army Building, National Archives)*

authorized one room, captains and chaplains two; majors and lieutenant-colonels three; colonels and brigadier-generals four; and major-generals five.

During the early years, Officers' Row contained three units, two north of the parade ground, and one to the east. The post surgeon reported in 1870:

> A large adobe building is used as quarters for unmarried officers; it is 60 by 36 feet, and 12 feet high to the eaves, and is divided into six rooms, the attic being unfinished. A plank building lined with adobe, 36 by 44 feet, and 10 feet to the eaves, is used as lieutenant's quarters; the rooms, three in each set, are nicely plastered and finished. A block of buildings, 116 by 30 feet, built of plank, lined with adobe, contains one set of major's and two sets of captain's quarters. A small log building, 26 by 20 feet, and 10 feet high, is occupied temporarily as officer's quarters.[14]

These four buildings stood, respectively, on the quadrangle's north side, on the northeast corner, on the east side, and finally the small log quarters was centered on the south side of the parade ground.

In September 1871, another set of quarters began to rise on the north row. Three years later the east row was filled out with the commanding officer's quarters on the southeast corner, and in 1875 the south side of the parade ground received the last officers' quarters built.

In May 1875, the post surgeon's yearly report described the seven buildings that were housing officers at that time:

> All except one are one and a half stories high, most of the attics finished; shingled, plastered, with verandas along front; paling fences in front, and high fences around yards. Buildings are yellow-washed; two are built of logs, one of adobe supported by studding, all other of boards lined with adobe. Three contain each two sets of quarters with separate halls; one contains five sets with out halls, two without kitchens. The commanding officer's quarters contain five rooms on the first and two on the upper story; the house is well finished and very comfortable, with pantries, closets, &c., and the necessary outhouses and stable (of adobe) in the yard. One set of quarters contains five rooms, besides hall and kitchen; rather low and small, but quite comfortable. As a whole, these buildings furnish sufficient, most of them fair, some of them good, quarters; those contained in the unpromising "log houses" are by no means the worst. The material for adobe is very superior; the thickness of the walls renders the rooms warm in winter. The kitchens are mostly roomy and all furnished with good stoves or ranges and all other necessaries; a root-cellar, shelved, is in each yard.

The surgeon went on, alluding to the "domino effect" mentioned earlier:

> Much of the comfort the officers are enjoying now may be due to the fact that three different sets were successively erected for quarters for the commanding officer. Still the quarters are called fair and good only in comparison with the average quarters on the frontier. Here, as almost everywhere, the results of green lumber and army mechanics are visible in wide cracks in roof, floor, window and door frames, admitting rain, drought, and (worst of all) dust. The chimneys will smoke, plaster will tumble down, and bed-bugs will defy the house-keeper. Two additional sets of captain's quarters are being built of logs.[15]

These were nearly complete by June 30, 1875, and described by Captain Gerhard L. Luhn: "A double set of officers quarters...is under roof, and partition walls are up and two rooms are lathed, floored and window casings in; the labor was nearly all preformed by daily duty men..."[16] Lathed, plastered, and painted during the fall, by September 29 they were done.[17] The inner walls were made of adobe as were the fireplaces and interior chimneys. Outside, the chimneys were and still are soft red brick. This building stands today and is used as the historic site museum.

**Post Headquarters.**    Fort Fetterman's post headquarters was its administrative nerve center. Here meetings were held, records were housed, and functionaries—such as the post adjutant who served as the commanding officer's secretary—worked. The original headquarters was a small log building erected in 1868 on the south side of the parade ground. Two years later a new, two-story building was framed next to it, with offices for the post adjutant, quartermaster, and commissary on the first floor, and rooms for the clerks and telegraph operator upstairs.[18] When it was completed on September 15, 1870, the old building was plastered and reverted to quarters for officers.[19] Three years later a third building was framed on the east side of the quadrangle, measuring 70 feet by 29 feet 5 inches; its walls were fourteen feet high. The offices for the post adjutant, commissary, quartermaster clerks, and telegraph operator then were transferred to this building.[20]

On January 5, 1880, a violent windstorm tore away the porch "that extended the entire west side of the headquarters building...the lumber composing it scattered in different directions."[21] Soldiers repaired it within three weeks.[22] This same windstorm broke some windows in the hospital and caused "a severe shaking of plaster of the walls in the row of officers quarters on the east side of the garrison—leaving the wall in some instances in such cracked condition that portions may fall inward upon the slightest provocation."

**Hospital.**    The hospital stood about 150 yards east of the parade ground's flagstaff. Its logs had been hauled from Fort Caspar in the fall of 1867, but by 1870 it still had not been completed. Measuring 92 by 20 feet, with 9-foot walls, the hospital had two rear wings, one 18 by 13 feet, the other 36 by 16 feet. Like the officers' quarters, the hospital had a picket fence around the front yard and a high plank fence enclosing the

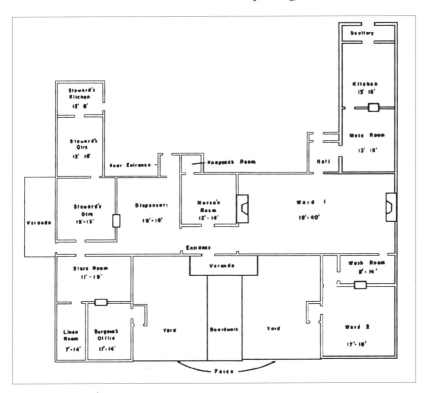

*Plans for the hospital.* (From the original drawings approved by the Office of the Quartermaster General. United States Army Building, National Archives)

rear yard and outbuildings. After touring the hospital with Assistant Post Surgeon Francis Le Baron Monroe, post commander Chambers reported to departmental headquarters in April 1870:

> I have inspected the Hospital and find that the building consists of logs, chinked and plastered. One large ward with no ceiling. No floor in the kitchen and though a generally ill arranged building for Hospital purposes, can be made comfortable for the sick by ceiling and plastering. This I purpose to have done as soon as necessary materials can be procured. I do not deem it necessary to build a new Hospital as I am of the opinion the present building can be made both convenient and comfortable by some alterations...[23]

The hospital was remodeled by late July, to make it habitable, as reported by Surgeon Monroe:

The plasterers finished on the 7th (July)—the carpenters yesterday the eighteenth, and today the painter puts on the final touches. One room is left untouched, the Com'g. Officer not wishing to do any work on it as it is only needed at present as waste room—one half of the shelving in the dispensary also remains to be put in at some future period. With these two exceptions, this Hospital will now compare favorably with any for convenience, suitability, and even elegance.[24]

In December Monroe and his colleague C. Makin noted both the progress and the problems :

The building is a second-hand affair... Until recently it has remained in its original condition, a mere shell, with no internal lining of any kind, or ceiling, and no flooring at all in some of the rooms. Owing to the wretched condition of the roof both light and snow were freely admitted, while the ventilation was more than could be desired... The ward, 20 by 40 feet, contains fifteen beds, with a cubic air space of 640 feet to each. There is no lavatory or bath-room, nor convenient latrine; the only structure of the latter kind is a board arrangement situated about 150 feet east of the building.[25]

Improvements were made gradually. The dispensary shelving and "waste room" were completed early in 1871. This room was then designated for use by the "matrons" who worked in the hospital as nurses.[26] Next came two additions to the front of the hospital: a new ward and steward's room on one side, and a storeroom on the other, each measuring 19 by 26 feet.[27] The additions were completed in June 1874.[28] The new ward room held an "earth-commode," apparently a removable box filled with dry earth with a lid-covered hole in the top. Intended for patients unable to make the trip to the privy, the earth-commode was, in the post surgeon's words, "used without bad effect."[29] A shed just east of the hospital housed one of the fort's few milk cows—purchased in 1874 for sixty-five dollars—so that patients might benefit from fresh milk, butter, and cheese.

Even when remodeled, the hospital continued to be a maintenance headache. Each year the post surgeons enumerated the repairs needed. In May 1875 he commented, "After much waste of ink and paper, the hospital has attained its present condition, which, however poor, would have made the earlier post-surgeons feel quite proud."[30] Post commander J.S.

POST·HOSPITAL·FT·FETTERMAN.

*This watercolor of the hospital was painted by Captain Bisbee while he was stationed at Fort Fetterman. In color, it shows attractive gold and blue trim on a barn red and white building.* (Courtesy Wyoming State Archives)

Mason said it succinctly in 1879: "It is old and shaky and has to be plastered every year. Sums required to repair it annually for a few years would build a new one." [31]

For everyday needs the hospital was adequate, but during the campaigns against the Sioux in 1876, more room was needed. In June the post surgeon requested that the barrack of Company F, Fourth Infantry, be used as a hospital ward for the wounded from General Crook's fight with the Indians on Rosebud Creek. [32] After the battle of Slim Buttes in September, the post surgeon was directed to prepare to receive wounded soldiers and again use a barrack if necessary. [33]

**Recreation Areas.**    A theater was built south of the cavalry barracks in 1873 as an entertainment area for the garrison. A plank-sided frame building 104 by 30 feet, it also housed the post library, school, and a "club room" for the enlisted personnel. At the post school, uneducated enlisted men, and the children of Fort Fetterman, could learn to read and write. By 1874 the post surgeon stated that the library's 250 books offered "as good a selection as could be expected in so small a collection". [34] The theater and stage occupied the southern two-thirds of the building. [35] As noted earlier, the first performance was given January 15, 1874. Several more productions—perhaps mostly "minstrel shows" by the enlisted men and their

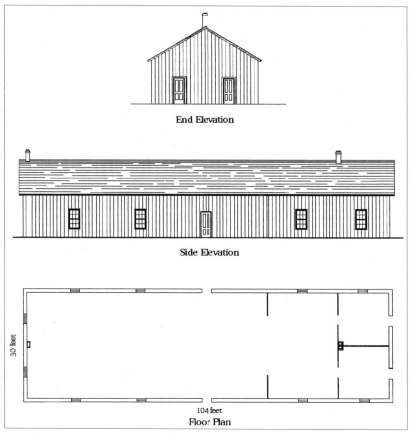

End Elevation

Side Elevation

30 feet

104 feet

Floor Plan

*This building, which first served Fort Fetterman's residents as a theater and school, later became the Sparhawk Opera House in 1886.* (From the original drawings approved by the Office of the Quartermaster General. United States Army Building, National Archives)

wives—followed over the next two years, with a rare treat in May 1875, when a touring troupe, the Pardeys, played Fort Fetterman.[36]

Another entertainment was horse racing, a sport quite popular during the nineteenth century. Built in the summer of 1870, Fort Fetterman's oval-shaped racetrack was one hundred yards northeast of the cemetery.[37] Later, when the post became the town of Fetterman, its citizens used this track extensively, generally ensuring that large sums of money changed hands.

**Post Trader's Store and Quarters.**    Southwest of the theater building stood the post trader's store, erected in 1868 and first owned by the firm of Wilson & Cobb. First Sergeant John O. Ward described it:

The post trader's store faced east. It was built of adobe and its length was about seventy-five feet. On the south end was the officer's clubroom, in which they had their sideboard, a billiard table, and several small tables for card playing. A colored man operated a barber chair in which the officers had their tonsorial work done. This Negro also attended to the janitor work of the room. On the north end of the store was the bar where enlisted men and the civilian population were served.[38]

Jules Ecoffey and I. N. Campbell took over the tradership in July 1870.[39] Three months later Ecoffey, a local entrepreneur who had previously built a billiard hall at the fort, moved it from its site near the commissary and quartermaster storehouses and attached it to his store.[40]

Ecoffey and Campbell were soon replaced by Ephraim Tillotson in January 1871. A retired army officer, Tillotson had been the acting assistant quartermaster at Fort Reno when that post had been abandoned. He probably received this position at Fort Fetterman in recognition of his military service.[41] Apparently Tillotson prospered; on May 27, 1874, he began raising the frame of his "new dwelling house."[42] But it seems he had not sought permission from the commanding officer and was shown the error of his ways. A week later post adjutant Lieutenant Robert A. Lovell responded to Tillotson:

> …in answer to your communication of the 7th inst. in regard to obtaining permission to erect a dwelling house in the vicinity of your store, that said permission is given you. He would suggest as a site for said building, a point about due South of the Post Guard House and about East of your store, at equal distance from both.[43]

The next year Lieutenant Colonel John Sanford Mason wrote that Tillotson left the fort:

> I have the honor to report that Mr. E. Tillotson Post Trader at this Post has left the Post with the intentions of not returning. That he has left his Traders Store in the hands of Mr. A. Jordan. In January Mr. A. Leighton the partner of Mr. Tillotson arrived at this Post bringing Mr. Jordan with him. An Inventory of Stock was taken at that time. Mr. Tillotson reported to me that he would continue as Trader, whilst it was given out generally that he had sold out and would retire. Mr. Jordan took charge of the business. On April Twenty-seventh Mr. Tillotson left

the post with his family stating that he would not return. In the meantime the store is conducted by Mr. Jordan although in the name of Mr.
Tillotson.[44]

Tillotson's continued absence caused the Adjutant General's Office to
write:

I am directed by the Secretary of War to inform you that if Mr. Tillotson does not return to his Post at the expiration of his leave of absence,
another trader will be appointed in his stead, you will please communicate the above to Mr. Tillotson and at the expiration of his leave,
inform this office whether he has returned.[45]

Tillotson finally returned to Fort Fetterman on December 2, 1875. He
remained at his business until he retired in August 1880, selling his store
and dwelling to E.K. Nichols.[46]

But Nichols's tenure was short, as his store caught fire and was consumed by the flames on October 3, 1881. Nichols saved most of his
inventory, but the building and $4,000 were lost.[47] Apparently he built
again, as his store and saloon became the focal point of the soon-to-be
Fetterman City.

**Quartermaster Corral, Stables, and Shops.**    The post's quartermaster
was responsible for the troops' food, wagons and carts, and post equipment. Care of horses and mules fell under his purview as well. Even before
Fort Fetterman's cavalry arrived in 1872, a corral had been laid out. This
corral was intended solely for government draft animals, a few quartermas-
ter-owned horses, and some horses privately owned by officers. (Officers
were supplied with army mounts, but most chose to buy their own.)

This corral stood at the fort's northeastern outskirts, where the bluffs
rose from the river. Built of adobe, the corral walls conformed to the
shape of the bluff and were flanked east and west by ravines. Irregular in
shape, the corral measured 450 feet along the north wall, and roughly
150 feet along the east and west walls, which angled inward to the 325-
foot southern wall. The walls were ten feet high, with sheds constructed
of overlapping wood slabs against the interior. Before the construction of
the cavalry stable, the shed along the north wall served the purpose, measuring 18 feet wide by 225 feet long. In the northwest corner was a small

*Fort Fetterman circa 1880. The hospital building is shown in the center, with the cavalry stable to the right and storehouses at top.* (Courtesy Wyoming State Pioneer Museum)

building housing grain for the animals and also the hospital's ambulance. In the northeast corner was a harness room that also housed ponies. In the southwest corner was another small stable, 15 by 20 feet, for the quartermaster mules. Attached to the south wall, but outside the enclosure, were the teamster's quarters which measured 25 by 100 feet, extending to the corral's southeast corner; on its west end a gate led into the stockade. A small adobe building, 15 by 19 feet, along the east ravine was used as quarters for the saddler and the stable guard. Three buildings outside the corral lined the western side of the ravine and were built as carpenter, wheelwright, and blacksmith shops. By 1879, an inspection report noted its "dilapidated tumble down condition."[48]

Authorization to build a stable for the mounts of the post's cavalry detachment was given in 1872. The chief quartermaster of the Department of the Platte forwarded instructions to his counterpart at Fort Fetterman:

> …The specifications are made for a stable 142 ft 4 inches long by 30 feet wide, but if it should be found that the length is not sufficient it can be increased a few feet. It will be observed that the plan is for stalls 9 ft wide, but the Department Commander deems it best to have them ten feet in width, to accommodate two horses in each stall more comfortably and safe. You will therefore have them erected ten feet wide.

You will please report to this office what material necessary for the construction of this stable can be procured in the vicinity of your post, with cost of same in detail ...[49]

Meanwhile, horses were sheltered at the quartermaster corral. By December 1872, work on the stable was being

... as rapidly pushed forward as the materials on hand will admit, the weather boarding for the sides is ready, and the window frames, door frames and doors nearly so. The frame will be commenced as soon as the logs can be obtained from the woods, which I expect will be in a few days, and all the carpenter's work possible will be gotten ready, so as to allow the lumber, all of which is green, a little time to season while the foundation is being built.[50]

Yet the stable remained unfinished for years; presumably, the horses were wintering in the corral, or perhaps other sheds were used. The stable was finally completed on September 5, 1877. In the meantime, the square footage had grown by fifty percent: at thirty-two feet wide, it now stood a full 225 feet long, resting on a stone foundation mortared with lime. Its eight-foot walls were built of split log panels fifteen feet long and joined with upright logs. There were ten-foot-square double doors and three windows on each end. The stalls were ten feet wide, and the partitions built of two-inch lumber. Each stall had a ten-foot manger, a feed box at each corner, and an air hole for ventilation.[51] The stable could house eighty-four horses; its total cost was $3,050.[52]

**Quartermaster and Commissary Storehouse.**　On the point of the bluff, about two hundred yards north of the parade ground, stood the quartermaster and commissary storehouses. The main storehouse, 150 by 32 feet, was described in 1870 "as built of adobe and two stories high."[53] A May 1872 inspection noted:

The *Quartermaster* storehouses at this post, are generally speaking, well fitted for their respective uses. The principal one needs a floor in its second story, and its northern end should be weather boarded to protect the adobes—of which material the building is constructed—from further injury by winter storms which beat with great violence against that portion of the building. No fires are permitted in or about them. They

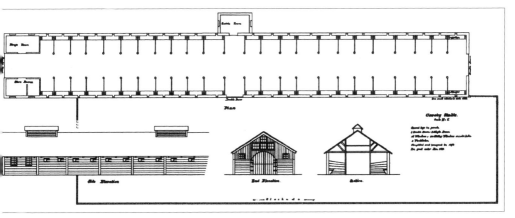

*Plans for the cavalry stable which was built of logs and completed September 5, 1877.* (From the original drawings approved by the Office of the Quartermaster General. United States Army Building, National Archives)

are guarded by a *Sentinel,* the windows have iron bars across them and doors are kept locked...[54]

A 1879 inspection revealed more winter wear: the adobe had "worn away and partially tumbled down... Two new store houses and one new forage house should be built, old buildings not worth repairing."[55] In January 1880, a severe windstorm damaged the quartermaster buildings beyond repair. A board of survey reported:

> The east wall of the Q. M. Storehouse is very much shaken, bulging outward throughout its entire extent, being one and a half feet out of plumb at its center—a corresponding inward bulging having taken place in the wall of the opposite side. Two windows at the north end have been blown in carrying with them the surrounding adobe bricks, forming two extensive openings... In addition to this damage, the S.W. corner of the structure has also been carried away from the eaves to the foundation. This leaning of the building and its shaken conditions is accompanied by cracks and separation adding the bricks of greater or less extent in all four walls. With these injuries in view, the Board arrived at the opinion that the Q. M. Storehouse was utterly unsafe and not a fit shelter for Gov't. property.[56]

Although estimates and plans for a new storehouse and granary were made quickly, they were not authorized before the post was abandoned in 1882. For over a year, stores were kept under canvas cover and guarded by sentries.

Foodstuffs were stored in the commissary storehouse. Built in 1869, it stood "100 by 36 feet, and 16 feet high, is built of plank lined with adobe; a fine root cellar underlies the building."[57] A May 1872 inspection deemed it:

> ...a suitable building for the purpose. The present floor which is of boards and slabs loosely laid down, should be replaced by one of boards properly joined and nailed down. It is dry and well ventilated. It stands near the *Quartermaster* storehouse and has similar security against loss by fire or theft; the same *Sentinel* guards both.[58]

Unfortunately for the garrison, potatoes stored in the cellar froze during the winter months. A new root cellar was built in 1873, its nine-foot log walls partially dug into the side of the bluff about one hundred yards north of the bakery. At 41 by 25 feet, it could store fifteen thousand pounds of vegetables.[59]

The slab floor criticized in the 1872 inspection report still had not been replaced by July 1876. The post commander wrote that the commissary

> ...is greatly in need of a new floor. The building itself is an excellent one, airy and roomy, but the floor is laid with slabs, the rough side up, which prevents the use of a truck, and in case of packages breaking[,] the loss of stores...[60]

A new floor of rough planks was finally laid in November 1876.[61] The building remained in good condition until the post was abandoned.

During the summer of 1869 two more quartermaster buildings were built near the adobe structure. Both were frame, sided with planks, and lined with adobe bricks. One stored grain and wagon parts; the other, 30 by 120 feet, housed goods and offices for the commissary and quartermaster departments.[62]

The granary, 17 by 85 feet, primarily housed the feed for the government horses and mules. Apparently its design was not rodent-proof; through the years it was infested by mice and rats. The post quartermaster's 1878 request for a new granary had not yet been acted on when a windstorm — the same one that demolished the storehouse in January 1880 — also damaged the granary. The board of survey reported: "The damage to the Q. M. grain room consists in the destruction of the large door at the west end of the building and a removal of a piece of the roof (6 ft x 24 ft) on the south side by the wind."[63] On February 11, 1880, authority and funding to replace it was received.[64] Nature had achieved results that the army was unable to obtain alone: a new granary! Specifications prepared in 1878 were now dusted off. They called for a building of "… one story, sat upon four rows of posts 16" diameter, 8 feet long—4 feet in ground—six feet apart, running lengthwise: one hundred feet long; thirty feet wide, walls ten feet high, roof one third pitch, shingled. Floor 2" matched boards. Double walls, the inner against which grain is to rest, to be three feet from the outer, leaving twenty-four feet in width, grain capacity. The outer wall to be studded and girthed, boards nailed on horizontally."[65] Meanwhile the existing granary was repaired temporarily.

That fall the new granary was built on the site of the old one by post trader Ephraim Tillotson, with materials provided by the quartermaster. Records show that some of the labor was donated: Tillotson "does not want to make any thing by the transaction"[66] and a Mr. Latta, who was employed by the quartermaster department, agreed to plane the flooring after his regular work hours at no extra charge.

**Guardhouse.**    A post's guardhouse served two purposes, to house the daily sentinels and to confine prisoners. Typically it had a prison room with both solitary and general confinement cells, and an adjoining guards' room with overnight quarters for greater security.

In Fort Fetterman's case, it also housed the post commander's office. The first guardhouse, built of logs in 1868 south of parade ground and behind the southern officers' quarters, was used for about five years. Standing 50 by 20 feet and one story high, it was divided into three apartments. The post commander's office and the guardroom were the same size, 14 by 18 feet, with ceilings 13 feet 9 inches high and windows for ventilation. The guardroom had two doors, one opening into the prison area. The prison room was divided into two portions; the first, a general confinement cell, was 17 by 7 feet, with a seven-foot ceiling. A seventeen-foot central hallway separated this room from a second cell block. Here were four windowless cells, each four feet wide, 6 feet 9 inches long and 7 feet 5 inches high, with a door into the hallway. The cells were unventilated, causing the prisoners to "knock out the plaster between the logs, so that the result is attained."[67] In October 1869, when the prison room was being used to store ordnance, the post commander had to direct that prisoner Private Wood of Company E, Fourth Infantry, be returned to duty as they could not confine him with the ordnance.[68]

Furnishings were spartan. The guards were provided with a group type bunk and an arms rack. All the rooms were heated with coal stoves and in 1869, four or five spittoons were furnished.[69] The guardroom also had a clock which evidently the guards tampered with, because the post commander directed "that a suitable box with glass front be made to enclose the Guard-House Clock, and lock it by a small padlock or otherwise—thus preventing the Guard from interfering with the clock."[70] In 1879, a requisition for twenty-five iron bunks was ordered for use in the guardhouse. This would indicate preparation for prisoners as well as for the guard.[71]

By 1872, the building was in poor repair, more expensive to fix than replace, and a new one was requested. On September 3, 1873, the frame for the new guardhouse had been completed. Finished by May 10, 1874, the new guardhouse was plank sided, whitewashed, and lined with adobe. This single-story building measured 36 by 51 feet with a low-pitched, shingled hip roof 18 feet high at the ridge, with no interior ceiling. The post surgeon reported in 1875:

> Owing to the unique interior arrangement, but little benefit from these dimensions accrues to the prisoners. The main building is occupied by the guard. The prisoners occupy separate rooms built of substantial plank within the main building; so as to have a free space around them; they have a plank ceiling; height to ceiling 10 feet. These rooms or cages communicate with the main room by means of a door and two gratings, 3 by 14 inches and 3 by 18 inches, 7 feet from the floor. One such room is at each end of the building; one, 14 by 10 feet, for general prisoners, (average occupancy, 12; greatest 21;) the other, 18 by 10 feet, for garrison prisoners, (average occupancy, 6; greatest, 10.) In the corner opposite to the general prisoners is the room for the non-commissioned officers of the guard, 11 by 15 feet. Adjacent to the other prisoners' room are three cells, 3 by 6 feet and 7 feet high, with ceilings consisting of grating, used for refractory prisoners and those sentenced to solitary confinement, rarely occupied. There are ten windows (3 by 2 ? feet, about 7 feet from the floor) and two doors (6 3/4 by 2 ? feet) in the main building, which is also perforated by numerous loop-holes,

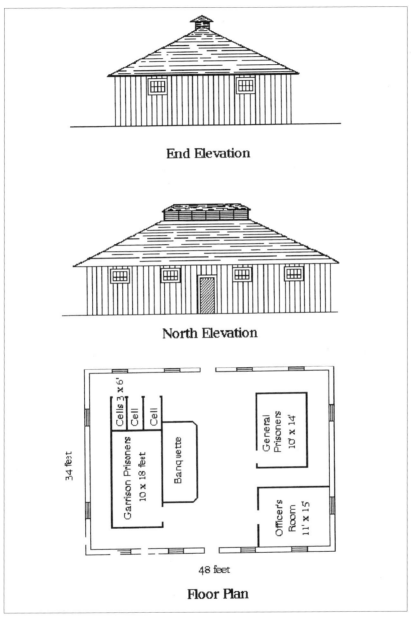

**End Elevation**

**North Elevation**

**Floor Plan**

*The second guardhouse was completed in May 1874. This building became the town jail during the civilian era and was the building where "Red" Capps was hanged.* (From the original drawing prepared by the Office of the Quartermaster General. United States Army Building, National Archives) (about 2 by 4 inches, now boarded up.) The prisoners sleep on the floor, no bed-sacks or bunks, and but two blankets to each prisoner, being allowed. The guards sleep on a platform along the outer wall of the room for the garrison prisoners. The whole building is well warmed by a wood-stove in the center. No special arrangement for ventilation. The whole is in good repair and kept well policed. This plan is certainly ingenious to prevent escape of prisoners.[72]

The old guardhouse was then removed to the quartermaster area next to the wheelwright's shop and made into a carpenter shop.[73]

**Magazine and Ordnance Storehouse.** Ideally, an army post's magazine was used only to store explosive materials such as powder, cannonballs, fuses, powder charges, and rifle and pistol ammunition. A separate ordnance storehouse was used for weapons such as Gatling guns, rifles, pistols, and cannons—so an explosion in the magazine would not destroy both the ammunition and the weapons.

During the early years at Fetterman, however, all these supplies were kept under one roof. The original magazine, a twenty-foot-square log structure south of the guardhouse, had a mixed review from the post commander in 1873:

> The Ordnance property and stores are sufficiently well covered and stored but the magazine is too small to be convenient, or to hold everything pertaining to the Department, which should be under roof. Neither is it fireproof, but is so situated as to be pretty well out of danger in that respect.[74]

Indeed, space seemed tight: ordnance equipment was sometimes kept in the quartermaster's warehouse, and even, as noted, in the guardhouse. In June of 1875, the magazine was "renovated, (replastered & whitewashed), Harness oiled, small arms cleaned & etc. during the month."[75]

In 1879, a new ordnance storehouse was completed just west of the new guardhouse. Post commander John S. Mason described its rammed earth walls:

> It is what is called a "Cohen" building made by pounding moist earth mixed with short hay into a box 6' x 20" x 20", the walls on the out and inside being plastered with cement, eight barrels of which were used. The building is the best at the Post, and has not cost the Government $275.[76]

Measuring 80 by 30 feet, it had double doors at each end flanked by two large windows, and four small windows on each side beneath the eaves. The flooring was made of two-inch rough planking nailed to the floor joists. Fort Fetterman finally had a storage building for all its ordnance supplies, including, in 1880, two .45-caliber Gatling guns and a twelve-pound mountain howitzer.[77]

**Bakery.**    The first bakery was located on the edge of the bluff north of the hospital. It was simple: an oven built around an iron arch which was in turn surrounded by adobe on a foundation of sandstone, which had been quarried three miles west of the fort.[78] The oven was enclosed with a frame building.[79] But the bakery's life was short. On May 11, 1869, a fire destroyed the entire building and about seven hundred pounds of flour. Only the oven survived, remaining in use, covered by a tent, until a new housing could be built of adobe bricks.[80]

A new bakery was constructed the next summer, this one 27 by 18 feet, with ovens at each end and work space in between. But this bakery, too, was short-lived. When a new granary was built in 1880, a new bakery was planned as well. On May 7, during a construction boom of sorts, the post commander requested additional troops be sent to Fort Fetterman as the men stationed at the post were busy cutting logs for the new bakery and granary.[81] A plan of the bakery was provided to the quartermaster general of the Department of the Platte stating that the building was of "Frame; vertical boarding and battens, outside; lathed and plastered inside. 4 Windows; 1 Door. Oven, 8' x 10' inside, built of stone (quarried near Post), and brick furnished by the Q.M. Dept. Completed 1880."[82]

**Laundress Quarters.**    Laundress quarters were often unofficially called Suds Row, both here and at other forts. Fort Fetterman's original laundress quarters, where the washerwomen and their soldier husbands were housed, were located below the bluff on the floodplain of the Platte River. The building had rooms for "(six sets) laundress and married soldiers" and measured 92 by 23 feet.[83] Attached to it was the post icehouse, a log structure 23 by 36 feet, with twelve-foot walls; it would be completely rebuilt in October 1873.[84] A second set of quarters was also built in the early 1870s north of the hospital. Originally intended as officers' quarters, this adobe structure stood 24 by 94 feet. Its eight apartments each 23 by 10 feet, with ten-foot

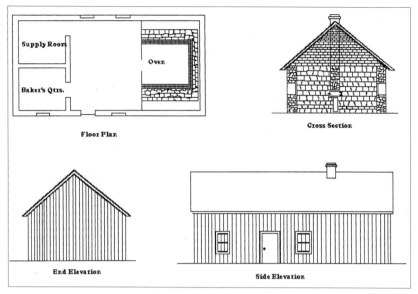

Supply Room

Oven

Baker's Qtrs.

Floor Plan

Cross Section

End Elevation

Side Elevation

*These plans show the design of the third bakery built at the fort. This frame and stone bakery was completed in 1880.* (From the original drawings approved by the Office of the Quartermaster General. United States Army Building, National Archives)

ceilings, were further divided by canvas into two rooms, each approximately ten feet square. Kitchens for each set were in tents in the rear.[85]

**Cemetery.**   The post cemetery was located east of the fort, on a plateau rising above the windswept bench. Later, rancher John Hunton remembered the fence around the cemetery:

> …The enclosure consisted of post set in the ground, two posts close together and poles attached by putting the ends of the poles between the posts. Some of the posts were held together by having pieces of plank or split poles nailed to them. I and my employees sometimes repaired this fence, after 1876, when my cattle were ranged in the country. When I last saw the enclosure, during the summer of 1881, most of the poles and posts were lying on the ground in a decayed condition.[86]

**Sawmill.**   While Fort Fetterman itself stood on a largely treeless plain, timber was not far away. Early in 1868 a steam-powered sawmill was built about ten miles to the southwest, in the wooded foothills of the Laramie Mountains—then known locally as the Black Hills—between Box Elder and Little Box Elder Creeks. But after just a few months, the sawmill was moved to the floodplain of LaPrele Creek, just west of the fort. This placed the lumber closer to the construction area, but now the raw logs had to travel twenty-two miles to the mill. Ten trips a week with ten six-mule teams barely kept it supplied. Captain Carlton wrote to department headquarters in November 1868:

> I would respectfully recommend that a train of fifty or more teams be sent here to remain until it has made four or five trips to the Black Hills: this should give us a sufficient number of logs to keep our carpenters employed all winter and enable us to saw and have seasoning the lumber necessary for the buildings to be erected next season.
>
> If this request is favorably considered the train should be sent at once as a snow storm would render our road to the Black Hills impassable."[87]

In August 1868 the sawmill from the abandoned Fort Reno was sent to Fetterman. It served well until it was reported in 1875 that the sawmill engine and boiler were in very poor condition. The quartermaster requested that a qualified engineer be employed to repair them.[88]

But the sawmill remained a dangerous place: three summers later an enlisted man was killed by a flyaway saw blade. The post surgeon recorded on June 7, 1878, that Private Louis P. Bauer, of Company C, Fourth Infantry, was "instantly killed by bursting of circular saw, while on fatigue duty sawing wood for his company."[89] Then the events took an even nastier turn. First Sergeant John Ward reported:

> The sawmill and its auxiliary, as well as the pumping plant, were under the supervision of a civilian named DeLay, assisted by Private Lamb. Pvt. Lamb had called attention to repair needs for the sawmill several times but DeLay only commented "Oh, if it kills anyone it will be only a soldier."

The men of the company held DeLay responsible for his careless remark and wanted to kill him. Ward kept his men in check temporarily, but in an anonymous letter he warned DeLay to leave the post in "twenty four hours or take the consequences." DeLay reported the threat to the post commander, Captain Edwin M. Coates (also commander of Company C, Fourth Infantry), who told him to arm himself and notify him of any further messages or attempts on his life. Several days later, DeLay was caught off guard, escorted from the post by the men of Company C, and told never to return. Coates was on a hunting trip at the time, leaving Lieutenant George Webster in charge of both the post and Company C. Webster directed an escort to return DeLay to the post. When Coates returned, he commissioned a board of inquiry to investigate the death of Private Bauer and the subsequent threats to DeLay.[90] On July 24 the board inspected the sawmill machinery and the "anonymous letters being sent out."[91] DeLay left the post following the inquiry, relieved of his duties.

A fire damaged the mill in early September 1878; the post quartermaster outlined the losses:

> One saw mill, no attachments, capacity for sawing ten thousand feet of lumber per day;
>
> The sawmill which contained the shingle, lath and crosscut saw has been burned by fire and a Board has been appointed to investigate and report upon same. The shingle machine, and lath machine are beyond doubt rendered entirely unserviceable. The engine and boiler are injured to some extent but to what an extent is unknown at present.[92]

By 1879, the equipment was fixed and operational, described by post commander John Sanford Mason as "an excellent saw and shingle mill and with our own ingenuity a lathe machine has been lately added. The finest lumber timber in this country 26 miles from here…"[93] Lumber became plentiful again at the fort, although most major construction was already complete.

**Water System.**    During the early years, most of the fort's water for drinking, bathing, washing, and other uses was hauled by wagon from the North Platte River. Impure and somewhat alkaline, the water was described by the post surgeon in 1874:

> … its flavor to one unaccustomed to it is disagreeable; but its influence upon the health of the garrison is not very marked… During 1873, 49 cases of acute diarrhoea and dysentery appeared on the reports, or about 11 per cent of all cases taken sick. The fact that the season of greatest frequency of these diseases does not correspond to the season of low water… does not disprove the effect of the water in their production. Though the water is more impure in winter and early summer, greater quantities of it are consumed in the hot season.[94]

LaPrele Creek, which flowed into the Platte, offered water with the same impurities, if not worse. The post surgeon explained:

> The slaughter-house is situated on the La Prele, about 1,200 yards distant. The refuse is carted to the banks of the same creek, about 500 yards above its mouth, and as the water-supply is derived from the Platte, a short distance below, it is sure to be contaminated, and more than ordinarily, during the floods in summer.[95]

A spring near the sawmill on the creek provided cool, sulphurous water which was extensively used in summer by the garrison, and especially the hospital, instead of the dirty Platte River water.[96] For some reason rain and snow water were not collected from the roofs of the buildings.

For seven years, the post managed this way, but in January 1875 permission was granted to build a water system and reservoir. Plans were drafted in February.[97] A steam-powered pump on the Platte's south bank would draw the water from a well and force it through an underground pipe two hundred yards uphill to a reservoir near the commissary storehouse. The force of gravity would then feed the water through more underground pipes to the garrison. Post Quartermaster Luhn did some research:

> …the pump required is for the following purposes; viz: To pump sufficient water to fill a tank with capacity for 15 barrels in one hour. It takes 30 barrels or 2 tanks full to supply the garrison each day. The spring from which we intend to supply the post is eighteen feet below the bank where the tank is to stand while being filled; it will therefore, require a pipe 25 feet long, throwing a 2 inch stream, a plunging rod the same length and 25 feet of hose, the same size as the pump spout to which it is to be attached. From what information I can gather of pumps, I would respectfully request that a double brake pump be furnished.[98]

Luhn's request was filled with a Shelden steam pump No. 4. But installation of the pump and piping required professional help. Post commander J.S. Mason wrote to A.C. Carn of New York City for guidance: "…We intend placing the Pump on the bank of the river and force water into a reservoir on top of the hill about one hundred feet above. Our Reservoir will be 15' x 15' x 6'."[99]

Construction began on June 25, 1875, with the survey of the line between the pump and reservoir. Civilian stonemasons from Laramie City, employed by the quartermaster department, began quarrying sandstone for the reservoir on "Commissary Hill." [100] By July 21 both the reservoir and the uphill ditch were almost ready, but the wrong-sized pipe had been delivered. [101] Nine days later the work was done, and even the collection well was nearly dug; next it would be lined with sandstone. [102] Finally, as the post surgeon stated, "Trenches are being dug for the accommodation of water pipes, which in connection with steam force pump, it is intended to supply water to the Barracks and Officers quarters, from a small well on the bank of the Platte." [103]

Starting September 28, "30 Recruits" toiled every day as ditch-diggers, under the eye of a sergeant. After ten days the detail was rotated until the trenches were done. [104] On November 4 the reservoir, a partly submerged 7520-gallon tank, was tested in concert with the pump. [105] By the end of the month the water system had been completed, just in time for winter. A small wood-heated structure was built over the reservoir to prevent freezing. [106] Water consumption seems to have been quite heavy as the quartermaster was ordered to fill the tank every Monday, Wednesday and Saturday. [107]

But by the next October the pump had nearly worn out. Requests to repair or replace it were denied. [108] In May 1877 quartermaster Luhn, apparently a gifted improviser, explained the problem and asked for some specific parts:

> The plunger-rings referred to are in two sections, a copper, or composition ring inside of a steel ring. The taking of sand has worn the cylinder unequally. The engineer now employed at the post says that the outer ring should have been the soft one instead of the steel.
>
> The rings do not seem to be worn, but the cylinder is worn from the action of sand so that it is at least 1/16 of an inch larger in the centre than at the ends in consequence of the outer ring being harder than the cylinder.
>
> About the 1st of December, last, the plunger rings were taken out entirely and hemp packing used in their stead, in this way the pump works very satisfactorily. Besides this, extra precautions were taken to prevent the taking of sand. Recently I have procured a piece of gauze wire which answers the purpose admirably.
>
> The following articles are required to place the pump and engine in thorough repair, viz: a new piston rod, four new cylinder cocks with

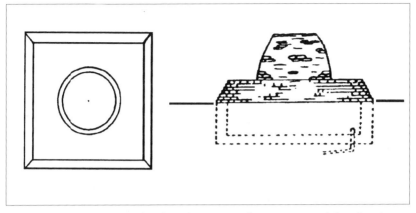

*Plans for water reservoir. The plans show two tanks, one on top of the other.* (From the original drawings approved by the Office of the Quartermaster General. United States Army Building, National Archives)

> couplings for water-pipes, 1 stuffing box for valve-stem, 4 new bolts for heads of steam chest, a piece, say one or two pounds, of gauze wire for strainers, such as enclosed sample.

Luhn had been learning on the job:

> Upon receipt of your communication about the time I was appointed Post Quartermaster, I had not sufficient experience with the pump to make an intelligent report upon it. As the engineer employed, I determined to give him an opportunity to see if some improvements in its working could not be made, and in consequence there seems to be no difficulty with its working, and with the articles asked for I think there will be no need of further expense for some time.[109]

That sand or sediment was being pumped into the reservoir is corroborated by the post surgeon in his monthly log. In January 1879, he reported that the "water is fairly good, contains considerable sediment."[110]

A second reservoir was built on top of the old one that summer. The new stone tank was circular—14 feet 6 inches in outside diameter—and held four feet of water, for a capacity of 5,980 gallons. (The old reservoir, fifteen feet square, with a depth underground of six feet of water, held 7,520 gallons.)[111] The Post surgeon noted that the water was "improved by an additional tank."[112] A year later, the pump again needed repair, and the garrison had to conserve water. At the end of 1880 post commander Powell

FORT FETTERMAN
FROM C.G COUTANT'S HISTORY OF WYOMING

*M.D. Houghton, an early Wyoming schoolteacher and artist, drew this pen illustration of Fort Fetterman as it appeared in 1880 at a later date for C.G. Coutant's* History of Wyoming. *He based the drawing on interviews, research, and trips to the site. Note the fountain in the center of the parade ground.* (Courtesy Wyoming State Museum)

ordered, "… the water will only be turned hereafter until further orders between the hours of 11 A.M. and 1 P.M."[113] This is the last reference to the water system in the military records.

Still, the system probably remained useful until the post was abandoned in 1882. In 1889, Merris C. Barrow, who started his newspaper *Bill Barlow's Budget* in the town of Fetterman in 1886, recalled the fort as it appeared in the early 1880s, mentioning the water system—which by then featured a fountain:

> …substantial buildings surrounding a parade ground in the center of which stood a fountain. Situated on a high plateau overlooking the Platte, with its system of waterworks, well-kept streets and walks and grassy lawns and parade, it was a beautiful spot, like unto an oasis in the desert.[114]

# FORT FETTERMAN
# BECOMES A TOWN 1882–1885

CHAPTER

# 8

DIMINISHING INDIAN troubles on the Wyoming frontier during the late 1870s increased white settlement in the Platte River valley of Wyoming Territory. The Bozeman Trail remained the major northern route through central Wyoming above the North Platte River, now safely traveled by the military and settlers alike. With the Indians on reservations and relative peace in the territory, Fort Fetterman faded in military importance and was abandoned in 1882.

Towards the end, the fort's personnel had dwindled to just two companies of the Fourth Infantry. When Company A was transferred on November 10, 1881, only Company G was left to occupy the waning post.[1] Six days later the post commander wrote:

> … in sending one man from this post to Omaha, Neb. in obedience to instructions from Dept. Hd Qr's of November Third 1881, there are but four (4) privates for duty at this post, and I deem it necessary to report, that with this number of men, no regular guard duty can be performed, and consequently the public stores and property cannot be sufficiently protected.[2]

Still, Company G kept the post in operation—barely—for another six months.

On May 11, 1882, post commander Major W. H. Powell received a telegram from Headquarters, Department of the Platte containing orders to abandon the post. That day Powell relayed the news to the troops:

> General Orders #9:
> In accordance with instruction from the Lieutenant General, the posts of Fort Fetterman and Fort Sanders, W. T., will be at once abandoned and the garrisons thereof will proceed to Fort D. A. Russell, W. T. and take station thereat…[3]

T. M. Anderson, the commanding officer of Fort McKinney, heard the news and telegraphed Powell: "Have you orders to abandon Fetterman? Will I have to send a guard. What will be done with [Fort] Washakie. Sorry to lose you for a neighbor."[4] (Fort Washakie, to the west in the Wind River range, would remain active as a post for twenty-seven more years.)

On May 16 Major Powell posted more specific orders for the garrison:

> In compliance with G. O. No. 9 Hdqrs Dept. of the Platte, the Post of Fort Fetterman, Wyo. will be abandoned on Saturday morning the 20th instant.
>
> Company "G" 4th Infantry will proceed to Fort D. A. Russell, Wyo. and there take station, reporting to the Commanding Officer on arrival. The public property at this post will be disposed of under the direction of the chiefs of the staff to which it pertains.
>
> Pending this disposition, 1st Lieut. C.W. Mason 4th Inf. with a guard of ten men, for Company "G" 4th Inf. will remain at the Post for the protection of the property. These men will be supplied with thirty days rations and one hundred rounds of ammunition per man.
>
> The records of the Post will be properly packed and turned over to Lieut. Mason for shipment to Headquarters Department of the Platte. The Post Fund and all property pertaining thereto, will be transferred to the Post Treasurer of Fort D.A. Russell, Wyo.[5]

Within thirty days this was accomplished, and the United States Army marched away from Fort Fetterman forever. Yet since the reservation remained under War Department control, a small military guard was detailed to protect the site temporarily. On September 29 the post's government buildings were sold at public auction for $1,052[6] and ownership of the military bridge was transferred to Albany County.[7]

But Fort Fetterman's military reservations—the land itself—was still War Department property, and would remain so for six more years. The buildings sold to private parties were supposed to be removed within a reasonable time. Some were, but with the guard detail gone and nobody enforcing their removal, many remained standing. And many soon had new occupants.

Almost immediately after the army left the post, a new town was born, retaining the military name, and attracting a variety of squatters, entrepreneurs, and other profit-seekers. Fort Fetterman soon grew into a wild cowtown, the once-vacant buildings housing a population as disorderly as its former one was orderly. Throughout the American West, communities had sprung up near military posts and eventually absorbed the posts when they were abandoned. The town of Fort Fetterman was one that actually rose from the shell of an abandoned post. For nearly a decade after the army departed, it was a trading center and rendezvous point for cattlemen, cowboys, gamblers, dance-hall girls, and kindred frontier personalities.

During the years 1882–1884, the civilian community grew out of the slowly rotting shells of the residences and offices that framed the old parade ground, and the outlying buildings as well. As the new owners took control of the buildings, and (illegally) of the grounds, their military tidiness vanished. Inexplicably, neither the War Department nor the federal civil authorities made any effort to remove these squatters. Here a few traders and other businessmen eked out a living from ranchers, outlaws, and travelers—but mostly from the hard-working cowboys who flocked to town from ranches far and near. Young and energetic, with their pockets full of money, they rode into Fort Fetterman by tens and twenties, then out again next morning, generally penniless but happy or hung over.

Indeed, ranches were prospering in Wyoming Territory. Following construction of the Union Pacific Railroad ranchers had slowly advanced north from the Cheyenne area toward Fort Fetterman during the early 1870s. As the military forced the Indians onto reservations, cattlemen moved into the North Platte River valley, settling first on its south bank and its smaller tributaries. These modest early ranches provided meat and other commodities to the garrison. Some unscrupulous ranchers even invaded the military hay reserves, illegally grazing their cattle and cutting valuable hay. By 1878 the Indian threat had diminished throughout Wyoming Territory enough that cattlemen began grazing their herds on the fertile grasslands north of the river.

༄ ༄

In these early years two businesses served the fledgling community of Fort Fetterman. One establishment, known as the Hog Ranch, had been serving liquor and women to soldiers and civilians alike since 1880. But its barroom brawls were soon rivaled by those at the old post trader's store and saloon, which perhaps was the heart of the new community. Its new owners, Altman & Webel, had purchased the business from Ephraim Tillotson in 1882, just before the post was abandoned. Altman & Webel's saloon was the scene of the first murder, and subsequent lynching, in a town destined to be known for its wild revelry and homicides. Rancher

John Hunton tersely recounted in his diary on Friday, October 13, 1882: "… Dick Elgin killed at Fetterman yesterday. Murderer hung. Nice day."[8]

That confrontation began when Searight's Goose Egg Ranch roundup crew came to Fetterman on October 12; they had just gathered and tallied a herd of cattle bought by the CY Ranch. Among the hard-drinking cowboys crowding the saloon were two men of quite different character but with one thing in common: both would be killed that night. One was Dick Elgin, known as a fine, upstanding man, who was employed as bookkeeper and paymaster for the Goose Egg Ranch. As he stood visiting with friends in the saloon, a Goose Egg cowboy by the name of "Red" or "Arkansas Red" Capps was drinking heavily at the bar. (The deputy sheriff later remembered Capps as "a big, red-headed, happy boy—but whiskey always made him half crazy."[9]) Elgin had started to tell a story when Red Capps staggered over, grabbed him by the arm, and spun him around, demanding money. The still-smiling Elgin told the drink-crazed cowboy that he had already overdrawn his wages, and he could not give him more money without authorization from Mr. Searight, the Goose Egg's owner. Suggesting that Capps call it a night, Elgin turned back to finish his conversation. Again Capps grabbed him, threatening to kill him if he did not supply more money, then gave him a violent shove and jumped backward. Capps's movement caused him to stumble and his revolver discharged, the bullet creasing his own hip. Apparently believing that Elgin had fired on him, Capps now drew and fired. The bullet entered Elgin's mouth and exited through the back of his head, killing him instantly. Realizing what he had done, Capps tried to escape on the first horse he found in front of the saloon—Elgin's. The horse began to buck and run, finally throwing Capps off before reaching the nearby Platte River.

Deputy sheriff Malcolm Campbell's moment had arrived; he had been appointed earlier that year to serve under Albany County sheriff Louis Miller. Campbell was not present when the shooting occurred, but his brother Dan and a man named Moore found Capps floundering around on foot near the Platte River bridge. When Campbell arrived in town, his brother and Moore were returning to Fetterman with their prisoner. The three locked him in a cell at the town jail—the abandoned military guardhouse. A man named Tom Walker was placed on guard to ensure Capps's safety as the deputy went home for supper. But before Campbell could finish his meal, Walker appeared and told him that he need not hurry, because he had been "surprised" and overpowered by a mob of Elgin's friends. When the deputy returned to the jail, Red Capps was hanging from the porch of the jail. The verdict of an inquest held by Justice of the Peace John O'Brien was inconclusive: Capps came to his death by parties unknown to the jury. In a gesture of idiosyncratic frontier justice, the very cowboys who had hanged Red Capps gave him a big and proper funeral.

ᔢ  ᔢ

Solely a purveyor of vice and scandal, the notorious Hog Ranch stood north of the Platte River on the Bozeman Trail, just outside the government-controlled reservation. The establishment earned its name not by the raising of swine, but for its downcast women of sport and its vile whiskey. Harrison Kane had built the Hog Ranch's two log structures about 1880 and did a profitable business with soldiers and teamsters at the fort. In 1883, John Lawrence and Jack Saunders bought the business and continued to cater to travelers and cowboys.[10] Technically it was the only legal business in the town of Fort Fetterman, as it was located off the military reservation and therefore under county jurisdiction. But it too existed only on "squatter's rights," as this land was not opened to settlement.

Other men opened saloons in town, such as Frank "Sod Corn" Gore, who sold out in 1884 to Billy Bacon. But the Hog Ranch was the real destination spot. The owners usually employed six to eight women, aged twenty-five to forty-five, whose "affections were negotiable."[11] Abe Abrahams, a cowboy and handyman employed there, recalled the facilities:

> …the main building comprised the dance-hall, bar, and separate rooms
> for the women. It was about 40 feet long and 18 feet wide, with a stand
> built on the north end for the fiddler. The south end of the bar opened
> into a room where Jack Saunders the proprietor, and his wife Vi slept.
> Across the road about 20 feet there was another log building. It housed
> the kitchen and dining room with a long table covered with oil cloth…
> which would seat about 20 people.[12]

Known as a hot-headed Irishman, John Saunders — known as Jack, his last name sometimes spelled Sanders — had worked as a cook for Searight's Goose Egg Ranch before his partnership with Lawrence.[13] Jack's notorious antics occasionally led to tragedy, but more often were simply humorous. One day Saunders appeared in the office of the town doctor, Amos Barber, and requested his teeth be cleaned. Dr. Barber advised him that he did not offer this service and recommended a certain tooth powder. Saunders then drew his revolver and told the doctor to clean his teeth or get shot. Barber cleaned Saunders's teeth with his personal toothbrush and charged him five dollars, to the satisfaction of both parties.[14]

One of the Hog Ranch's bloodier dramas began on August 29, 1884, when three drunken cowboys, John Fenex, "Pretty Frank" Wallace, and Harry Crosby, shot up the Hog Ranch barroom and chastised its prostitutes. Sheriff Malcolm Campbell recalled that they

> ...had shot out the windows, put bullets through the mirrors back of the bar, and had terrorized the women of the resort...Jack Saunders and John Lawrence were the proprietors of the Hog Ranch and on the day of the disorder they had finally put the three drunken men out and stated that if they ever returned there would be serious trouble.[15]

Several weeks passed and the three cowboys again came into Fetterman for some pleasure before going into winter employment at the E S Ranch. After drinking heavily at Billy Bacon's saloon, they crossed the river to the Hog Ranch. Gunfire soon was heard from that direction. Then Fenex and Crosby galloped into the fort, Fenex having been shot in the abdomen. While the facts are uncertain, presumably Saunders and Lawrence had fired on the three. Wallace had been shot in the face and the two owners must have presumed him dead, otherwise they likely would have finished the job. Instead they pursued Fenex and Crosby, and Wallace made his escape soon after.

Saunders and Lawrence were soon at the fort wanting to finish Fenex and Crosby off, but were calmed down before any more blood could be shed. Lawrence had been wounded in the shoulder and one of the working women, variously reported to be named Ella Wilson or Ella Watson (perhaps making her the notorious Cattle Kate), who was present in the barroom, was similarly injured. Fenex's wound proved fatal, and though Lawrence is credited with killing him, both he and Saunders had fired at the man. Deputy Sheriff Campbell took the participants' testimony, including Fenex's deathbed statement. Lawrence was taken to Laramie for trial where he was acquitted. Later in October, John Lawrence, Jack Saunders, and Ella Wilson (Watson) charged "Pretty Frank" Wallace with attempted murder, but nothing came of the trial due to lack of witnesses.[16]

Late in life Abe Abrahams recalled that at one point, Saunders and his future business partner Billy Bacon owned about thirty horses together:

They ranged on the north side of the river. They were nice cow ponies…
But any way Jack Sanders came over to Fetterman one day and said to
me Kid are you doing any thing now. I told him no… He said I have a
bunch of horses over on Sage Creek. I want you to bring them in. I will
pay you for it he said. So the next morning I went over to the H.R.
where there was a saddle horse in the barn. I started out and I found the
horses about 9 miles from the ranch. It was then about 10 o'clock. Haz-
ing them into the ranch twisting my rope just as I came to the hill leading down to the ranch I heard a shot. The horses heard it too for they
stopped suddenly and started to turn back. I rode over the brow of the
hill and I saw where a cow was shot down. There were several cattle of
different brands ranging round there. I let the horses mosey back a little
ways and waited till I saw the cow butchered and carried away. When all
was clear I drove the horses into the corrall just a log one.

Abrahams' discretion, and good timing, won him an early look at the
trigger-happy habits of Saunders. He went on:

It seems I was just in time for breakfast…the girls did not get up very
early, and I of course joined them being young and always hungry. Jack
Sanders was sitting at the head of the table with Vi along side. There
were two other men beside myself and as I remember 6 girls? It was a
real nice meal, baking powder biscuits, *fried meat* Arbuckles coffee etc…
The meat was on one large platter and was passed around, after eating
awhile some one said, please pass the beef. When Jack Sanders heard this
he said this is elk…Pretty soon some one at the other end of the table
said please pass the *beef*. Pulling out his six gun and shooting into the
ceiling he said *I said this is elk*, and from the end of the table came a calm
voice saying, would you please pass me the elk…Jack Sanders may have
had an impediment in his speech but there was no impediment in his
trigger finger and theres lots of fellows who might *now* say that Sanders
was this and that would not have said it if he were alive.[17]

The Hog Ranch rapidly was gaining the reputation as one of Wyoming's roughest establishments. In 1884 Lawrence and Saunders moved it
across the river into one of the old military buildings.[18] They sold the old
buildings back to Harrison Kane, who continued to operate a business of a
similar nature.[19]

Abrahams saw his boss kill another man on October 26, 1884, on the heels of the Fenex-Crosby-Wallace affair. Abrahams recalled that a man named Ed Schloss had been sent to Fetterman to deliver some papers to the Hog Ranch's owners. On his way, Schloss met up with a friend, Thomas Diamond; according to Schloss, Diamond was in a bad mood and looking for trouble. They went over to the Hog Ranch where Schloss delivered the papers, then joined his friend in the saloon. It seems that Diamond began to insult Saunders. Saunders seemed to take all the insults while the two were present, but after Schloss left, Saunders killed Thomas Diamond.[20]

Two versions of this killing have been recorded, but they concur that Diamond had been gambling and had acquired a substantial debt. The question was: was it murder, or self-defense as the coroner's jury pronounced? The jury determined that both men had drawn their guns with intent to kill. But one jurist, Frank "Sod Corn" Gore, owner of another saloon in Fort Fetterman, felt the killing was the "most cowardly, cold-blooded murder I ever saw," claiming that Diamond was not a gambler nor was he carrying a gun.[21]

Late in 1884 saloon owner William "Billy" Bacon decided to broaden his business holdings. He bought out Lawrence and became Saunders's partner in a new "Hotel de Joy," as it was proclaimed by Sod Corn Gore, in one of the abandoned military buildings. Soon it was a popular place; Gore disclosed that there were always enough saloon customers to "make up a square dance or two at night."[22] Viola Saunders, Jack's wife, was a very pretty woman who attracted the interests of the cowboys who frequented the saloon. According to Malcolm Campbell, Vi would talk to any cowboy as long as he bought drinks for both of them. A waiter would bring the couple three glasses on the tray, one dark frosted glass ostensibly a "chaser" of water for Vi. The sly woman would take a shot of whiskey, hold it in her mouth, then pick up the frosted "chaser" glass and discreetly spit the alcohol into it. Vi could drink all night without getting drunk, while keeping the liquor flowing to the cowboys.[23]

On December 8, 1885, Saunders and Bacon exchanged fire in a gunfight; both men would die. This double homicide only boosted Fort Fetterman's reputation for lawlessness. The ever-present Abe Abrahams recalled the story years later:

> It was in the new Hog Ranch on the Fort side of the river that Bacon and Sander went into partnership... It was the headquarters for the cowboys

*In 1940 Abe Abrahams wrote letters recalling the early days at Fetterman City. Shown here as a younger man, Abrahams was present during much of the rowdy action of the town.* (Author's collection)

and incidentally the gamblers, I have seen poker games for big stakes played there. But it was also a rule that when a person sat in the game he had to leave his gun behind the bar for reason that were obvious. One night there was a 5 handed poker game in which were playing Jack Sanders, Charlie Cobb, Geo. Goodrich, a cowboy named "Blondie" and another whom I have forgotten, Cobb was sitting next to Sanders I remember on his left. During the game Cobb made some remark to Sanders which evidently got under his skin for he immediately, with the back of his hand slapped Cobb across the cheek. A hush fell over the other players but Cobb did not resent it. He was too cowardly, the game went on as usual but at that time was born a plan of revenge. Cobb used to tend bar occasionly for Billy Bacon and seeing Sanders gun (which was ivory handled) amongst the others managed some way to extract the cartridges that were in Sanders gun and replace them with cartridges from which he had previously extracted the powder and replaced the bullets.

Having laid the trap, Cobb now had to lure Saunders into it—at the proper time:

The cowboys in that country were paid with checks good at the Hog Ranch and at the saloon. Bacon would make periodical trips to Cheyenne to cash them. On the last trip from Cheyenne Cobb told Bacon that Sanders had been accusing Bacon of holding out on him which of course was not true. Sanders was tough all right but he was honest. It was 3 or 4 o'clock in the afternoon when Bacon went over to the Hog Ranch. Sanders was seated on a stool near a box stove which stood in the center of the dance hall, on entering he walked toward Sanders and said "Jack what have you been saying about me?" Sanders answered "I don't know what you are talking about." All the time they were speaking Bacon had his hand on his gun. "You're a dam liar" he said and commenced shooting. The bullet struck Sanders in the belly and he fell to the floor. Pulling his gun while leaning on one arm his gun snapped 4 times and the last shot went "puff," I can describe the sound and the bullet from Sanders gun struck Bacon under the chin and lodged some where near his throat. Bacon then walked out and went to his saloon. Throwing his 45 down Sanders went to his room where he and Vi slept and came out with a double barrel shot gun (even tho he was shot in the guts) and started to walk over to Bacon's saloon. He had gone about 20 feet when he reeled and fell to the ground. Boom went the shot gun. Yes I helped pick him up and carried him to his room undressed him while Vi bathed his wound.

Now the story took an ironic turn:

Dr. Watkins who lived in Buffalo was soon brought to Fetterman and after seeing Sanders condition saw that it was a matter of only a few hours and after giving him a hypo went over to Bacon to attend to him. Bacon was playing poker at the time. He had a handkerchief tied around his throat. So going to Bacon's room, undressed him laid him on the bed and administered ether. He had a kit of tools with him which he placed on a chair. He intended to cut out the bullet while the cone was still over his face. Bacon gave a cough and commenced to struggle. The bullet went down his wind pipe and Bacon choked to death. The irony of it was that he died a few hours before Sanders did. The boys couldn't figure out how it was that a 45 cartridge fired from a 45 Colts would fire a bullet that would merely penetrate the skin under his chin, until they got (to) examining the cartridges in Sanders gun and found them devoid of powder. They figured that one cartridge must have had a little powder in it which was evidently caked and didn't empty when Cobb faked those cartridges. Whether Bacon knew that Sanders gun was fixed I don't know but suspicion pointed strongly to Cobb who left the country soon after.

Those are the facts not hearsay for I saw it from the time Bacon walked in the Hog Ranch until he died.[24]

When news of yet another Fort Fetterman shooting spree reached the Wyoming town of Buffalo, the *Big Horn Sentinel* noted:

Jack Sanders was well known in Buffalo, having been a fire warden and deputy sheriff here 2 years ago for a short time. He was a mule skinner in Montana, a foot racer at Ft. Maginnis, a tin horn gambler and a partner of the notorious Dick Buckley, who died with his boots on at Sheridan a short time ago, and lastly proprietor of the Ft. Fetterman Hog Ranch. Sanders' character has been bad for years, and he seemed to court the reputation of 'bad man.' While in Buffalo he was twice arrested with intent to kill, but by some means managed to escape prosecution. His violent death created no surprise here.[25]

The *Cheyenne Democratic Leader* commented:

The settlement of Fort Fetterman is establishing a reputation as one of the worst spots in Wyoming Territory. Nine people have been slaughtered there in the last five years. If Bacon dies, there will be two bad men less in Fetterman. But there is no reason why such a plague spot should be allowed to exist.

It is the government reservation, and if the authorities of Albany County are powerless to remedy the evil, the military authorities at that point owe to themselves that this 'hog ranch' shall be broken up and the hogs driven away.[26]

*William and Frances Bacon came to the Fetterman area about 1879. Bacon owned a saloon in Fetterman and in late 1884 he and John Saunders became partners in a bawdyhouse known as the Hog Ranch at Fetterman. In 1885 Bacon choked to death on a bullet, after an altercation with Saunders.* (Courtesy Wyoming Pioneer Museum)

Indeed, Bacon was marked as a bad man who lived a wild and transient life. In the late 1870s, he and his wife Frances had owned a road ranch between the Laramie and North Laramie Rivers near Uva, Wyoming on the Cheyenne-Deadwood stage road. Johnny Gordon settled nearby with his family, and disliking the gambling, drinking, and hellraising conducted at Bacon's, Gordon bought him out for $1,000 in 1878. Next the Bacons settled on LaBonte Creek in 1879, where they opened another road ranch at the crossing of the Platte River Road. Bacon then sold his squatter's rights for $5,000 to a Mr. Pollard in the spring of 1883 and lived in Cheyenne with his wife for several months, reportedly drinking and gambling, until friends encouraged them to leave. They returned to LaBonte Creek and bought some cows. In June 1884 they took the herd to what would be called Bacon Park, built a cabin, and remained for a short time. Later that year Bacon traded his hundred head of cattle to Frank Gore for Gore's saloon in Fetterman. Soon Bacon and Saunders became partners in the "New Hog Ranch."[27] He occasionally worked as a cowboy for John Hunton and other local ranchers during his abbreviated life.[28]

Bacon left his holdings to his wife, who remained at Fetterman after his death. A public notice was printed in the town's newspaper, *Bill Barlow's Budget*, on July 21, 1886:

> Parties indebted to the estate of the Late Wm. L. Bacon are requested to call upon Collins & Greene and settle. Mrs. Francis Bacon has placed all books and accounts in their hands that all outstanding debts may be promptly collected.

The *Budget* reported that Mrs. Bacon was going into the lodging business: she was having the old military barracks removed and the ground leveled for a new boardinghouse to be run in connection with Erben's restaurant.[29] Later that year, on December 10, she remarried to J. M. Abney, a stock detective for the Wyoming Stock Growers Association, Fetterman district.[30]

Characters such as Billy Bacon kept lawman Malcolm Campbell busy in the Fetterman area. Sometimes the lawbreakers were truly notorious. In the winter of 1883, while serving as deputy sheriff, Campbell arrested the famed "cannibal" Alfred (sometimes spelled Alferd) Packer, who had eaten the remains of five miners in his party in Colorado ten years earlier. Under the alias John Swartz, Packer was now prospecting the hills south of Fetterman, based in a cabin on Wagon Hound Creek. Another prospector, Frenchy Cazabon, recognized Packer drinking in one of the Fetterman saloons and reported his discovery to Deputy Campbell. Campbell telegraphed authorities in Colorado who were eager to apprehend the outlaw and requested Campbell to do so. Campbell and his brother made the arrest on Wagon Hound and brought the fugitive back to Fetterman where they locked him in the old guardhouse overnight. The next morning Campbell took the prisoner to Laramie, where he was jailed, then turned over to Colorado authorities. Alfred Packer was hanged in Colorado in May 1883.[31]

*Malcolm Campbell first came to Fort Fetterman in 1872 working as a freighter for*
*John Hunton. Later he held his own government contracts. But he was best known*
*as a lawman, first as a deputy sheriff, then as the sheriff of Converse County, later*
*chief of police at Douglas. He and his wife ran a boarding house near Fetterman.*
(Courtesy Wyoming State Museum)

When Malcolm Campbell died in 1932, both his time as a lawman
and his early days had been filled with adventure. The Canadian-born
Campbell was not afraid of work, and had worked as a bullwhacker, railroad construction worker and tie cutter, and cowboy. After serving as
deputy sheriff in Albany County, he became the first sheriff of Converse
County in 1888, while the town of Fetterman was being replaced by
Douglas as the center of activity. The reputation he had acquired while
deputy sheriff at Fetterman gained him high respect in the area, helping
him become one of the new county's most respected citizens and lawmen.

# THE RISE AND FALL
# OF "DRYBONE" 1885–1890

CHAPTER

**9**

WESTERN NOVELIST Owen Wister visited Wyoming on doctor's orders in 1895 to reclaim his health after a long illness. Wister's Philadelphia physician, S. Weir Mitchell, had asked his friend Amos Barber—former surgeon at Fort Fetterman—to recommend a retreat where Wister could rest in isolation. Frank Wolcott, a rancher on the North Platte River near present-day Glenrock, offered his ranch, and Wister accepted.

While in Wyoming, Wister became interested in collecting stories about Fort Fetterman in its cowtown heyday, which had been about ten years earlier. He drew on many of these tales in his novels and short stories in later years. In Wister's fiction he named it Drybone,[1] and some of its characters are recognizable citizens of Fort Fetterman.

In the 1907 novel *Lin McLean*, Wister described approaching Drybone on a night of revelry:

> Upstream they could make out the light of Drybone bridge, but not the bridge itself; and two lights on the further bank showed where stood the hog-ranch opposite Drybone. They went on over the table-land, and reached the next herald of the town, Drybone's chief historian, the graveyard. Beneath its slanting head-boards and wind-shifted sand lay many more people than lived in Drybone. They passed by the fence of this shelterless acre on the hill and shoutings and high music began to reach them. At the foot of the hill they saw the sparse lights and shapes of the town... Drybone had known a wholesome adventurous youth, where manly lives and deaths were plenty. It had been an army post. It had seen horse and foot, and heard the trumpet. Brave wives had kept house for their captains upon its bluffs. Winter and summer they had made the best of it. When the War Department ordered the captains to catch Indians, the wives bade them God-speed. When the Interior

*Dr. Amos W. Barber was surgeon in charge of the hospital of the Fetterman Hospital Association. He moved his practice to Douglas but still visited the Fetterman Hospital daily. He later served as acting Governor.* (Courtesy Wyoming State Archives)

Department ordered the captains to let the Indians go again, still they made the best of it...

Then, Wister continued, "the soldiers were taken away," and

...into these empty barracks came to dwell and to do business every joy that made the cowpuncher's holiday, and every hunted person who was baffling the sheriff...

The captain's quarters were a saloon now; professional cards were going on in the adjutant's quarters night and day; and the commissary building made a good dance-hall and hotel. Instead of guard-mounting, you would see a horse-race on the parade ground, and there was no provost-sergeant to gather up the broken bottles and old boots. Heaps

*Fort Fetterman as a town in 1886, viewed from the southwest. Note that the infantry barracks on the west side of the parade ground have been removed. The guardhouse and ordnance storehouse are in the upper right of the photograph. The post trader's store (Bolln and Rastaetter's store when this image was taken) is the large building in center. At the top edge of the photo, is the old officers' row, its buildings now serving as (left to right) the Fetterman Hospital Association's first hospital building, an unknown business, the Metcalf & Williams Store, the Meat Market and Dick's Place.* (Photographer, Ned Nearing. Courtesy of the Wyoming State Archives)

of these choked the rusty fountain. In the tufts of yellow ragged grass that dotted the place plentifully were lodged as many aces and queens and ten-spots, which the Drybone wind had blown wide from the doors out of which they had been thrown when a new pack was called for inside. Among the grass tufts would line visitors who had applied for beds too late at the dance-hall, frankly sleeping their whiskey off in the morning air.[2]

Wister depicted Drybone, rough-hewn as it was, during its glory days. At Fort Fetterman those glory days, prosperous but numbered, were in 1885–86. The town's prospects had brightened with the news that the Fremont, Elkhorn and Missouri Valley Railroad would extend westward from Chadron, Nebraska, into the Platte River Valley in 1886. Speculators bet that somewhere in the Fetterman vicinity a town would be located as a terminus; the existing settlement seemed the logical choice. By spring of 1886 Fort Fetterman was booming. It even had a newspaper, known as *Bill Barlow's Budget*. Newspaperman Merris C. Barrow, who used the name Bill Barlow in his writings, later recalled the 1886 population boom:

> ...probably twenty-five or thirty houses—some of them quite pretentious and all in good repair. All had been sold to private parties, and when the writer reached there on May 22d all were occupied...Fetterman at that time numbered possibly 500 souls. Everybody had money in plenty—prices were altitudinous, and rents sky-high. There was a daily stage from Rock Creek on the Union Pacific and on north to Buffalo and (Fort) McKinney, and already adventurous freighters were breaking a trail from Chadron along the survey of the proposed railroad and along which were numerous grading camps.[3]

While Barrow was optimistic that the town would flourish, writers for the *Cheyenne Mirror* noted the pitfalls. Not only did Fetterman have a reputation as a resort for crime, it also lacked any legal right to exist as a town. The U.S. government still owned the reservation on which it stood. The *Mirror's* correspondent pointed out, "The liquor dealers are trembling in their boots for fear that their licenses will be recalled and they be ordered off the reservation. We will wait and see what Uncle Sam will do in the matter."[4]

Barrow, too, saw Fort Fetterman's precarious situation. In his newspaper's first issue, on June 9, 1886, he noted:

> ...the reservation, embracing sixty square miles of Wyoming's choicest land, has not yet been thrown open for settlement, and the present town of Fort Fetterman therefore is subject to removal and total obliteration at the will of Uncle Sam. Most of the buildings built by the military still remain, and many more have been erected recently and are now in process of construction—all occupied as either business houses or residences...[5]

A week later he updated his readers:

> The Fort Fetterman reservation will not, in all probability, be thrown open for settlement for sometime...the latest instruction from the

*Merris C. Barrow established central Wyoming's first newspaper,* Bill Barlow's Budget, *with the first issue published on June 9, 1886 in Fetterman. Barrow used the pseudonym Bill Barlow in his writing.* (Courtesy Wyoming State Pioneer Museum)

interior department to the surveyor general of Wyoming is that no more surveys are to be made until those of several years previously have been examined. As the necessary preliminary to the opening of a reservation is its survey, it becomes at once apparent that, with others, Fort Fetterman will probably remain for some time as now, the property of Uncle Sam.[6]

Interestingly, while Fort Fetterman's town status was unofficial, the U.S. Postal Department maintained the old military post office in a supposedly non-existent town.

But many citizens remained optimistic, and launched enterprises to serve a legitimate town. Fort Fetterman was changing rapidly. In 1885, a

*The western officers' quarters on the north side of the parade ground became the first hospital for the Fetterman Hospital Association in 1885. Note the man on the porch with his arm in a sling.* (Photographer, Ned Nearing. Courtesy of the Wyoming State Pioneer Museum)

soldier passing through saw a town consisting "… simply of a couple of saloons (so different these western ranch-bars to the magnificent affairs in peopled States,) and a government agency."[7] By 1886, in addition to many saloons, gambling halls, and houses of prostitution, Fort Fetterman sported hotels and restaurants, a bank, dry-goods and grocery stores, a blacksmith shop, and an opera house.

It also had a community-funded institution: a hospital. In November 1885, the newly created Fetterman Hospital Association opened a medical facility in the old officers' quarters on the northwest corner of the old parade ground. (The old post hospital east of the quadrangle was already being used as the "New Hog Ranch" at this time.) Amos Barber was re-employed as the hospital surgeon. Medical care was free to those who joined the association for a dollar a month; non-members were charged separately for service. The next spring several responsible citizens and nearby ranchers used a form letter to sell more memberships, raising dues at the same time:

Fort Fetterman, Wyoming, April 25, 1886

Mr.:

Dear Sir:

    A year ago at the General meeting of the Stockmen held at Fort

Fetterman, the Fetterman Hospital Association was organized for the purpose of furnishing medical attendance, board and lodging to all men who would subscribe one dollar ($1.00) per month to the Hospital Fund. The executive committee secured the services of Dr. A. W. Barber of Pennsylvania Hospital, Philadelphia. The hospital was opened and conduced until November 1885, with a degree of success that has warranted a reorganization for the year 1886. The services of Dr. Barber have again been secured and we trust the purposes for which the hospital association was organized meets with your approval. The subscription fees will be from April 1, 1886 ten dollars ($10.00).

You are respectfully solicited to become a subscriber and to use your influence in inducing all the men in your employment to do the same, and to forward a list of names together with their subscriptions to the secretary, who will furnish you a printed receipt for the same.

Donations thankfully received,

W. C. Sampson, Secretary

Fort Fetterman, Wyoming

| | |
|---|---|
| D. H. Andrews | A. A. Falknor |
| W. S. Weaver | Alex. Cox |
| Alex. Bowie | Jas. Bury |
| Philip Dater | Lee Moore |
| W. E. Guthrie | C. Rasteatter *Committee* |
| H. E. Teschmacher | |

The association held a business meeting on the first Monday of each month. Barrow wrote of the July 5 meeting:

> …quite a number of the cowboys in this section—especially among the new hands—have not yet become members of this benevolent institution. It would seem as though every man in the business would cheerfully pay the small amount asked, and thereby secure the best medical treatment, careful nursing and the comforts of a home in case he met with any of the accidents peculiar to his mode of life.[8]

Apparently the first hospital building was too small; after the deaths of Billy Bacon and Jack Saunders, Vi Saunders sold the "New Hog Ranch" building to the association in 1886.

*Another view of the Fetterman Hospital Association building, with Doctor Amos Barber, his horse and dog. Note the square shaped medical saddle bags attached to the cantle and the cantina saddle pockets attached to the horn.* (Photographer, Ned Nearing. Courtesy Wyoming State Archives)

In his July 14 edition Barrow announced that the hospital had three patients: Sam Miller of the 74 Ranch with a chronic abscess, O. J. Brennen, a carpenter from Douglas who had tick or "mountain fever," and J. Crook Verden, a VR Ranch cowboy with a badly sprained ankle.[9]

A month later, Barrow reported that Albany County officials had contracted with the association to "provide for caring for all the county's paupers " in the central region.[10] More sardonically, the *Cheyenne Mirror* noted that the county had "provided for a hospital at this point for paupers and insane persons. It will soon be needed."[11] As it turned out, this arrangement ensured that the hospital would continue to operate at Fort Fetterman—for a time—even after the town's fortunes had turned.

The hospital never was short of patients, as Barrow reported that same month under the headline "A Chapter of Accidents." All the incidents involved firearms and all were self-inflicted. In one case E.C. Johnson, son of the railroad grading crew contractor, overturned in his buggy and the fall discharged his revolver. Wounded in the lower leg, Johnson pushed the buggy upright and drove himself to Fetterman where Dr. Barber treated him at the hospital. Next, local rancher John Arnold was loading his gun in preparation for a hunting trip when a cartridge exploded and put out an eye. Arnold rode his horse to Fetterman where Dr. Barber, Dr. Van Norman, and Mr. W.C. Sampson removed the "mangled optic." On the very same day young Norvill Goodynoontz of the Anvil Ranch was hunting antelope when a cartridge exploded prematurely, putting one eye out and badly burning the other. Barber and Sampson had just finished removing Arnold's eye when they were called to the Anvil Ranch to work on the boy. After the surgery Dr. Barber said that while the boy lost one eye, the other would recover in time.[12] Fate was against young Norvill, who died in Greeley, Colorado, of typhoid fever a few weeks later.[13]

Amos Barber took a leave of absence from Fetterman on October 27 to go east to seek medical help for a severe eye infection of his own. Dr. Wilson assumed Barber's duties.[14] That November and December, typhoid fever ravaged Fort Fetterman and its new neighboring town of Douglas, causing several deaths in each community.[15] On January 3, 1887, Barber returned having recovered almost entirely from his eye trouble.

Weekly columns in the *Budget* reveal an average daily census of four patients during the last three months of 1886. Most patients had broken limbs or other common but acute ailments.

Merris Barrow visited the hospital on December 2, during the typhoid scare, and was favorably impressed:

> The county authorities have certainly done a wise thing in making arrangements for patients to be admitted to this institution upon orders issued by our justices of the peace. The house is clean and neat, and the wards occupied by patients are made as pleasant and comfortable as such places can possibly be made. With so much sickness in our midst the Fetterman Hospital is a very boon to this community, and deserves the liberal support of our citizens. Those among us who are so unfortunate as to be ill and unable to pay for the services of a physical certainly need feel no shame in applying to Judge Clay or to his associate justices for admitting orders to the Fetterman Hospital. Women are not treated in the hospital building, but arrangements are made for their care and treatment by the hospital surgeon—so there is no need for anyone in our young community to suffer for want of proper medical treatment.

This institution is the philanthropic undertaking of private parties originally and ostensibly for the benefit of cow-boys, but by the
wise and timely action of our county commissioners is made available
to all who are in need of it. The expenses of the hospital are very great,
and often greater than the income, yet no complaint is heard but the
deficiencies are generously contributed by our cattlemen. It would
seem that the merchants who derive their best trade from the cattlemen of this section might surely assist materially in the support of the
institution...[16]

Despite the excellent facilities there were some patients the doctors
could not save. One poignant story was that of Mrs. Sophia Schaus, who
died on August 15, 1886 of inflammation of the bowels, leaving her husband Julius with two children, one only two months old. She was buried
the next day in the Fetterman cemetery.[17] Fate was not finished with
Julius, however; two weeks later his infant son died unexpectedly.[18]

Fetterman boasted three hotels: the Wyoming House, the Valley
House, and the Fetterman Hotel. The last, perhaps, could be proclaimed
first-class considering the remoteness of the community. The Wyoming
House—a boarding house and restaurant—was owned and operated by
Mrs. Ellen Slaymaker whose husband Samuel, known as Judge "Sammy"
Slaymaker, served as justice of the peace.

Ellen Slaymaker ran a successful enterprise, augmenting her restaurant
fare with occasional dances. It may have been during one of these dances
that a woman named Mary Potter died from an overdose of laudanum, an
extract of opium commonly available at the time.[19] Perhaps Mary Potter
was the mysterious woman described by both Malcolm Campbell and
Owen Wister in separate accounts—one fact, the other fiction—of a
death by laudanum in July 1885.

Campbell's version appears in Robert B. David's book *Malcolm Campbell, Sheriff*. Although he did not name her, the sheriff recalled a married
woman for whom Dr. Barber was the attending physician. While the poor
woman was "dead drunk" with laudanum and dying, her husband threatened to kill the doctor if he could not save her. The woman died but the
grief-stricken husband failed to follow through with his murderous threat.
According to Campbell, the woman was very popular with the cowboys

*Judge Samuel Slaymaker came to Fort Fetterman in 1875 as a commissary sergeant. He stayed in the area after his discharge, running the Buckshot road ranch. Later he served in several county offices including justice of the peace which brought him the title "Judge" Slaymaker.* (Courtesy Wyoming State Pioneer Museum)

and they decided to give her a grand funeral. At the old abandoned military cemetery they found an "old soldier's coffin" and brought it to the fort. They "lined it inside with muslin, black calico and cushions" and placed her body in it, attired in her wedding dress. A wagon was produced and the body taken to the cemetery, surrounded by "yelling, shooting cowboys, who were half drunk."[20]

Ben Merchant Vorpahl, in his study of the Frederic Remington and Owen Wister letters, points out that Amos Barber related this story to Wister during his summer stay in Wyoming in 1895. Wister fictionalized it in "Burial of the Biscuit Shooter," a short story that later became the last chapter of his novel *Lin McLean*.[21] In that chapter, retitled "Destiny at Drybone," Amos Barber appears as Amory W. Barker and the Slaymakers

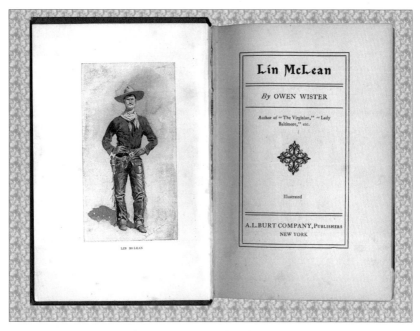

*Owen Wister's 1897 novel* Lin McLean *was based on the town of Fetterman, which the book called Drybone.*(High Plains Press collection)

as the Slaghammers. The hero, Lin McLean, arrives in Drybone on a riotous night, Wister wrote:

> Tonight the innocents had certainly come to town, and Drybone was furnishing to them all its joys. Their many horses stood tied at every post and corner—patient, experienced cow-ponies, well knowing it was an all-night affair. The talk and laughter of the riders was in the saloons; they leaned joking over the bars, they sat behind their cards at the tables, they strolled to the post-trader's to buy presents for their easy sweethearts, the boots were keeping audible time with the fiddle at Mrs. Slaghammer's.

A woman from McLean's past, Katy Lusk, is there, and although they are estranged, McLean feels responsible for her. At Mrs. Slaghammer's dance, Katy collapses, having taken six ounces of laudanum. When the doctor asks McLean to keep her awake and moving to shake off the laudanum he dutifully obeys. "Her words came through deeper and deeper veils, fearless, defiant, a challenge inarticulate, a continuous mutter...as he struggled to move with her dragging weight." Next, Katy's deranged husband, encouraged with drink, threatens Dr. Barker with his pistol and assaults McLean with a rifle. Finally, after several hours, Katy dies and the coroner is summoned. Wister named the coroner Judge Slaghammer (Samuel Slaymaker had been enacted as Fetterman's coroner during this time) and noted that the coroner's jury were all drunk, probably another true-to-life touch.

Learning of Katy's death, two cowboys ride up to the graveyard where they search "among the old dug-up graves on the hill," rope "a light, halfrotted coffin" and return to the "post trader's store." Several other cowboys, with names like Chalkeye and Limber Jim, find "cloth and chintz" to line the coffin, and a surreal, drunken funeral follows:

> Stuffs were unrolled and flung aside until many folds and colors... unmeasured yards of this drab chintz were ripped off, money treble its worth was thumped upon the counter, and they returned, bearing it like a streamer to the coffin. While the noise of hammers filled the room, the hearse came tottering to the door, pulled and pushed by twenty men. It was an ambulance left behind by the soldiers, and of the old-fashioned shape, concave of body, its top blown away in winds of long ago; and as they revolved its wheels dished in and out like hoops about to fall. While some made harness from ropes, and throwing the saddles off two ponies backed them to the vehicle, the body was put in the coffin, now covered with chintz. But the laudanum upon the front of her dress revolted those who remembered their holidays with her, and, turning the woman on her face, they looked their last upon her flashing, colored ribbons, and nailed the lid down. They carried her out, but the concave body of the hearse was too short for the coffin; the end reached out, and it might have fallen. But Limber Jim, taking the reins, sat upon the other end, waiting and smoking. For all Drybone was making ready to follow in some way. They had sought the husband, the chief mourner. He, however, still lay in the grass of the quadrangle, and despising him as she had done, they left him to wake when he should choose. Those men who could sit in their saddles rode escort, the old friends nearest, and four held the heads of the frightened cowponies who were to draw the hearse. They had never known harness before, and they plunged with the men who held them. Behind the hearse the women followed in a large ranch-wagon, this moment

arrived in town. Two mares drew this, and their foals gamboled around them. The great flat-topped dray for hauling poles came last, with its four government mules. The cow-boys had caught sight of it and captured it. Rushing to the post-trader's, they carried the sleeping men from the counter and laid them on the dray. Then, searching Drybone outside and in for any more incapable of following, they brought them, and the dray was piled.

Limber Jim called for another drink, and, with his cigar between his teeth, cracked his long bull-whacker whip. The ponies, terrified, sprang away, scattering the men that held them, and the swaying hearse leaped past the husband, over the stones and the many playing-cards in the grass. Masterfully steered it came safe to an open level, while the throng cheered the unmoved driver on his coffin, his cigar between his teeth.

"Stay with it Jim!" they shouted. "You're a king!"

A steep ditch lay across the flat where he was veering, abrupt and nearly hidden; but his eye caught the danger in time, and swinging from it leftward so that two wheels of the leaning coach were in the air, he faced the open again, safe, as the rescue swooped down upon him. The horsemen came at the ditch, a body of daring, a sultry blast of youth. Wheeling at the brink, they turned, whirling their long ropes. The skillful nooses flew, and the ponies, caught by the neck and foot, were dragged back to the quadrangle and held in line... So they went up the hill. When the riders reached the tilted gate of the graveyard, they sprang off and scattered among the hillocks, stumbling and eager ...and began choosing among the open, weather-drifted graves from which the soldiers had been taken. The figures went up and down the uneven ridges, calling and comparing.

The sand-hills became clamorous with voices until they arrived at a choice, when some one with a spade quickly squared the rain-washed opening. With lariats looping the coffin round, they brought it and were about to lower it, when Chalkeye, too near the edge, fell in, and one end of the box rested upon him. He could not rise by himself, and they pulled the ropes helplessly above...[22]

After her burial (Chalkeye survived it), the funeral-goers return to the fort to continue their drinking spree.

*The Fetterman Hotel was owned by Bury and Nichols in 1886, the year of this photograph. It stood on the east side of the parade ground and was originally a triplex of officers' quarters for the army. Note the striped "barbers pole" at the right.* (Photographer, Ned Nearing. Courtesy Wyoming State Archives)

Such were the misadventures that might begin in Fort Fetterman's hotels. Perhaps the clientele proved too wild for Ellen Slaymaker, for in 1886, after just a year in business, she sold the Wyoming House to C.T. Camp. It changed hands several times: Camp retired in October of that year and was succeeded by a J.H. Van Meter.[23] By March Van Meter was already advertising the building for sale or rent.[24] The Wyoming House reopened in April 1887, under the management of new owners Doggett & Cox.[25]

Little is known about the establishment called the Valley House; the only mention was in an October 1886 issue of the *Cheyenne Mirror*: "Lovers of the terpsichorean art anticipate a pleasant time at the masquerade to be given by the Valley house on Christmas eve."[26] Short-lived at Fort Fetterman, it apparently moved to the growing community of Douglas, where the *Douglas Budget* (a later incarnation of Barrow's paper) later referred to a business by that name.

Lastly, the Fetterman Hotel and dining hall was, by most accounts, the best of the three hotels. Owners James H. Bury and William Nichols established it in 1885 in the former large triplex officers' quarters on the east side of the parade ground, and it soon became the business and cultural center for the community. Its large dining room was in demand for both social and religious gatherings, as Fort Fetterman had no church. The hotel even hosted weddings; in its parlor Joe Black married Mary Jaycox on New Year's Day in 1886,[27] and James E. Wallace, of Johnson County, Wyoming, wed Miss M. V. Seade of Carlisle, Illinois, on July 15 of the next year. Judge Madison had barely finished the ceremony when he "imprinted an affectionate kiss on her off cheek—an act that was lustily cheered by the boys." The newlyweds were fifty years old.[28]

Church services were conducted at the hotel in August 1886 by two young theological students. In September Reverends Richardson and Conrad, Congregationalists, held Sunday services in the dining room. They moved later that month into a new church in Douglas, a shack-tent known as the "Tabernacle."[29] But apparently religion had not entirely departed Fetterman; three o'clock Sunday services were led by a Mr. Stanton on April 24, 1887.

But merry-making was more typical at the hotel. The *Cheyenne Mirror* reported in December 1886; "The Fetterman hotel will give a dance on the 30, in their dining room. Supper will be served after the dance."[30] The *Budget* reported that seventy-five couples attended, including a dozen from Douglas, and that the success of the "affair was due to Mr. F. M. Clarke, the gentlemanly clerk of the house, who was untiring in his efforts to make everybody feel at home, and to enjoy themselves."[31]

Not every encounter was gentlemanly at the hotel saloon, where M.E. "Smoky" James tended bar. On the morning of August 26, 1886, after an argument with H.T. Blair, James shot Blair with a .45-caliber Colt revolver. Later James's friends said he shot in self-defense, but other witnesses contradicted their statement.[32] At the inquest held by Judge Clay, who had succeeded Samuel Slaymaker, witnesses claimed the shooting was unprovoked. The prisoner was refused bail and, as Blair was still alive, James was charged with attempted murder. Deputy Sheriff J.T. Williams ordered him to await trial at the Territorial Prison in Laramie.[33] By the end of November, Blair had miraculously recovered from his wound, and James was found guilty of attempted murder.

In February 1887, Bury and Nichols enticed Miss Lou Baily, cook at the Valley House—now in Douglas—into their employ, "to the great satisfaction of the many patrons of that well conducted house."[34] The next issue of the *Budget* reported that Miss Minnie Craw, the pastry cook for the Valley House, also switched her employment to the Fetterman Hotel.[35]

*The Metcalf & Williams store and post office, shown here in 1886, was located on the northeast corner of the parade ground in a building originally used as an officers' quarters. Like most of the officers' quarters, it was a duplex, intended to house two individual, lower-ranking officers. Presumably, the interior center partition was removed to make a single large storeroom for the general store and post office. This would account for the removal of the chimney stack between the two dormer windows. The individuals in the photograph are unidentified.* (Photographer, Ned Nearing. Courtesy Wyoming State Archives)

Soon after, Nichols retired and Bury acquired a new partner, W.C. Sampson.[36] The Fetterman Hotel's success continued for about a year. Although unannounced, the hotel seems to have closed in the spring of 1888, when all advertisements in the *Budget* ceased. No other reference to the hotel exists after that time.

Many restaurants opened their doors briefly at Fort Fetterman, but besides the hotel dining rooms, evidence of only one remains. In late August 1886, J.H. Van Meter (who also briefly owned the Wyoming House) leased space from a man named Urban in a building on the west side of the old parade ground. Here, presumably in one of the old military mess halls,[37] Van Meter opened a restaurant which he called a bakery and oyster house. The oysters may have been questionable, but the bakery was much needed. A month after opening, Van Meter's bakery was threatened by a fire. It started in the kitchen but the flames were quenched before it had done much damage.[38] It is uncertain how long the bakery lasted thereafter.

*Elizabeth and John T. Williams were prominent Fetterman citizens. He was a partner in the Metcalf & Williams general store. They later moved to Douglas and became involved in ranching. He held many public offices including serving two years in the Wyoming State Senate. (Courtesy Wyoming State Pioneer Museum)*

Fort Fetterman also briefly boasted a lending institution, the Maverick Bank, named with the cowboy term for an unbranded calf. It opened early in 1886, but operated only until the end of June, when a branch office was built in Douglas. For a few months Mr. H. T. Blackburn, an assistant cashier, continued bank hours at Fetterman while the president, Mr. C. M. Garver, presided in Douglas,[39] but by September the Maverick Bank closed its doors at Fort Fetterman."[40]

Grocery and clothing stores are important to any frontier community; Fort Fetterman had several. The Blue Front was established on the north side of the parade ground in the eastern officers' quarters in late 1884 by George W. Metcalf. Metcalf advertised his wares in the *Budget:* "Seaside Library…Stetson hats…Lemons seventy five cents a dozen…Golden Spike cigars."[41] July 7, 1886, found the Blue Front under a new name, Metcalf & Williams, John T. Williams having bought a half interest in the business. In Barrow's words, "They make a strong team."[42]

The store also housed the post office, which was the scene of a scuffle that both the *Budget* and the *Cheyenne Mirror* found newsworthy:

*For health reasons George Metcalf came to Fort Fetterman as a civilian quartermaster agent. Later he became postmaster of Fetterman and a partner in the Metcalf & Williams general store. He and his wife Susan later moved to Douglas.* (Courtesy Wyoming State Pioneer Museum)

> Miss Mattie Harnett, a young lady employee of the Fetterman Hotel, entered the post office accompanied by a lady friend, and proceeded to apply a rawhide to Mr. Pease's shoulders, but he grasped the rawhide and wrenched it from her. She drew another from some mysterious recess, and began again. Pease caught her hands and both fell struggling to the floor, when they were separated. Miss Hartnett claims that Pease had been circulating false reports injurious to her character, and she resorted to the rawhide as a means of redress. She failed in accomplishing her object, but her intentions were good.[43]

This episode, while humorous in print, certainly was not considered so by Miss Harnett or Mr. Pease.

In 1886 the *Mirror* reported on Metcalf's annual trip to Chicago: "Metcalf & Williams are bringing on a stock of clothing to stock their store in the post office building."[44] In July Metcalf went east again for inventory, but Barrow reported another motive: "Postmaster Metcalf has gone east after a wife. He will purchase incidently a big stock of clothing for Metcalf & Williams Douglas store."[45]

*George Bolln came to Fetterman as a merchant, establishing a grocery store with his partner Charles Rastaetter. Later they opened a second store in Douglas which Bolln ran. In 1887 he married Paulene Muegel and built a brick home in Douglas.* (Courtesy Wyoming State Pioneer Museum)

But that firm, too, would decide that the future lay in the new town of Douglas. That October, the partners opened a second store there and turned the management of the Fetterman store and post office over to Mr. Pease, a long-time resident in central Albany County. Pease had been the assistant postmaster at Fetterman and was appointed as postmaster after Metcalf left. But within months he died of typhoid fever and was buried in the Fetterman cemetery on January 11, 1887.[46] Williams moved back to Fetterman to take charge of the store. Barrow reported that "Douglasites will miss him."[47] Thus the Metcalf & Williams store continued to serve Fetterman as the U.S. Post Office until the summer of 1887, when William Werner became postmaster.

While living at Fetterman, John T. Williams also served one year as deputy sheriff. Barrow wrote: "While in Fetterman last week Sheriff Jamison revoked the commission of Mr. C. Reid as his deputy and appointed John T. Williams. Mr. Williams will make Douglas his headquarters."[48] He was replaced when a new Albany County sheriff was elected.

The old post trader's store and saloon, sold by Ephraim Tillotson in 1882 to Altman & Webel, was sold again in 1886 to George Bolln and

*William Werner and his wife Mary Pfeifer Werner were the last known residents of Fetterman. They homesteaded on the abandoned Fort Fetterman reservation and he served as Fetterman's postmaster. In 1893 they moved from the nearly deserted town of Fetterman to live on the homestead.* (Courtesy Howard Apel)

Charles Rastaetter. They converted it into a grocery and dry-goods store. After two successful years they opened a second store in Douglas in September 1888. George Bolln supervised the new shop while Charles Rastaetter remained at Fetterman with the old one.[49] The split was fateful. Bolln became one of Douglas's leading merchants, later serving as Albany County commissioner, city councilman, and mayor, while Rastaetter apparently absconded from the Fetterman store with the company funds and disappeared in 1889.[50]

In earlier days Bolln and Rastaetter had also owned an icehouse at Fetterman, which by 1887 they had sold to James Bury & Company. During that cold January, the new owners put up ninety tons of ice in it, in addition to ninety-five in their existing icehouse. Other citizens were busy with ice-cutting too; Joe Barker put away fifty tons and Judge F. H. Sparhawk cut three hundred tons. Lacking an icehouse, Sparhawk left his haul on the banks of the Platte below the town.[51]

In the blacksmith, carpenter, and wagon repair shop he opened in 1886, Harold Peterson made bits and spurs for such Wyoming personalities as Senator John Kendrick and F.A. Meanea, the famous Cheyenne saddler.

*Archie Faulkner's restaurant at Fetterman had a short business life of less than one year in 1886. The building was presumably located east of Dick's Place, north of the Fetterman Hotel. Hand painted above the door is "Archie." None of the individuals are identified.* (Photographer, Ned Nearing. Courtesy Wyoming State Pioneer Museum)

Phares C. Hubbard built the shop, a frame structure with an adjoining sleeping apartment, completing it on August 5, 1886. However, when Peterson failed to pay, Hubbard placed a lien on the shop, forcing him to sell out the following February. The property was valued at about $225.00, of which $113.00 was owed Hubbard.[52] Apparently, with the extra cash, Peterson rented another storefront and stayed in business, as he continued to advertise in the *Budget* through March 1888. A month later he moved to the new Wyoming town of Bessemer where he plied his blacksmithing trade. Later, when he gained steady work on the Pathfinder Dam west of Casper, he rarely returned to his shop at Fetterman.[53]

Entrepreneur Archie Faulkner operated several businesses in Fetterman including a saloon just east of the Metcalf & Williams store. Faulkner and his partner Richard Moses named it Dick's Place. Their ad noted that they specialized in mixed drinks during the summer months. With John T. Williams as partner, Faulkner also opened a butcher shop, the Meat Market, and advertised its location in the *Budget:* "First door east of post

*The Meat Market, owned by John T. Williams and Archie Faulkner, was located immediately east of the Metcalf & Williams store. Dick's Place, one of the many saloons at Fetterman in 1886, was owned by Archie Faulkner and Richard Moses. Neither of these buildings was constructed by the army, but most likely were built with lumber salvaged from military buildings. The picket fence indicates that the photograph was taken inside the north fence of the Fetterman Hotel. Dr. Amos Barber, the only man indentified, is on horseback in the foreground, his medical saddle bags clearly visible behind the cantle. Curiously, a number of the men have their pistols drawn in what seems to be posed gunplay.* (Photographer, Ned Nearing. Courtesy Wyoming State Pioneer Museum)

office, north side of parade ground."[54] He also briefly owned a restaurant, which closed in October 1886.[55] Later, Faulkner would remain at Fetterman when many others moved to Douglas. In January 1887 he even built a new home on "Hospital Avenue."[56] The Faulkner and Moses partnership dissolved in March 1887, and in the same month Faulkner advertised in the *Budget* that all personal debtors should pay W.C. Sampson at the Fetterman Hotel.

Dick Moses continued to run his saloon while Faulkner was closing all his interests at Fetterman.[57] On June 8, 1887, Ed Lynn fired two shots into Moses's saloon, solely because he considered himself a "bad man," and fatally wounded an elderly man named William H. Parks. Parks had earlier been a partner in another Fetterman saloon, the Arcade. He was attended in the hospital by Dr. Barber, but died the following day and was buried in the Fetterman cemetery. Lynn was arrested in Douglas by Deputy Sheriff Campbell and given a hearing by Judge Mecum, who bound him over in Laramie for trial.[58]

Dick Moses had added a restaurant to his saloon that January, advertising that the "hungry will be served with the best the market affords."[59] He borrowed the money for the addition from C. C. P. Webel, with the saloon itself as collateral. But Moses's timing was off; the town's fortunes had turned. Slow business forced Webel to foreclose on Moses. The loan of $300 plus interest came due on October 5, and Moses was unable to pay. He therefore advertised his business closure and defaulted to Webel, who took his property and inventory as payment. The building was listed as a "One frame building located near the northeast corner of the public square, or old parade grounds, at Ft. Fetterman."[60]

Fort Fetterman had saloons aplenty, though most were short-lived. The *Cheyenne Mirror* on December 23, 1886, noted that a "slight disturbance took place at Borker's saloon Saturday night. Some of the railroad men from the camp near town attempted to run the place, but they were quieted after they had received a few black eyes."[61]

The same issue reported that "twenty retail liquor licenses were issued to Fetterman parties last week. A bull train pulled in from Rock creek yesterday loaded with liquors and cigars for *Idelman Bros*."[62] For those who bought their liquor by the bottle, Idelman Brothers of Cheyenne had opened a wholesale liquor and tobacco store in Fetterman on July 7 of that year, with Phil Idelman as the manager.[63] But this well-known firm quickly sold out when Fetterman's fortunes waned.

ᔑᑎ ᑎᐤ

Fetterman's cultural events were held at Sparhawk's Opera House, run by Frank Sparhawk in the old military theater building. On September 9, 1886, a somewhat chaotic performance was described in the *Cheyenne Mirror:*

> …a very enjoyable affair. The company was very select. No improper characters were admitted, and those who were there complimented the management very highly for the orderly and quiet manner in which it was conducted. The ball was managed by the Tudor Comedy company, who played here for the last time Saturday night, and the house was crowded to such an extent that there was standing room only. Toward

*Shown here in 1886, these officers' quarters stood on the southeast corner of the parade ground. How the building was used during the town days is unknown, but it appears it was a private residence. This building is presently the museum at Fort Fetterman State Historic Site.* (Photographer, Ned Nearing. Courtesy Wyoming State Archives)

the close of the entertainment the rear seats, which were constructed in a temporary manner of rough lumber, fell to the floor with a crash, precipitating the occupants into a sprawling mass of humanity, and causing quite an uproar. Fortunately no one was hurt, and those who failed to procure reserved seats stood up during the remainder of the entertainment. A number of cowboys raised a small disturbance in the rear of the house, but they were requested to be quiet and the racket ceased.[64]

In December the *Mirror* reported:

The fine weather was taken advantage of by a number of the young people of Fetterman and Douglas, to have a grand ball at Sparhawk's opera house on Friday. In all, about twenty-five couples were present. Dancing commenced early and continued until 12 o'clock; when the party repaired to the Wyoming house restaurant and partook of a substantial supper, after which they returned and enjoyed themselves until 3 o'clock when they returned home, perfectly satisfied that Fetterman is the right place to come to receive good treatment and enjoy a pleasant time.[65]

Frank Sparhawk closed his opera house sometime in 1887, when he left town and opened the Fetterman Coal mines about six miles to the east. These now-abandoned coal mines are on the map today as Inez.[66]

Like the soldiers before them, Fetterman's citizens enjoyed horse racing as well as theater. During the summer of 1887, they revived the military's oval racetrack on the hill northeast of the cemetery. The first race was between Benjamin Wheelock's "B.C. Tommy" and Madison and Whitt's "S. M. Fetterman Belle." Wheelock's horse was favored, with $150 and $200 bets placed, but its rival took the day, winning by a head. Gamblers on both sides were dissatisfied with the race and vowed to have a rematch. When this race was run on July 13, "Fetterman Belle" won again. After the main event came a donkey race, to the onlookers' amusement, but it was never finished as both "animals bolted and took to the old parade ground, where the grass is in very good condition." Fifty dollars had been staked but with no winner, the money was refunded and spent by all the gamblers at the various saloons in town.[67]

Yet much of Fort Fetterman's newfound prosperity was built on sand —and all too soon those sands shifted. As Owen Wister put it years later:

> To-day, Drybone has altogether returned to the dust. Even in that day its hour could be heard beginning to sound, but its inhabitants were rather deaf. Gamblers, saloon-keepers, murderers, outlaws, male and female, all were so busy with their cards, their lovers, and their bottles as to make the place seem young and vigorous; but it was second childhood which had set in.[68]

Fort Fetterman's citizens and investors had been gambling that the railroad would soon link it to other population centers, but those hopes first began to dissolve in the spring of 1886. Rumors circulated, later confirmed, that the rails would pass Fetterman by. The Pioneer Townsite Company, a subsidiary of the Fremont, Elkhorn and Missouri Valley Railroad, announced that a new town, as yet unnamed, would be established east of Fetterman as the railroad terminus in late summer of 1886. Fetterman's citizens looked eastward as the rails approached.

By July 5, the tracks had reached the town of Lusk, at the eastern edge of Wyoming Territory, and were advancing toward the new town site at the rate of two miles a day. Yet although the railroad was to bypass Fetterman itself, its route fell within the limits of the old military reservation. The railroad company needed a right-of-way from the U.S. government. And certainly the railroad magnates and their investors had more sway with Congress than

*The southeast officers' quarters continued to be used as a home. In the 1930s when this photograph was taken, it was being used as a ranch house. Now it serves as the museum at the Fort Fetterman State Historic Site.* (Author's collection)

Fort Fetterman's citizens did. In August, during the first session of the Forty-eighth Congress, a bill was passed granting railroads right of way through military and Indian reservations. This new law cleared the way for the Fremont, Elkhorn and Missouri in the Fetterman area. However, only a right-of-way was granted, not the right to build a town; this forced the Pioneer Townsite Company to seek a terminus off the military reservation.

The rush was on. In the spring of 1886, those speculators and businessmen from Fort Fetterman who saw the writing on the wall began moving to the vicinity of the town-to-be, eight miles east. Presently a small tent town flourished along the small watercourse called Antelope Creek. C.H. King pitched a tent at the creek's mouth and opened a store. The tent next door became the office of a surveyor named Wattles, and in a small shack two cowpunchers named Blaisdell and Mosley opened a saloon. From this meager beginning the town of Antelope grew rapidly, although Fetterman still attracted more travelers: Fetterman's population peaked that same summer with a thousand hardy souls. Then the Pioneer Townsite Company surprised the entrepreneurs yet again; they surveyed the new town on a site south of Antelope Creek, naming it Douglas.[69] Douglas was nothing but a sagebrush-covered plain before July, but after it was surveyed and platted, lots were offered for sale and a town sprang into existence by the end of summer. For now, it would serve as the railroad terminus.

The name choice pleased no one, Barrow noted in the June 16 *Budget*.

> The railway magnates have dubbed the new Fetterman "Douglas." The *Budget* does not like the name nor has it yet found a man who does. A thousand other more appropriate names pertaining to the country and having some local significance could have been selected. Everybody wanted the "future great" called Fetterman, but the post office department would not give us a post office of that name, claiming that with the present office of Fort Fetterman still in existence a confusion of mail would result...[70]

The graders were within sight of the new town by the end of June. Its name became official on July 5, when Justice Clay swore Douglas's new postmaster, Mr. McReynolds, into office. The tracks reached Douglas on Saturday, August 22. Within two days the rails were laid to the stockyards north of town, which became the terminus for the railroad for about a year. By November the U.S. mail route from Bordeaux to Fort Fetterman was terminated; all mail was routed through Douglas. By now, most Fetterman residents must have felt the local center of gravity shifting—about eight miles east, to Douglas.

Nature dealt another blow. The winter of 1886–1887 marked the demise of many of Wyoming's large range cattle companies, and ultimately ended the open-range system. An extremely harsh winter, coupled with an overstocked range, resulted in a ranchers' nightmare. When spring arrived, most of the range cattle in Wyoming had starved to death, and many cattlemen went bankrupt. Those around Fetterman and Douglas suffered great losses as well. Barrow wrote in the *Budget* in February, "There is no denying the fact that a large number of range cattle are dying these days. This weather is a 'corker'... The winter, thus far, has been very severe all over the west—much more than common ... more snow has fallen already than usually falls to our share..."[71]

But the cattle industry was not dead: that spring the regular Fetterman area roundup, number 6, took place, terminating at Fort Fetterman near the end of June. "Missou" Hines was foreman and William "Billy" Jaycox assistant foreman. In addition to this big gather, William Jaycox, foreman

*By the 1930s when this photo was taken, this ordnance building had been converted to a livestock barn. A shed was added to the east side of the building, and the roof was raised to create a hay loft by either the rancher or the previous owner, a livery stable operator, during the Fetterman City period. Today the building has been restored and is one of two original buildings remaining at the Fort Fetterman State Historic Site.* (Author's collection)

of the Three Circle Ranch, arrived with three thousand head of cattle he was driving north. In the herd were nearly 150 head of calves that needed branding. The ex-cowboys living at Fetterman turned out en masse and made short work of the job. The ropers and wrestlers included Charles Cobb, saloon owner Dick Moses, and sometime deputy sheriff John T. Williams (of Metcalf & Williams), while Dan Mitchell kept the irons hot in the fire. Ned Nearing, the Douglas photographer, joined in, taking various roundup views.[72]

Fort Fetterman's versatile cowboy-entrepreneurs could still rise to any occasion. But their town, now slowly emptying, remained in limbo. Albany County surveyor W.O. Owens and his crew arrived on June 6, 1887, and began to survey the military reservation into sections. These sections would be opened for sale in 1888 by the Department of Interior. They had just completed surveying the Fort Fetterman hay reservation on Deer Creek, where another new town, Glenrock, was established.[73]

The track graders for the railroad had advanced past Fetterman to what would become the town of Casper by the end of August 1886.[74] Working with mule teams and manual labor, the graders had the slow, tough work;

*First, the army built the rectangular stone water reservoir (remains in the foreground). Later they constructed the curved tank, shown as stone remains in the background of this 1930s photo. Only the lower tank exists today.* (Author's collection)

however, the rail-laying was relatively quick. But the "big cut" south of Fort Fetterman took 125 men working in two shifts over a month to dig and was not completed until June 1887.[75] The railroad company built stockyards one mile north of Douglas in 1886, anticipating that the town would become a major shipping point. Not until 1888 did the Fort Fetterman military reservations open to the public for sale and the railroad continue to advance westward. By that date Douglas had become well established.

Fetterman's hospital shared in the history unfolding in the area. Dr. Barber moved to Douglas in January 1886 to serve as surgeon for the Fremont, Elkhorn and Missouri Valley Railroad.[76] But he remained the surgeon of record for the Fetterman Hospital, which he visited daily between ten A.M. and four P.M.[77] On June 13, 1888, the town's Hospital Association purchased the Treat warehouse in Douglas, west of the new tracks, and carpenters began remodeling it for medical use. When Barber moved his Fetterman patients there,[78] the Fetterman Hospital was abandoned. Its association existed in Douglas nearly one year longer until it was dissolved in 1889.

Fetterman not only ceased to be the Mecca for incoming settlers; its resident population also fell. A subscriber to the *Budget* stated in April 1887, "A visit to old Fetterman discloses the fact that there has occurred many changes since a year ago; old faces have disappeared and new ones have taken their place." The majority of the town's residents had moved to Douglas by the fall of 1887. Now the largest population center in central Wyoming, Douglas became the county seat when the Wyoming Territorial Legislature created Converse County in March 1888. Fort Fetterman's fate was sealed.

However, one more time, a flicker of hope returned: as the rails continued westward, Fetterman might yet become a station. But it was not to be. Fort Fetterman took its final death blows when the railroad passed it a mile to the south. Rumors briefly spread that a new town site named Fetterman was to be surveyed there, but in fact, only a siding was established.

By 1890, the year Wyoming won statehood, Fort Fetterman was composed of only a few hangers-on. Malcolm Campbell saw "practically nothing but a wayside post office, and William Werner held undisputed sway at the place, being owner of the shoe repair shop, store and post office."[79] By 1907 most of the remaining buildings at Fort Fetterman were moved to Douglas, or were torn down for the building materials.

ᔡ ᔢ

Fort Fetterman had been built during a time of turmoil by a government trying to civilize an untamed territory. Created on the barren bluff above the North Platte River in 1867, the fort witnessed the closing of the Bozeman Trail, which it was built to protect. It survived the Great Sioux War of 1876 and the revitalization of the Bozeman Trail by freighters, travelers, and ranchers in the years that followed. The soldiers who built Fort Fetterman and lived there ultimately succeeded in their assigned task of making the country, of which the fort was the center, a productive area where settlers and ranchers could live in safety. Like many posts on the American frontier, its holdings were opened for settlement after it had outlived its military usefulness. But unlike any other post, Fort Fetterman also enjoyed a brief heyday as a notorious cowtown—one that would be immortalized by Owen Wister as a town he called Drybone.

Only two of the original buildings of the military garrison and the civilian town remain today, the ordnance storehouse and a captains' quarters built of log. These two structures survived solely because they served as a private ranch house and barn until the State of Wyoming acquired the property in 1962.

But echoes from the past can be heard in the wind by any visitor with ears to hear. The building foundations around the parade ground beckon the passer-by to listen to the stories of yesterday, a day no one living can remember. Fort Fetterman is now a state historic site under the management of the Wyoming State Department of Parks and Cultural Resources as a tribute to Wyoming's history, and those who lived and died at Fort Fetterman.

# BIOGRAPHIES OF PROMINENT FETTERMAN CITIZENS

**A** **Abe Abrahams** was born in London, England, on August 20, 1860. By his own admission "a free lance with an itchy foot," Abe pursued many and varied occupations. He was a cowboy, handy-man, bailiff for the U.S. District Court in Wyoming's Sheridan County, and, at the time of his death, a florist in Sheridan. Abe left a record of events as he saw them while living at Fort Fetterman in the form of various letters, many of which have been previously published in part. He died in Sheridan on January 17, 1952 at the age of ninety-one.

**James M. Abney** was born in Savannah, Missouri, on January 20, 1860. He married Frances Bacon, the widow of Billy Bacon, on December 10, 1886; she died on July 20, 1927. He married Opal Entzminger on October 2, 1929. Abney died on June 9, 1930, in Douglas. His occupation was listed in his obituary as a rancher[1] and he had earlier worked as a range detective for the Wyoming Stock Growers Association, Fetterman district.

**Billy and Frances Bacon** are first mentioned in Wyoming history in the late 1870s as the owners of a road ranch (an establishment generally consisting of a boarding house and saloon) near Uva, Wyoming. Bacon worked as a cowboy, but many labeled him as a bad man or outlaw. It is true that he tended to be wild of spirit and associated with notorious individuals, but he was never a criminal. Soon Johnny Gordon and his family settled nearby, and Gordon didn't like the gambling, drinking, and hell-raising at Bacons, so he bought out the establishment for $1,000 in 1878.

The Bacons settled on LaBonte Creek in 1879, where they opened another road ranch at the crossing of the early immigrant trail. In the spring of 1883, they sold their squatter's rights for $5,000 to a Mr. Pollard and moved to Cheyenne for several months. Bacon reportedly continued drinking and gambling there, until friends encouraged them to leave. They returned to LaBonte Creek, grazing some cattle at what became known as Bacon Park in June 1884, where they built a cabin.

Later in that year Bacon traded his cattle to Frank Gore for Frank's saloon in the newly created town of Fetterman. While in Fetterman he became a partner with John Saunders in the "New Hog Ranch," while continuing to work occasionally for John Hunton and other area ranchers.[2] After Bacon and Saunders died in the fracas at the hog ranch, Bacon's holdings were left to his wife Frances.[3]

Frances Bacon was born on October 17, 1859, in Pennsylvania, the daughter of John and Margaret Gill. It is not known how she met Billy, nor the exact date of their marriage. In 1880 the two were in Omaha and adopted her niece Eula E. Erben after she was abandoned by her parents. After Billy's death, Frances started a lodging business at Fetterman.[4] On December 10, 1886, she married James M. Abney.[5] James and Frances homesteaded on Little Boxelder Creek west of Fort Fetterman where they remained until Frances's death on July 20, 1927.

**Doctor Amos W. Barber** was born at Doylestown, Pennsylvania, April 26, 1861. In 1883 he graduated from the University of Pennsylvania in both the medical and literary departments. For nearly two years he served as a staff physician at the Pennsylvania Hospital.

In November 1885, Barber was appointed surgeon in charge of the Fetterman Hospital Association at Fort Fetterman. In January 1886 he moved to Douglas, taking the position of the surgeon for the Fremont, Elkhorn, and Missouri Railroad, with his office in the Stimpson Building on Center Street. He remained the surgeon of record for the Fetterman Hospital and visited the hospital daily.

He soon left Douglas to practice medicine in Cheyenne. On September 11, 1890, he was elected Wyoming's first secretary of state during Francis E. Warren's term as the first governor of Wyoming. His term was to be from November 1890 to January 1896. But fate intervened when Warren was elected to the U. S. Senate by the state legislature and resigned as governor. Barber automatically became acting governor, a position he held from November 1890 until January 1893, a timespan which placed him in the middle of one of Wyoming's most infamous events—the Johnson County Cattle War. After his brief political career, Barber volunteered to serve in the army during the Spanish-American War as an assistant surgeon.

Amos W. Barber died at Rochester, Minnesota in 1915. At his request his body was interred in the Cheyenne cemetery.

**Merris Clark Barrow** was one of the more influential characters to arrive at Fetterman and help shape the community's destiny. He was born in Canton, Pennsylvania, on October 4, 1857, Robert and Helen Barrow's first son. His father was a simple farmer who devoted himself to the study of the Bible and eventually became an evangelist. The family moved from Pennsylvania in the late 1860s to Missouri, and in 1865 moved to London, Nebraska. They settled in Tecumseh, Nebraska where Merris began work at the age of nineteen as the editor of the *Tecumseh Chieftain* in 1876.

On March 17, 1877, Barrow married Minnie Florence Combs. The next year he left the newspaper business to become a United States postal clerk in Nebraska. Later in 1878 he was transferred to Laramie, Wyoming with the Postal Department. He held this position until January 1879, when he was accused of robbing the mail. Barrow was legally acquitted of any guilt, but the incident left him unemployed. To provide for his family during his trial, he worked for the *Laramie Daily Times* as a reporter and in 1881 he assisted Bill Nye in establishing and printing the first issue of the *Laramie Boomerang*. Barrow continued with the *Boomerang* until September 1884, when he moved his family to Rawlins, Wyoming and established a newspaper named The *Wyoming Tribune*.[6] Feeling some inner urge to relocate, Barrow and family moved to Fort Fetterman in a light wagon, where he arrived on the night of the May 22, 1886, and began to set up a new newspaper office in a small "rough-board shack a little better than a shed." Ten days later a freight team arrived with his printing press and on the evening of June 9, central Wyoming's first newspaper began, known as *Bill Barlow's Budget*.[7] Barrow continued to publish the *Budget* at Fetterman until shortly after the town of Douglas, Wyoming was established. There he relocated his newspaper business but retained the name. For two years he listed both Fort Fetterman and Douglas on the front page as the headquarters of the newspaper, but by the end of 1888 Barrow had found a home in Douglas. The newspaper exists today but is known as the *Douglas Budget*.

**George Bolln** was born in Hamburg, Germany in 1847. He immigrated to the United States and in 1870, at the age of twenty-three, settled in Cheyenne. For six years he was employed as a baker. Bolln joined the Black Hills gold rush in 1876 but returned to Cheyenne a year later, without having found his fortune. He then moved to Fetterman and with his new partner Charles Rastaetter bought the old post trader's store from Altman & Webel in 1886 and converted it into a grocery store. In 1888, the partners opened a second store in Douglas which Bolln operated while Rastaetter managed the Fetterman store. It appears that Charles Rastaetter absconded with the company monies and left the country. Bolln then closed the Fetterman store, keeping the Douglas store as his business.

In 1887 he married Pauline Muegel and built her the first brick home in Douglas. They had a son, Henry. In 1903, he made a trip to his old home in Germany with Henry. On the return trip George became critically ill, died, and was buried at sea.[8] His business remained a family enterprise in Douglas until the turn of the twenty-first century.

**James H. Bury** was born in Pennsylvania in April 1847 and became a resident of Wyoming in 1867. In 1885 he became the part owner, with William Nichols, of the Fetterman Hotel, until they dissolved the partnership in 1887. W. C. Sampson then became Bury's partner, and they kept the hotel operating until 1888 when they closed the business. In 1891 Bury moved to Casper, Wyoming and opened a real estate office which he operated until his death.

In 1889 Bury married Jennie Dater and they had a daughter named Mary, who married C. S. McDonald of Diamondville, Wyoming.[9]

**Malcolm Campbell** was born near London, Ontario, Canada in June 1839. He moved with his family to Dewitt, Iowa when he was twenty-five. In 1865 he started a freighting company based out of Beatrice, Nebraska. For several years he worked as a freighter and "tie hack" for the fledgling Union Pacific Railroad. Then in 1872 he began to work for John Hunton supplying firewood for Fort Fetterman, until he eventually began his own business as a government contractor at the fort.

On December 22, 1879 he married Priscilla Noble. They lived at Fort Fetterman where he became a deputy sheriff, first for Albany County under N. K. Boswell and later for Lew Miller. He was named constable of Albany County on three separate occasions. He was appointed the first Sheriff of Converse County when it was created in 1888. While he was deputy sheriff at Fort Fetterman he and his brother arrested Alfred Packer. Later, Malcolm served for many years as the Chief of Police in Douglas.

*Lea Marie Levasseur married George Cross in 1884 and moved to the Braehead Ranch where they witnessed the rise and decline of the town of Fetterman.* (Courtesy Wyoming State Pioneer Museum)

He moved his family to Casper, Wyoming in 1920 where he was employed as a watchman at an oil refinery. Malcolm died in Casper on July 20, 1932.[10]

**George Harry Cross** was born in Montreal, Canada, on September 15, 1854, to Scottish parents. He was well educated, attending Upper Canada College in Toronto and Nicollet college in Quebec. Seeking adventure, he and two friends moved to Colorado in 1874 where he learned the cowboy trade at the Dowling Ranch in eastern Colorado.

In the spring of 1876 he and his traveling companion Alex Wilson joined ranks with Charley Campbell, William Daily, Clint Graham and Joe and Andy Sullivan, the owners of the LaBonte Ranch. While at the LaBonte Ranch George met what was left of the Heck Reel wagon train which had been ambushed by Indians the day before. Two years later in 1877 he and Alex Wilson were running the LaBonte Ranch. In the spring of 1883 he filed a homestead and began his own ranching enterprise.on Red Canyon Creek, which he named "Braehead" after his ancestral home in Scotland.

On January 30, 1884, he married Lea Marie Levasseur whom he had known since childhood in Canada, and they immediately moved to the new ranch. They had two daughters; Margaret, born November 28, 1884, and Julia born October 16, 1887. Both daughters died of diphtheria in 1889 while the family was visiting relatives in Canada. They had nine more children after this tragedy.

Besides his ranching interests, he became interested in public affairs and was elected a member of Converse County's first board of county commissioners in 1888 and in 1894 was elected from Converse County to the state senate for two terms.[11]

The Cross family witnessed the army occupation of Fort Fetterman, the life and death of the town of Fetterman with the arrival of the railroad, and the beginning of Douglas.

Lea Cross died on October 10, 1940, and George died on November 28, 1946.[12]

**A. A. "Archie" Faulkner** led a life that touched only his closest friends and his visibility on the pages of Wyoming history is quite limited. He was born on February 22, 1854, but the place of his birth is unknown. He had moved into Fort Fetterman by October 1886 and established a saloon with Richard Moses known as Dick's Place. He also operated a butcher shop, the Meat Market, with John T. Williams. For a brief period he ran a restaurant at Fetterman and built a home in the town on "Hospital Avenue" in January 1887. Faulkner later established a ranch on upper LaPrele Creek where he died of a protracted illness on August 14, 1901. He was buried in the town of Douglas's first cemetery.[13]

**George W. Metcalf** was born on January 21, 1855, in Northfield, Vermont where he lived until attending college at the University of Vermont and Norwich University. In the spring of 1880, for the benefit of his health, he came west to Fort Fetterman, where he was employed as a civilian quartermaster agent until its abandonment in 1881.[14] Metcalf stayed in the area and was appointed postmaster in 1884, which was an added source of revenue. He retained that position for the four years he remained at Fetterman. In partnership with John T. Williams he opened a general mercantile store in 1885 at the town of Fetterman. In 1888, he married Susie Webel from Chicago. The new couple made their residence briefly in the town of Fetterman, moving later that year to Douglas, where he and Williams had previously established a store in that town as well as Casper.

Metcalf helped organize the Commercial Bank and Trust of Douglas in February 1914 and engaged in the livestock business as owner of the Metcalf Land and Livestock Company. George Metcalf died in 1938.[15]

**George Powell** was born in Jefferson County, Iowa on February 22, 1847. In 1865 he traveled west to Denver, where he ran a freighting business. For two years he logged in the Colorado mountains and then moved to Fort Laramie and became a civilian employee for the army. He remained there for one year, then began logging in the Elk Mountain area for a few months. Tiring of logging, he began his own bull freighting company, making deliveries to Fort Fetterman. He operated as a freighter until 1877 when he established his ranch in what became Converse County, Wyoming. On March 27, 1878, Powell married Maggie Skogland, by whom he had two daughters.[16]

**Samuel Slaymaker** was born June 6, 1846, in Lancaster, Pennsylvania, where he spent his childhood. In 1864, he joined Company B, Seventy-ninth Pennsylvania Volunteers, and fought for the Union Army during the Civil War. After the war he was mustered out of the service on April 12, 1865. In 1866 he re-enlisted with the Regular Army, assigned to Company F, Thirty-third Infantry regiment as first sergeant under the command of Captain Charles Wheaton. Upon the expiration of his second enlistment he "re-upped" and joined Company H, Twenty-second Infantry under command of Captain D. C. Poole. Again he was promoted to the rank of first sergeant. He remained with the Twenty-second Infantry until 1874, when he was given an honorable discharge—but his military career did not end then. In November 1875 he received a commission by the Secretary of War as a commissary sergeant at Fort Fetterman. He closed his Regular Army career at Fort Fetterman in 1881 when he resigned from the service. In 1891 he was appointed adjutant of the First Regiment of the Wyoming National Guard by the governor and served in that post until his death.[17]

After he received his military discharge, he built a road ranch on upper LaPrele Creek, on the military road between Fort Fetterman and Rock Creek on the Union Pacific Railroad. He later moved his establishment, called "Buckshot," above Spring Canyon. On March 23, 1872, while in the service, he married Ellen Howard, who was popularly known to the community of Fort Fetterman as "Mammy." Slaymaker divorced Ellen in

1892 and was married to Flora L. Hobbs on February 7, 1893.[18] Samuel served as justice of the peace and county coroner for northern Albany County from 1885 until 1889 when he was appointed Converse County's first assessor and later its first clerk of court. In 1906 he was appointed to the position of receiver of the U. S. Land Office. Samuel Slaymaker died on December 28, 1911.[19]

Uneducated in formal law, "Judge" Slaymaker ruled during his court sessions with simple, common-sense justice that generally did not conform to legal standards of the day. By his own admission he had disdain for lawyers when he stated:

> ... times was when we used to deal out justice, till the lawyers got in with their technicalities, and made us follow the law, then we resigned ... Yes, things changed when the railroads and the lawyers came. I remember the first case where lawyers interfered with administrating of justice, as they always do. An old codger named "Necessity Emors"—we called him Necessity because "necessity knows no law"—was plaintiff's lawyer and a young lawyer—I called them lyres, a sort of musical instrument, you know—from Douglas was the defendant's lawyer. I heard the plaintiff's side and decided the case for him.
>
> "Hold on!" says the young Douglas lawyer. "We haven't told our side yet". He argued from Blackstone, the Bible, Webster's First Reader, and threatened to put the county seat at Lusk until I gave in deciding for the defendant. Old Necessity stepped up to me and whispered in my ear: "Judge, this plaintiff is a poor honest man with 13 children." Now it was understood one of my court mottos was, "the fine may be remitted but the costs must be paid," so I had changed again, and decided for the plaintiff. The young sprig just raved and said I couldn't do it. I leaned over and said "young fellow, I want you to understand this court is like a wagon, it runs forwards and backwards". That settled him.[20]

**William Werner** was born in Aachen Baden, Germany on May 11, 1854, as William Worner, one of ten children born to Franz Ignaz and Catharina Straur Worner. Family records indicate that William may have immigrated to the United States in 1874 at the age of twenty, and may have been a skilled shoemaker. He moved to Cincinnati, Ohio in 1880 where on July 27, 1880, William enlisted in the United States Army and eventually was assigned to the cavalry. His shoemaking trade soon advanced him to company saddler in Company K, Fifth Cavalry. Werner's enlistment ended on July 26, 1885, when he received his discharge at Fort Reno, Indian Territory. Then he traveled to Fort Laramie, Wyoming where he joined the Fort Laramie Odd Fellows (I.O.O.F.) Lodge. Some time after his move to Fort Laramie he married Mary Anna Pfeifer and the couple moved to the town of Fetterman. In November 1890 the Werners filed a homestead three miles west of the fort on the abandoned Fort Fetterman reservation. While "proving up" on his homestead, William was employed as Fetterman's postmaster. In 1893 the family left Fetterman and began life on their homestead, where they became involved in the livestock industry.

**Benjamin Wheelock** was born in North Brookfield, Massachusetts on March 21, 1860. His father was a U.S. Army soldier who transferred to Fort D. A. Russell in 1875, bringing his family west. His father's company was then assigned to Forts Laramie and Washakie. While at Fort Washakie Ben studied and learned the Arapaho and Shoshoni languages and eventually became an interpreter for the army at Fort Washakie in 1883 and 1884. Ben's father was assigned for duty at Fort Fetterman in 1879. When the army abandoned Fort Fetterman, Ben remained and in 1885 bought a saloon when it was speculated that the railroad would pass through the town. When the railroad bypassed Fetterman and went to Glenrock, Ben sold his saloon in 1887 and bought another in Glenrock, called "The Maverick." He sold that saloon later that year to Tom Bird and Matt McGrath and went to Deadwood, South Dakota as a gambler. He arrived in Douglas, Wyoming in 1893 and ran a roulette wheel in Abe Daniel's saloon. He next went into partnership in a saloon on Second Street in Douglas, but eventually sold his share and began ranching. Ben had two brothers, Frank and Joe, and a sister who died in 1886. Benjamin Wheelock died on February 21, 1909 at age eighty-three.[21]

**John T. Williams** moved to Wyoming from Monroe, Wisconsin at the age of nineteen in 1878. Prior to entering into business with George Metcalf, Williams worked as a cowboy and a freighter between Rock River and Buffalo. After leaving Fetterman for Douglas, Williams became a partner in the Ogallala Sheep and Cattle Company. He purchased the Duck Creek and Sage Creek ranches north of Fetterman, which became known as the John T. Williams Sheep Company. In 1887, he married Elizabeth P. Ragsdale.

Merris Barrow wrote of the wedding:

At Cheyenne, on Thursday last, J. T. Williams and Miss Lizzie Ragsdale were united in marriage by Rev. Williams at the home of the Brides sister. The newly made husband and wife arrived on Sunday, and only await the completion of repairs now in progress, to begin housekeeping in a cosy and comfortable home provided by the groom at Fetterman. Mr. Williams, as ex-deputy sheriff, stockman and business man, is well and favorably known throughout central Wyoming, while his bride, during her residence at Fetterman, won the respect and esteem of all who have made her acquaintance, and is a deserved favorite in the social circles of both Douglas and Fetterman.[22]

Later that year the couple moved to Douglas. John T. Williams went on to hold many public offices including two terms in the Wyoming State Senate.[23]

# B | Children Born at Fetterman as a Military Post

| Date of birth | Sex | Parents' names, if known |
|---|---|---|
| June 10, 1869 | M | Captain and Mrs. (Louisa Davison) Henry W. Patterson, Co. E, 4th Inf., child named Alfred Patterson, Jr.[1] |
| Mar. 31, 1871 | F | Private and Mrs. Cotter, Co. H, 4th Inf.[2] |
| Nov. 4, 1871 | F | Colonel and Mrs. Woodward[3] |
| Oct. 10, 1874 | F | Lieutenant and Mrs. Gerhard L. Luhn, 4th Inf.[4] |
| Nov. 15, 1874 | M | Sergeant and Mrs. Russell, Co. H, 4th Inf.[5] |
| April 5, 1875 | M | Sergeant and Mrs. John D. O'Brian, Co. F, 4th Inf.[6] |
| Nov. 13, 1876 | F | Sergeant and Mrs. John D. O'Brian, Co. F, 4th Inf.[7] |
| Aug. 14, 1877 | M | Lieutenant and Mrs. Gerhard L. Luhn, 4th Inf.[8] |
| Oct. 12, 1877 | M | Mrs. Bridget Doolan (the hospital matron)[9] |
| Feb. 15, 1878 | M | Mr. and Mrs. O'Hara, musician (?) in Co. C, 4th Inf.[10] |
| Jan. 18, 1879 | F | Mr. and Mrs. Charles Hogerson (employed as post wheelwright)[11] |
| Feb. 1, 1879 | M | Sergeant and Mrs. John O. Ward, 4th Inf.[12] |
| Mar. 1, 1879 | F | Mr. and Mrs. John D. O'Brian (formerly sergeant, now owner of Six Mile Road Ranch)[13] |
| Mar. 30, 1879 | M | Second Lieutenant and Mrs. George N. Chase, 4th Inf.[14] |
| Sept. 6, 1879 | F | Mr. and Mrs. George Powell (well-known freighter and hay contractor)[15] |
| Sept. 26, 1879 | M | Second Lieutenant and Mrs. G.K. Hunter, 3rd Cavalry[16] |
| Oct. 15, 1879 | M | Private and Mrs. Dague, Co. A, 4th Inf.[17] |
| Oct. 16, 1879 | M | First Sergeant and Mrs. Conrad Bahr, Co. G, 4th Inf.[18] |
| Nov. 17, 1879 | M | Private and Mrs. K.W. Sheldon, Co. A, 4th Inf.[19] |
| Nov. 29, 1879 | F | Mr. and Mrs. C.C. Bushnell (rancher living six miles west of the post)[20] |
| Nov. 29, 1879 | F | Mr. and Mrs. E.C. Smith (employed at Benjamin Ranch)[21] |
| Dec. 2, 1880 | F | Mr. and Mrs. Charles Handy (hospital steward; birth occurred ten days before his discharge due to expired enlistment)[22] |
| Nov. 19, 1881 | F | Captain and Mrs. James H. Spencer, 4th Inf.[23] |

# C | COMPANIES AND POST COMMANDERS STATIONED AT FORT FETTERMAN 1867–1882

| Dates of Service | Companies | Regiments | | Post Commander* |
|---|---|---|---|---|
| July 1867–Nov. 1867 | A, C, H & I | 4th | Infantry | Dye |
| Nov. 1867–May 1868 | A, D, F, H, K & Band | 19th | Infantry | Wessells |
| May 1868–April 1869 | A, C, E & I | 4th | Infantry | Dye |
| April 1869–Oct. 1869 | A & E | 4th | Infantry | |
| Oct. 1869–Jan. 1870 | K | 2nd | Cavalry | Chambers |
| Oct. 1869–March 1871 | A, E & H | 4th | Infantry | |
| March 1871–July 1871 | D, F & G | 14th | Infantry | Woodward |
| July 1871–Sept. 1873 | D, E, F & G | 14th | Infantry | |
| Dec. 1872–Sept.1873 | C | 3rd | Cavalry | |
| Sept. 1873–Jan. 1874 | D & G | 14th | Infantry | |
| | A & F | 4th | Infantry | |
| | C | 3rd | Cavalry | |
| Jan. 1874–March 1874 | D & G | 14th | Infantry | J.S. Mason |
| | A & F | 4th | Infantry | |
| | C | 2nd | Cavalry | |
| March 1874–July 1874 | A, C, F & I | 4th | Infantry | Cain |
| | C | 3rd | Cavalry | |
| July 1874–Nov. 1875 | C, F & I | 4th | Infantry | J.S. Mason |
| Oct. 1875–Nov. 1875 | A | 2nd | Cavalry | |
| Nov. 1875–July 1876 | C & I | 4th | Infantry | Chambers |
| July 1876–Jan. 1877 | C & F | 4th | Infantry | Coates |
| | I | 2nd | Cavalry | |
| Jan. 1877–Oct. 1877 | C | 4th | Infantry | |
| Jan. 1877–April 1879 | I | 3rd | Cavalry | |
| Oct. 1877–Nov. 1878 | A | 4th | Infantry | |
| Nov. 1878–April 1879 | A & G | 4th | Infantry | |
| April 1879–June 1879 | A & G | 4th | Infantry | J. S. Mason |
| | B | 3rd | Cavalry | |
| June 1879–May 1882 | G | 4th | Infantry | Powell |
| May 1882–June 1882 | 10 enlisted men | 3rd | Cavalry | C.W. Mason |

* This list does not include acting or interim commanders.

# Biographies of Selected Officers at Fort Fetterman

**D**

**John Wilson Bubb** began his military career in 1861 as a private in Company E, First Battalion, Twelfth U. S. Infantry. By April 24, 1866, he had been promoted through the enlisted ranks to first sergeant. In 1866 Bubb was promoted to second lieutenant and on February 5, 1866 he became a first lieutenant in the Twelfth Infantry. He transferred to the Thirtieth Infantry on September 21, 1866, and then to the Fourth Infantry on March 23, 1869. He served as regimental quartermaster of the Fourth Infantry between April 1, 1872, and June 1, 1875. General Crook appointed him commissary of subsistence officer at Fort Fetterman prior to the Centennial Campaigns of 1876. Bubb was promoted to captain on March 16, 1879, major on April 26, 1898, and lieutenant colonel of the Twelfth Infantry on October 20, 1899. He was next assigned to the Twenty-fourth Infantry as colonel on July 1, 1901. On August 12, 1901, he transferred back to the Twelfth Infantry.[1]

**Caleb Henry Carlton** graduated from West Point eighteenth in his class on July 1, 1854. As was the custom of the time, he was unassigned from 1854 until July 1, 1859, when he received a brevet rank of second lieutenant in the Seventh Infantry. On October 12, 1859, he was promoted to the rank of second lieutenant in the Fourth Infantry and obtained the rank of first lieutenant in the Fourth Infantry on May 14, 1861. On June 30, 1862, Carlton obtained the rank of captain in the Fourth Infantry. Seeking rapid promotion during the Civil War, he transferred to the Eighty-ninth Ohio Infantry on July 7, 1863. He served with this regiment during the remainder of the war at the rank of colonel, and was honorably discharged from the volunteer service on June 23, 1865. During the war he became a brevet major on July 4, 1862, for gallant and meritorious service during the Peninsular campaign, and lieutenant colonel on September 30, 1863, for gallant and meritorious service during the battle of Chickamauga, Georgia. By Janaury 1869 he was at Fort Fetterman where he often served as acting and interim post commander. On December 15, 1870, when he was placed in the Tenth Cavalry as a captain. He was next promoted to major in the Third Cavalry on May 17, 1876, at which rank he served while stationed at Fort Fetterman. On April 11, 1889, he was promoted to lieutenant colonel in the Seventh Cavalry and remained with this regiment until January 30, 1892, when he earned the rank of colonel in the Eighth Cavalry. He became a brigadier general on June 28, 1897, and retired from the service two days later.[2]

**Alexander Chambers** was born in New York and graduated from West Point forty-third in his class of July 1849. He was placed in the Fifth Infantry as brevet second lieutenant on July 1, 1853. Two years later he achieved the rank of second lieutenant and on January 19, 1859, was promoted to first lieutenant in the Fifth Infantry. From June 9, 1857, to August 7, 1861, he held the post of regimental adjutant. With the outbreak of the Civil War, Chambers was appointed to captain of the Eighteenth U. S. Infantry on May 14, 1861. Between March 15, 1862, and September 22, 1863, he served with the Sixteenth Iowa Volunteer Infantry, first as a colonel and then, as of August 11, 1863, as brigadier general. Chambers earned the rank of brevet major on April 7, 1862, after the battle of Shiloh, Tennessee, and made lieutenant colonel on September 19, 1862, for gallant and meritorious service in the battle of Iuka, Mississippi. He was again breveted to colonel for gallant and meritorious service during the siege of Vicksburg, Mississippi on July 4, 1863. His appointment as brigadier general of the Volunteers was revoked on April 6, 1864. He was breveted brigadier general of volunteers for his participation during the battles of Champion Hills and Meridian, Mississippi on March 13, 1865. At the end of the Civil War he was transferred back into the Eighteenth Infantry at his former rank of captain. Chambers transferred to the Twenty-seventh Infantry on September 21, 1866. He was promoted to major in the Twenty-second Infantry on March 5, 1867 and two years later transferred into the Tenth Infantry where he served until June 24, 1869. On February 4, 1870, he was assigned to the Fourth Infantry where he remained until October 22, 1876, when he was promoted to lieutenant colonel of the Twenty-first Infantry. It was during his tour with the Fourth

Infantry that he served twice as Fort Fetterman's post commander: from October 1869 through March 1871, and from November 1875 to July 1876. On March 1, 1886, he was advanced to colonel of the Seventeenth Infantry. He died on January 2, 1888.[3]

**Edwin Mortimer Coates** was born in New York on August 1, 1846. He began his military career as a first lieutenant in the Eleventh New York Infantry on May 7, 1861. He resigned his commission in this New York regiment on August 4, 1861, to join the Second U. S. Cavalry as a second lieutenant the following day. He transferred to the Twelfth U. S. Infantry on October 20, 1861, and was promoted four days later to the rank of first lieutenant. During the Civil War, Coates was given the honorary rank of captain for gallant and meritorious service during the Battle of the Wilderness and during the campaign before Richmond, Virginia. He was promoted to captain on April 11, 1865, and continued to serve with the Twelfth Infantry until September 21, 1866, when he transferred to the Thirtieth Infantry. On March 23, 1869, he transferred to the Fourth Infantry and served this regiment while stationed at Fort Fetterman as post commander. On July 14, 1890, he was promoted to major in the Nineteenth Infantry and on November 23, 1893, reached the rank of lieutenant colonel in the Sixteenth Infantry. On July 23, 1893, he was promoted to colonel in the Seventh Infantry. He closed his military career on January 29, 1900, when he retired.[4]

**Patrick Edward Connor** was born in Ireland in 1820 and eventually emigrated to California where, in 1846, he was made a first lieutenant of the Independent Company of Texas Volunteers during the Mexican War. He was promoted to captain of the Texas Company in which he served until February 12, 1847, when he resigned. Connor was wounded at Buena Vista during the Mexican War. When the Civil War began he was instrumental in raising the Third California Infantry in 1861, in which regiment he was promoted to colonel. The Third California Infantry fought the Civil War in the western states and territories while the Regular Army was involved in the conflict in the eastern states. He participated in actions against the Mormons and Indians in Washington Territory from 1861 to 1863. On March 30, 1863, he was promoted to brigadier general of Volunteers and placed in command of the Utah District. Connor was ordered to lead a military force into Powder River country in the summer of 1865 to punish the Indians who had attacked miners prospecting in Montana. At the end of the Civil War the Regular Army was again assigned the role of protecting the western frontier. No longer needed for frontier duties, the Third California was mustered out of service in 1866. After Connor left the service on April 30, 1866, he settled in Utah and started that state's first newspaper. While residing in Utah, he established a silver mine, authored the state's first mining laws, established the town of Stockton, and introduced navigation on the Great Salt Lake. Connor died on December 17, 1891.[5]

**Philip St. George Cooke** graduated from West Point Military Academy on July 1, 1923. He was breveted a second lieutenant of infantry upon graduation and made second lieutenant on July 1, 1827. By 1833 he was a first lieutenant of Dragoons, rising to the rank of colonel of Dragoons on June 14, 1858. Cooke served with the second regiment of cavalry at the beginning of the Civil War and received several promotions before obtaining the rank of brigadier general on November 12, 1861. He retired from military service on October 29, 1873 and died March 20, 1895.[6]

**George Crook** graduated from West Point on July 1, 1848, ranked thirty-eighth in his class. He was breveted a second lieutenant in the Fourth Infantry on July 1, 1852, and became a second lieutenant in July the following year. He was promoted to first lieutenant on March 11, 1856, and made captain on May 14, 1861. Crook became colonel of the Thirty-sixth Ohio Volunteer Infantry on September 13, 1861. By September 7, 1862, he was elevated to the rank of brigadier general of Volunteers and on October 21, 1864, he was promoted to major general of Volunteers. He received brevet ranks for gallant and meritorious service at the battles of Lewisburg, Virginia; Antietam, Maryland; and Farmington, Tennessee. He was cited again for his action during the campaign of 1864 in West Virginia, and the battle of Fisher Hill, Virginia. Crook was honorably mustered out of the Volunteer Service on January 15, 1866, and after a six-month leave was promoted to the rank of major in the Third Infantry of the Regular Army. He was elevated to the rank of lieutenant colonel in the Twenty-third Infantry on July 28, 1866, and became a brigadier general on October 23, 1873. General Crook led the second column of the 1876 attack against the Cheyenne and Sioux which advanced north from Fort Fetterman. On April 6, 1888, he achieved the rank of major general, at which rank he died on

March 20, 1890. General Crook was instrumental in defeating the Apache and the Sioux Indians during his service on the American frontier.[7]

**George Augustus Drew** started his military career on October 11, 1862, as a captain in the Sixth Michigan Volunteer Cavalry. By September 24, 1863, he had attained the rank of major. He was breveted lieutenant colonel of Volunteers for highly distinguished and meritorious service in the Shenandoah Valley, and was promoted to colonel for highly distinguished service in the campaign against Richmond, Virginia. Drew was honorably mustered out of Volunteer Service on October 11, 1865, and was assigned to the Tenth U. S. Infantry as a second lieutenant on May 15, 1866. He received the rank of first lieutenant on March 26, 1868. He was unassigned between May 1869 and December 31, 1870, after which he joined the Third Cavalry and was stationed at Fort Fetterman. He was regimental quartermaster from August 15, 1875, until March 20, 1879, at which time he was promoted to captain. Drew retired from the service as a captain on March 15, 1896.[8]

**William McEntire Dye** graduated from West Point on July 1, 1849, ranked thirty-second in his class. His first assignment was as a brevet second lieutenant in the Fourth Infantry on July 1, 1853. He was promoted to second lieutenant on November 9, 1854, in the Eighth Infantry, and first lieutenant on February 1, 1856. Dye served as regimental adjutant of the Eighth Infantry from October 1, 1855, until October 10, 1859. He was then appointed regimental quartermaster, serving from October 10, 1859, to May 14, 1861, at which time he was promoted to captain. On August 25, 1862, he left the Regular Army to become a colonel in the Twentieth Iowa Infantry. During the Civil War he was breveted as a major and lieutenant colonel for gallant and meritorious service during the siege of Vicksburg, Virginia; the Red River Campaign; and the campaign against Mobile, Alabama. He was honorably mustered out of the Volunteer Service on July 8, 1865, and was assigned as major in the Fourth Infantry on January 14, 1866. In July 1867, Dye was instrumental in the establishment of Fort Fetterman, serving as its first post commander. On February 4, 1870 he was unassigned and on September 30, 1870, he received an honorable discharge at his own request. He died on November 13, 1899.[9]

**Captain James "Teddy" Egan** began his military career in 1856 as a private in Company H, Second Cavalry. During the Civil War, he worked his way through the ranks to that of lieutenant and in 1868 was promoted to captain of cavalry. In 1876 he was the commanding officer of Company K, Second Cavalry, stationed at Fort Laramie. He was stationed at Fort Fetterman during the Centennial Campaign of 1876. He retired from the military in May 1879, and died April 14, 1883.[10]

**Cuvier Grover** graduated fourth in his class from West Point in July 1846. On July 1, 1850, he was breveted a second lieutenant in the Fourth Artillery. He made second lieutenant on September 16, 1850, and served with his regiment until March 3, 1855, when he was promoted to first lieutenant of the Tenth Infantry. On September 17, 1858, he advanced to the rank of captain. In April 1862, he became a brigadier general of Volunteers. He left the Volunteer Service and was assigned to the rank of major of the Third U. S. Infantry on August 31, 1863. During the Civil War he was breveted for gallant and meritorious service during the battles of Williamsburg, Fair Oaks, Cedar Creek, Fisher Hill, Winchester, and in the campaign of the Shenandoah Valley, Virginia. He was mustered out of Volunteer Service on August 24, 1865, and was assigned to the Thirty-eight Infantry on July 28, 1866. On March 15, 1869, he was transferred to the Twenty-fourth Infantry. Between April 1869 and December 1870, he was unassigned while the army went through reorganization. On December 15, 1870 he was assigned to the Second Cavalry as a colonel. He served with the Second Cavalry at Fetterman as the company commander. He died while on active duty on June 6, 1885.[11]

**Guy Vernor Henry** began his military career after graduating from West Point in 1856. He made the rank of second lieutenant on May 6, 1861, in the First Artillery. Eight days later he was promoted to first lieutenant. He left the Regular Army on November 9, 1863, and joined the Fortieth Massachusetts Volunteers at the rank of colonel. At the end of the civil war he was discharged from Volunteer Service and on December 1, 1865, he reentered the Regular Army as a captain of the First Artillery. He transferred to the Third Cavalry fourteen days later. He served as captain in the Third Cavalry until June 26, 1881, when he was assigned as a major with the Ninetieth Cavalry. The wound he received during the Rosebud engagement was a serious head wound. He survived a long trip from the battlefield, traveling first by mule to Fort Fetterman. He then went by ambulance to Medicine Bow, Wyoming where he was placed on a Union Pacific train and taken to the hospital (and his wife) at Fort D. A. Russell near Cheyenne.[12]He became lieutenant colonel of the Seventh Cavalry on June 30, 1892. He transferred back to the Third Cavalry and commanded that regiment until October 14, 1897. He served in various other command positions until his retirement from the military as a brigadier general on October 11, 1898, after which he also commanded a volunteer regiment during the Spanish-American War. General Henry died on October 27, 1899.

**Gerhard L. Luhn** emigrated from Germany and joined the United States Army. He was assigned to Company E, Sixth Infantry on January 10, 1853, and reached the rank of first sergeant of that company on November 16, 1862. Luhn received a promotion to second lieutenant in the Fourth Infantry on February 19, 1863, and was advanced to first lieutenant on June 29, 1864. He was breveted a captain on April 2, 1865, for gallant and meritorious service during the combat at Petersburg, Virginia. After the Civil War he served as regimental quartermaster of the Fourth Infantry from January 31, 1869, until January 1, 1871. He was promoted to captain on December 31, 1875, while he was at Fort Fetterman. He served as post quartermaster there. Luhn retired from the military on February 19, 1895.[13]

**John Sanford Mason** was born in Ohio and graduated from West Point, ranked ninth in his class of July 1843. In 1847 he was made a second lieutenant of the Third Artillery and three years later, on September 7, 1850, was promoted to first lieutenant. While with the Third Artillery he acted as the regimental quartermaster between June 27, 1854, and June 1, 1858. He became a captain in the Eleventh Infantry on May 14, 1861. He joined the Fourth Ohio Infantry as colonel on October 3, 1861, and was promoted to brigadier general of Volunteers on November 29, 1862, at which rank he served until October 17, 1864, when he transferred to the Seventeenth U. S. Infantry and was promoted to major. He was breveted a major for gallant and meritorious service in the battle of Antietam, Maryland; a lieutenant colonel for services at Fredericksburg, Virginia; and ultimately brevet colonel for his actions during the war. At the conclusion of the Civil War he was mustered out of Volunteer Service on April 30, 1866. He transferred to the Thirty-fifth Infantry on September 21, 1866. On March 15, 1869, he transferred to the Fifteenth Infantry, and remained with this regiment until December 11, 1873, when he was promoted to lieutenant colonel of the Fourth Infantry. He served as post commander at

Fort Fetterman during January, February, and March 1874; again from July 1874 to November 1875; and a third time in April, May, and June of 1879. He remained with the Fourth Infantry until February 25, 1881, when he transferred to the Twentieth Infantry. On April 2, 1883, he transferred to the Ninth Infantry and was advanced to colonel of the regiment. He retired from the service on August 21, 1888, and died on November 29, 1897.[14]

**John Joseph O'Brien** was born in Kildare, Ireland on May 8, 1838. As a young man he emigrated to the United States in 1848. He joined Company F, Fourth Artillery on September 1, 1854 as a private and was a sergeant by September 1, 1859. At the outbreak of the Civil War he joined the First New York Cavalry and served in Companies B, K, and F between 1861 and 1864. On April 1, 1864, he was appointed to second lieutenant, and on December 27, 1864, he was promoted to captain. He was honorably mustered out of Volunteer Service on June 27, 1865. After the war, on July 29, 1865, he again enlisted in the Regular Army as a private in Company F, Twelfth Infantry. By May 6, 1867, he had made the rank of sergeant and on that date he received a commission as second lieutenant in the Thirtieth Infantry. He transferred to the Fourth Infantry on March 23, 1869. O'Brien remained with the Fourth Infantry the remainder of his military career. He made first lieutenant on March 16, 1879, and captain on September 14, 1892. On April 22, 1896, he retired from the service.[15]

**William Henry Powell** began his military career at the bottom of the enlisted ranks, serving as a private in Company B, Fourth Battalion of the District of Columbia militia from April 17 until July 17, 1861. Four months later he was promoted to second lieutenant in the Fourth Infantry. On September 16, 1862, he reached the rank of first lieutenant, and served as regimental adjutant between March 1, 1862, and January 29, 1863. He was breveted a captain on September 17, 1862, for gallant and meritorious service in the battle of Antietam, Maryland. On April 2, 1865, he received the breveted rank of major for gallant and meritorious service at Petersburg, Virginia. He was promoted to captain on February 2, 1865, in the Fourth Infantry. From June 1879 until May 1882 he served as commander of Company G, Fourth Infantry and post commander at Fort Fetterman. On August 5, 1888, he was promoted to the rank of major. On May 4, 1892, he reached the rank of lieutenant colonel in the Eleventh Infantry, and on June 27, 1897, he transferred into the Ninth Infantry as a colonel. Powell retired from military service on April 25, 1899, and died on November 16, 1901.[16]

**Joseph Jones Reynolds** graduated from West Point in 1839, ranked tenth in his class. He was breveted a second lieutenant in the Fourth Artillery on July 1, 1843. He became a second lieutenant in the Third Artillery on May 11, 1846, and resigned from military service on February 28, 1857. At the beginning of the Civil War he became a colonel in the Tenth Indiana Infantry on April 25, 1861. By May 1861 he was a brigadier general of Volunteers. On November 29, 1862, he was promoted to major general of Volunteers. Reynolds was honorably mustered out of Volunteer Service on September 1, 1866, after accepting a Regular Army commission as colonel in the Twenty-sixth Infantry on July 28, 1866. On January 8, 1870, he was assigned to the Twenty-fifth Infantry, and transferred to the Third Cavalry in December 1870. He commanded the first expedition north out of Fort Fetterman in the Campaign of 1876. Reynolds retired from the service on June 25, 1877, after General Crook brought court-martial proceedings against him for allowing an Indian horse herd to be recaptured during the battle at Crazy Horse's village on Powder River on March 17, 1876. He died on February 25, 1899.[17]

**Ephraim Tillotson** began his military career as a private in Company G, Third New York Artillery, during the Civil War. He entered service on March 23, 1864, and by June 12, 1865, had attained the rank of sergeant. On August 10, 1865, he was promoted to second lieutenant of the "United States Colored Infantry." He was honorably mustered out of the service on February 8, 1866, only to return as a second lieutenant of the Twenty-seventh Infantry on May 6, 1867. In 1868, he was promoted to first lieutenant and by June 14, 1869, he was listed as "not assigned" to any regiment. Upon his own request, Tillotson was honorably discharged from the service on December 31, 1870. By April 1871, he was at Fort Fetterman as the post trader. He died January 5, 1885.[18]

**Frederick Van Vliet** was appointed to the Third Cavalry on August 5, 1861, as a second lieutenant. On July 17, 1862, he was promoted to first lieutenant. He was regimental adjutant of the Third Cavalry between July 12, 1862, and January 9, 1863. For gallant and meritorious service during the battles of the campaign from the Rapidan to Petersburg, Virginia, he was breveted a captain. After the Civil War he gained the rank of captain on July 28, 1866. On Christmas Day 1872, he arrived at Fort Fetterman as commander of its first permanent cavalry detachment. He served with the Third Cavalry until June 26, 1882, when he was promoted to major in the Tenth Cavalry. Van Vliet died on March 8, 1891.[19]

**Anthony Wayne Vodges** joined the Hundredth New York Volunteer Infantry as a second lieutenant on August 13, 1863, and served with this regiment during the Civil War. He was honorably mustered out as first lieutenant on August 28, 1865. He was appointed second lieutenant of the Fourth Infantry on April 26, 1866, and achieved the rank of first lieutenant in that regiment on May 15, 1867. He remained with the Fourth Infantry until May 22, 1875, when he transferred into the Fifth Artillery. While with the Fourth Infantry he was stationed for two years at Fort Fetterman and it was during this time that his wife Ada recorded life at the fort in her diary. He remained with the Fifth Artillery until February 2, 1901, when he was assigned to the Artillery Corps as a major. On July 30, 1902, he was promoted to lieutenant colonel.[20]

**George Ogilvie Webster** graduated from West Point thirtieth in his class on September 1, 1861. He apparently did not serve during the Civil War because it was not until June 18, 1866, that he was appointed second lieutenant in the Fourth Infantry. While at Fort Fetterman he received his commission as first lieutenant on November 25, 1873. He first served as regimental adjutant between November 15, 1867, and May 6, 1875. Eleven years later he was again assigned as regimental adjutant of the Fourth Infantry and served in that position between October 1, 1886, and October 30, 1887. On August 5, 1888, he was promoted to captain. He served his entire military career with the Fourth Infantry. He reached the rank of major on March 2, 1899, retired on September 8, and died on October 10, 1899.[21]

**Eugene Wells** was commissioned into the army on May 14, 1861, as a first lieutenant and by September 9, 1863, had attained the rank of captain. After the Civil War he remained in the army and transferred to the Thirtieth Infantry on September 21, 1866. He was unassigned during the reductions and reorganization of the army in 1869, but on April 10, 1869, was appointed to the Fourth Infantry. While serving at Fort Fetterman he became involved in an altercation in the post trader's store with

Lieutenant Carl Teitenheimer of the Fourth Infantry. Court-martial charges were filed against the two officers and Wells tendered his resignation on September 6, 1870. Following Wells's resignation, the charges against Teitenheimer were dropped by post commander Alexander Chambers on October 13, 1870. Wells rejoined the army on July 6, 1875, as a second lieutenant in the First Artillery, but was dismissed from the service on October 13, 1877.[22]

**Henry Walton Wessells** was ranked twenty-ninth in his class when he graduated from West Point in 1829. He was breveted to second lieutenant of the Second Infantry on July 1, 1833, and became a second lieutenant on June 28, 1836. Two years later, on July 7, 1838, he advanced to first lieutenant and was promoted to captain on February 16, 1847. During the Mexican War he was breveted to the honorary rank of major for gallant and meritorious service in the battles of Contreras and Churubusco, Mexico. Wessells transferred to the Sixth Infantry with a promotion to major on June 6, 1861. On September 29, 1861, he became a colonel in the Eighth Kansas Infantry, but resigned from the Volunteer Service on February 7, 1862. For gallant and meritorious service during the battle of Fair Oaks, Virginia, he was breveted lieutenant colonel. He was breveted to colonel for gallant and meritorious service during the attack on Plymouth, North Carolina, and for his gallant service during the entirety of the Civil War he was breveted brigadier general on March 13, 1865. He was given the rank of brigadier general of Volunteers on April 25, 1862, and served in that capacity until mustered out at the end of the Civil War on January 15, 1866. On February 16, 1865, he was reinstated into the Regular Army as a lieutenant colonel, retaining that rank until he retired from the military on January 1, 1871. He served with the 18th Infantry as Fort Fetterman's post commander from November 1867 to May 1868. Wessells died on January 12, 1889.[23]

**George Abisha Woodward** joined the military on May 27, 1861, as a captain in the Second Pennsylvania Infantry. By December 4, 1863, he had obtained the rank of colonel. He was breveted a colonel for gallant and meritorious service during the battle of Gettysburg. At the conclusion of the Civil War he was honorably mustered out of service on July 20, 1866. Woodward became a major in the Fourteenth Infantry on March 15, 1869. It was during his time with the Fourteenth Infantry that he was

Fort Fetterman's post commander, between 1871 and 1873. On January 10, 1876, he was promoted to colonel in the Fifteenth Infantry. He retired from the service on March 20, 1879.[24]

# NOTES

**Abbreviations**

CCF = Consolidated Correspondence File    MH = Medical History

DP = Department of the Platte    NA = National Archives

FF = Fort Fetterman    PJ = Post Journal

GO = General Orders    PQ = Post Quartermaster

GPO = Government Printing Office    ROE = Record of Events

LR = Letters Received    SGO = Surgeon General's Office

LS = Letters Sent    SO = Special Orders

MF = Microfilm Roll    TR = Telegrams Received

     TSR = Telegrams Sent and Received

     WPCR = Wyoming State Department of Parks & Cultural Resources

     WPHS = Wyoming State Parks and Historic Sites

## 1. Opening the Bozeman Trail

1.  Grace Raymond Hebard, *The Pathbreakers from River to Ocean* (Chicago: The Lakeside Press, 1913), 167-170.

2.  Dee Brown, *Fort Phil Kearny: An American Saga* (Lincoln, NE: University of Nebraska Press, 1962), 13-16.

3.  Robert M. Utley, *Frontier Regulars: The United States Army and the Indian Wars, 1866-1890* (New York: Macmillan, 1973), 99.

4.  Utley, *Frontier Regulars*, 103.

5.  Fort Phil Kearny was named in honor of Major General Philip Kearny, who was killed September 1, 1862, at the Civil War battle of Chantilly, Virginia.

6.  Fort C. F. Smith was named in honor of Colonel Charles Ferguson Smith, who served gallantly during the Mexican War.

7.  Utley, *Frontier Regulars*, 107-111.

8.  Ibid., 125.

9.  Wister depicted the town of Drybone in his short story "Burial of the Biscuit Shooter" which he later incorporated into the novel *Lin McLean*. Drybone also appears in *The Virginian*.

## 2. Building a Post 1867 – 1869

1. Post letter book, Fort Fetterman (FF), Records of the War Department, Department of the Platte (DP), Wyoming State Department of Parks & Cultural Resources (WPCR), Microfilm roll (MF) # 803-1.

2. Circular Number 4, *Report on Barracks and Hospitals of the United States Army* War Department, Surgeon General's Office (SGO), Washington D. C.: Government Printing Office (GPO), 350.

3. Post letter book (FF, DP, Aug. 10, 1867, WPCR), MF #803-1.

4. General Orders (GO), (FF, DP, April 10, 1868), MF #803-6.

5 Captain Dye to DP, FF, Aug. 18, 1868, MF #803-1.

6. Copy of map in the Wyoming State Archives, FF Map and building blueprint files.

7. Letters Sent (LS) and Endorsements, FF (WPCR, Record Group 98), MF #803-1.

8. LS, FF, Oct. 1, 1867, (WPCR), MF #801-1.

9. Ibid.

10. Copies of the H. S. Searle letters were provided by Newell Searle who retains the original copies. Letter Oct. 23, 1867.

11. LS, FF, Nov. 5, 1867, (WPCR), MF # 803-1.

12. LS, FF, Nov. 6, 1867, (WPCR), MF #803-1.

13. LS, FF, Nov. 20, 1867, (WPCR), MF # 803-1.

14. GO, FF, Dec. 1867, (WPCR), MF #803-5.

15. Circular Number 4, *Report on Barracks and Hospitals of the United States Army* (War Department, SGO, Washington D.C.: GPO), 351.

16. LS, FF, March 1, 1869, (WPCR), MF #803-1.

17. Post Journal (PJ), FF, May 11, 1869, (WPCR), MF #H-76.

18. LS, FF, Oct. 21, 1868, (WPCR), MF #803-1.

19. PJ, FF, July 16, 1869, (WPCR), MF #H-76.

20. Medical History (MH), FF, May 1869, (WPCR), MF #H-120b.

21. LS, FF, Oct. 25, 1869, (WPCR), MF #803-1.

22. Consolidated Correspondence File (CCF), FF, Jan. 22, 1874, (WPCR), MF #H-134.

## 3. Transportation and Communications

1. H. S. Searle letter Oct. 23, 1867.

2. LS, FF, May 25, 1868, (WPCR), MF #803-1.

3. LS, FF, June 4, 1877, (WPCR), MF #803-1.

4. LS, FF, July 29, 1877, (WPCR), MF #803-1.

5. Telegrams Sent & Received (TSR), FF, July 26, 1878, (WPCR), MF #803-4.

6. John Hunton, *John Hunton's Diaries*, ed. L. G. Flannery, Vol. 3, 1878-1879 (Lingle, Wyoming: Guide-Review Press, 1956) 50-51.

7. LS, FF, May 2, 1879, (WPCR), MF #803-2.

8. Circular Number 8 (War Department, SGO, Washington D.C.: GPO, May 1, 1875), 352.

9. PJ, FF, Jan. 29, 1874, (WPCR), MF #803-5.

10. LS, FF, Aug. 2, 1874, (WPCR), MF #803-1.

11. LS, FF, Dec. 14, 1874, (WPCR), MF #803-1.

12. PJ, FF, June 30 & July 7, 1875, (WPCR), MF #803-5.

13. LS, FF, Dec. 15, 1878 & May 10, 1879, (WPCR), MF #803-2.

14. LS, FF, April 25, 1870, (WPCR), MF #803-1.

15. Circulars, FF, June 1, 1868, (WPCR), MF #803-6.

16. LS, FF, June 1, 1868, (WPCR), MF #803-1.

17. TSR, FF, Jan. 15, 1877, (WPCR), MF #803-4.

18. Post Quartermaster (PQ) Letters, FF, June 15, 1878, (WPCR), MF #803-10.

19. LS, FF, June 30, & July 20, 1879, (WPCR), MF #803-2.

20. Telegrams Sent, FF, Oct. 30, 1879, (WPCR), MF #803-4.

21. Record Of Events (ROE), FF, Sept. 5, 1879 (Annual Inspection Report, J. S. Mason, WPCR), MF #803-5.

22. PQ LS, FF, Nov. 22, 1879, (WPCR), MF #803-10.

23. LS, FF, Oct. 1 & 23, 1867, (WPCR), MF #801-1.

24. LS, FF, March 29, 1868, (WPCR), MF #803-1.

25. PJ, FF, Feb. 28, 1873 & March 14, 1873, (WPCR), MF #803-5.

26. Circular, FF, Oct. 9, 1874, (WPCR), MF #803-7.

27. LS, FF, Oct. 11, 1876, (WPCR), MF #803-1.

28. LS, FF, June 29, 1878, (WPCR), MF #803-2.

29. LS, FF, Oct. 20, 1877, (WPCR), MF #803-1.

30. LR, FF, Dec. 23, 1877, (WPCR), MF #803-14.

31. LS, FF, July 17, 1880, (WPCR), MF #803-2.

32. LS, FF, April 20, 1880, (WPCR), MF #803-2.

33. LS, FF, May 7, 1882, (WPCR), MF #803-2.

## 4. The Peace Treaty of 1868 and Its Aftermath

1. *Secretary of War Report, 1867–1868*, Serial No. 1324, Vol. 1, 40th Congress, Second Session, 28.

2. Ibid.

3. LS, FF, June 4, 1868, (WPCR), MF 803-1.

4. David Heib, *Fort Laramie, National Park Service Historical Handbook Series, No. 20* (Washington, D. C.: GPO), 22-23.

5. *Secretary of War Report, 1867–68*, Serial 1324, Vol. 1, 40th Congress, Second Session, 65-67.

6. Ibid.

7. Robert B. David, *Finn Burnett, Frontiersman* (Glendale, California: Arthur H. Clark Company, 1937).

8. LS, FF, Nov. 18, 1867, (WPCR), MF # 803-1.

9. LS, FF, Nov. 21, 1867, (WPCR), MF #803-1.

10. LS, FF, Nov. 30, 1867, (WPCR), MF # 803-1.

11. LS, FF, Feb. 18, 1868, (WPCR), MF # 803-1.

12. LS, FF, March 2, 1868, (WPCR), MF #803-1.

13. LS, FF, March 12 (WPCR), MF # 803-1.

14. LS, FF, March 19, 1867, (WPCR), MF #803-1.

15. LS, FF, Aug. 29, 1868, (WPCR), MF #803-1.

16. LS, FF, March 10, 1868, (WPCR), MF #803-1.

17. LS, FF, July 4, 1868, (WPCR), MF # 803-1.

18. LS, FF, July 22, 1868 & July 29, 1868, (WPCR), MF # 803-1.

19. Dye to General Slemmer at Ft. Laramie, FF, Aug. 24, 1868, (WPCR), MF# 803-1.

20. LS, FF, Aug. 25 & 28, 1868, (WPCR), MF # 803-1.

21. Letter Sent, FF, Aug.-Sept., 1868, (WPCR), MF # 803-1.

22. General Sherman to General Augur, DP, FF, Dec. 4, 1868, (WPCR), MF #803-1.

23. LS, FF, Jan. 19, 1869, (WPCR), MF # 803-1.

24. Ada Vodges, *Ada Vodges' Diary,* Jan. 5 & 6, 1870 (Original in the collection of the Huntington Library, San Marino, California), 138.

25. Vodges, *Diary,* April 2, 1870, 150.

26. Vodges, *Diary,* April 2, 1870, 151.

27. PJ, FF, April 24, 1870, (WPCR), MF #803-5.

28. Vodges, *Diary,* April 26, 1870, 155.

29. Vodges, *Diary,* April 27, 1870, 156.

30. Vodges, *Diary,* April 26, 1870, 155-156.

31. MH, FF, May 4, 1870, (WPCR), MF # H-120b.

32. Colonel Chambers commanding FF to General Flint commanding Fort Laramie, Telegraph, July 30, 1870, (WPCR), MF #803-4.

33. MH, FF, May 4, 1870, (WPCR), MF #H-120b.

34. Vodges, *Diary*, May 4, 1870, 160.

35. MH, FF, May 10, 1870, (WPCR), MF #H-120b.

36. TSR, FF, July 8, 1870, (WPCR), MF #803-4; MH, FF, July 13, 1870, (WPCR), MF #H-120b.

37. Vodges, *Diary*, July 14, 1870, 161.

38. Vodges, *Diary*, July 14, 1870, 162.

39. MH, FF, July 24, 1870, (WPCR), MF #H-120b.

40. MH, FF, Aug. 31, 1870, (WPCR), MF #H-120b.

41. Vodges, *Diary*, Sept. 8, 1870, 164.

42. Vodges, *Diary*, Oct. 19, 1870, 165.

43. TSR, FF, Dec. 4, 1870, (WPCR), MF #803-4.

44. MH, FF, Aug. 29, 1871, (WPCR), MF #H120b.

45. TSR, FF, Jan. 12, 1871, (WPCR), MF #803-4.

46. Post GO, FF, Circular, March 29, 1871, (WPCR), MF #803-7.

47. Vodges, *Diary*, Feb. 24, 1871, 173.

48. Vodges, *Diary*, Feb. 24, 1871, 175-176.

49. MH, FF, Aug. 29, 1871, (WPCR), MF #H-120b.

50. Vodges, *Diary*, Sept. 1869, 128.

51. John B. Sanborn, Office of Indian Affairs, Washington D.C., to N.G. Taylor, Commissioner of Indian Affairs, Feb. 22, 1869.

52. LS, FF, Sept. 9, 1869, (WPCR), MF #803-1.

53. Vodges, *Diary*, Sept. 10, 1869, 130.

54. Brian Jones, "John Richard, Jr. and the Killing at Fetterman," *Annals of Wyoming*, Vol. 43, No 2 (Fall 1971), 242-243.

55. *Secretary of War Report*, Vol. 1, 1869-70, No. 1412, 41st Congress, 2nd Session; Augur's Report, Oct. 23, 1869, 73.

56. Vodges, *Diary*, Oct. 21, 1869, 131.

57. Jones, "John Richard," *Annals*, Vol. 43, No. 2 (Fall 1971), 256-257

## 5. Fort Fetterman and and the Centennial Campaigns

1. LS, FF, Jan. 20, 1869, (WPCR), MF #803-1.

2. PJ, FF, March 23 & 25, April 3-9, 1869, (WPCR), MF #803-5.

3. TSR, FF, April 6, 9, & 17, 1869, (WPCR), MF #803-4.

4. LS, FF, Oct. 14, 1869, (WPCR), MF #803-1.

5. TSR, FF, Oct. 29, 1869, (WPCR), MF #803-4; Sharon Lass Field, *Fort Fetterman's Cemetery* (Privately published, 1970).

6. LS, FF, Dec. 7, 1869, (WPCR), MF #803-1.

7. TSR, FF, Jan. 1, 1870, (WPCR), MF #803-4.

8. Vodges, *Diary*, Jan. 11, 1870, 139.

9. TSR, FF, April 12, 1870, (WPCR), MF #803-4.

10. MH, FF, April 27, 1870, (WPCR), MF #H-120b.

11. MH, FF, June 28, 1870, (WPCR) MF #H-120b; TSR, FF, June 29, 1870, (WPCR) MF # 803-4.

12. MH, FF, Dec. 3, 1871, (WPCR), MF #H-120b; TSR, FF, Dec. 4, 1871, (WPCR), MF #803-4.

13. MH, FF, May 1, 1872, (WPCR), MF #H-120b.

14. LS, FF, May 5, 1872, (WPCR), MF #803-1.

15. TSR, FF, Oct. 29, 1872, (WPCR), MF #803-4.

16. MH, FF, Oct. 1872, (WPCR), MF #H-120b.

17. ROE, FF, Dec. 25, 1872, (WPCR), MF #803-5.

18. LS, FF, March 5, 1873, (WPCR), MF #803-1.

19. PJ, FF, Feb. 10, 1874, (WPCR), MF #803-5.

20. MH, FF, March 22, 1874, (WPCR), MF #H-120b.

21. MH, FF, March 28, 1874, (WPCR), MF #H-120b; TSR, FF, April 27, 1874, (WPCR), MF #803-4.

22. LS, FF, Sept. 19, 1874, (WPCR), MF #803-1.

23. MH, FF, July 2 and 11, 1874, MF #H-120b, WPCR. Also, TSR, FF, July 2, 1874, MF #803-4, WPCR.

24. MH, FF, July 16, 1874, (WPCR), MF #H-120b.

25. LS, FF, July 18, 1874, (WPCR), MF #803-1.

26. Field, *Fort Fetterman's Cemetery*, 13.

27. MH, FF, July 29, 1874, (WPCR), MF #H-120b.

28. PJ, FF, Dec. 10, 1874, (WPCR), MF #803-5.

29. LS, FF, Feb. 24 & 25, 1875, (WPCR), MF #803-1.

30. PJ, FF, June 7, 1875, (WPCR), MF #803-5.

31. PJ, FF, Sept. 30, & Oct. 3, 1875, (WPCR), MF #803-5.

32. "The Majors and the Miners: The Role of the U.S. Army in the Black Hills Gold Rush," *Journal of the West*, Vol. XI, No. 1, Jan., 1972, 99.

33. "The Majors and the Miners," *Journal of the West*, 101.

34. Utley, *Frontier Regulars*, 251-253.

35. Special Orders (SO), FF, March 29, 1875, (WPCR), MF #803-8.

36. MH, FF, June 21 and 23, 1875, (WPCR), MF #H-120b.

37. Utley, *Frontier Regulars*, 254-255.

38. John G. Bourke, *On The Border With Crook,* (Lincoln, NE: University of Nebraska Press, 1971), 288-291.

39. TSR, FF, May 29, 1876, (WPCR), MF #803-4.

40. TSR, FF, June 6, 1876, (WPCR), MF #803-4.

41. PJ, FF, June 20, 1876, (WPCR), MF #803-5.

42. MH, FF, June 27, 1876, (WPCR), MF #H-120b.

43. TSR, FF, June 21, 1876, (WPCR), MF #803-4.

44. MH, FF, June 30, 1876, (WPCR), MF #H-120b.

45. MH, FF, Dec. 6, 1876, (WPCR), MF #H-120b.

46. Virginia Trenholm, *Footprints on the Frontier,* Douglas, WY: Douglas Enterprise Co., 1935, 111-113.

47. TSR, FF, Aug. 2 and 3, 1876, (WPCR), MF #803-4.

48. TSR, FF, Aug. 8, 1876, (WPCR), MF #803-4.

49. TSR, FF, Aug. 5, 1876, (WPCR), MF #803-4.

50. PJ, FF, Oct. 7 and 18, 1876, (WPCR), MF #803-5.

51. PJ, FF, Oct. 16, 1876, (WPCR), MF #803-5.

## 6. Garrison Life at Fort Fetterman

1. Vodges, *Diary,* April 30, 1869, 120.

2. Vodges, *Diary,* April 30, 1869, 120.

3. PJ, FF, Aug. 27, 1869, (WPCR), MF #H-76.

4. Vodges, *Diary,* Aug., 1869, 124.

5. PJ, FF, Oct. 11, 1869, (WPCR), MF #H-76.

6. Vodges, *Diary,* Nov. 14, 1869, 135.

7. ROE, FF, Dec. 31, 1869, (WPCR), MF #803-1.

8. Vodges, *Diary,* Dec. 21, 1869, 136.

9. Vodges, *Diary,* Dec. 25, 1869, 137.

10. Vodges, *Diary,* Jan. 16, 1870, 139 -140.

11. PJ, FF, Jan. 16, 1870, (WPCR), MF #803-5.

12. Vodges, *Diary,* Jan. 19, 1870, 141.

13. Vodges, Diary, March 9, March 30, & April 30, 1870, 147, 149 & 158.

14. GO, FF, Jan. 17, 1870, (WPCR), MF #803-7.

15. Vodges, *Diary,* Jan. 18, 1870, 140-141.

16. Vodges, *Diary,* Jan. 26, 1871, 170.

17. A "striker" was an enlisted man serving as a butler for an officer. This prestigious role held rewards such as a private room in the officer's residence, often better prepared food than that served in the barracks, and extra pay.

18. Vodges, *Diary*, March 7, 1871, 177.

19. Vodges, *Diary*, Sept. 4, 1869, 127.

20. Thomas J. Caperton and LoRheda Fry, *Old West Army Cookbook, 1865 – 1900* (Museum of New Mexico, 1974), 3-6.

21. Jerome A. Greene, *Historic Furnishing Study, Fort Laramie Restored 1876, Old Bakery,* (Denver, CO: National Park Service, United States Department of Interior, Denver Service Center), 1-13.

22. PJ, FF, April 28 & May 18, 1869, (WPCR), MF #803-5.

23. Dr. F. V. Hayden, U.S. Geological Survey of Wyoming and Contiguous Territory, 1870, 22.

24. MH, FF, May 28, 1870, (WPCR), MF #H-120b.

25. Vodges, *Diary*, April 23, 1870, 154.

26. MH, FF, March 1872, (WPCR), MF #H-120b.

27. LS, FF, March 7, 1874, (WPCR), MF #803-1.

28. MH, FF, May, June, and July 1874, (WPCR), MF #H-120b.

29. PJ, FF, Aug. 8, 1875, (WPCR), MF #803-5.

30. LS, FF, Feb. 14, 1879, (WPCR), MF #803-2.

31. ROE, Sept. 5, 1879, (WPCR), MF #803-5.

32. MH, FF, Dec. 26, 1870 & Jan. 19, 1871, (WPCR), MF #H-120b.

33. Oliver Knight, *Life and Manners in the Frontier Army*, (Norman: University of Oklahoma Press, 1978).

34. LS, FF, May 7, 1877, (WPCR), MF #803-2.

35. Knight, *Life and Manners in the Frontier Army*, 6, 67-70.

36. LS, FF, July 6, 1878, (WPCR), MF #803-2.

37. Knight, *Life and Manners in the Frontier Army,* 70.

38. MH, FF, May 31, 1870, (WPCR), MF #H-120b.

39. MH, FF, Aug. 15, 1870, (WPCR) MF #H-120b.

40. PJ, FF, June 18, 1870, (WPCR), MF #803-5.

41. LS, FF, Nov. 20, 1867, (WPCR), MF #803-1.

42. LS, FF, July 6, 1867, (WPCR), MF #803-1.

43. LS, FF, July 9, 1868, (WPCR), MF #803-1.

44. LS, FF, Aug. 24, 1868, (WPCR), MF #803-1.

45. LS, FF, Sept. 28, 1868, (WPCR), MF #803-1.

46. LS, FF, June 24, & July 1, 1868, (WPCR), MF #803-1.

47. LS, FF, June 7, 1869, (WPCR), MF #803-1.

48. GO, FF, June 7, 1869, (WPCR), MF #803-6.

49. LS, FF, Oct. 27, 1869, (WPCR), MF #803-1.

50. LS, FF, April 20, 1871, (WPCR), MF #803-1.

51. MH, FF, Jan. 30, 1874, (WPCR), MF #H-120b.

52. MH, FF, Jan. 31, 1874, (WPCR), MF #H-120b.

53. MH, FF, March 7, 1874, (WPCR), MF #H-120b.

54. LS, FF, Sept. 7, 1874, (WPCR), MF #803-1.

55. TSR, FF, July 29, 1869, (WPCR), MF #803-4.

56. PJ, FF, Feb. 15, 1870, (WPCR), MF #803-5.

57. MH, FF, July 4, 1870, (WPCR), MF #H-120b.

58. MH, FF, July 4, 1871, (WPCR), MF #H-120b.

59. ROE, FF, July 4, 1875, (WPCR), MF #803-5.

60. Circulars, FF, Dec. 15, 1880, (WPCR), MF # 803-10.

61. Circulars, FF, Dec. 24, 1880, (WPCR), MF # 803-10.

62. GO, FF, March 25, 1869, (WPCR), MF #803-6.

63. MH, FF, Aug. 19, 1872, (WPCR), MF #H-120b.

64. GO, FF, Sept. 9, 1872, (WPCR), MF #803-7.

65. PJ, FF, Jan. 15 & 30, 1874, (WPCR), MF #803-5.

66. PJ, FF, May 10 & 11, 1875, (WPCR), MF #803-5.

67. LS, FF, Jan. 19, 1875, (WPCR), MF #802-1.

68. LS, FF, Feb. 23, 1875, (WPCR), MF #803-1.

69. LS, FF, June 19, 1868, (WPCR), MF #803-1.

70. MH, FF, March 1, 1871, (WPCR), MF #H-120b; Field, *Fort Fetterman's Cemetery*, 12.

71. MH, FF, Feb. 2, & April 12, 1875, (WPCR), MF #H-120b.

72. ROE, FF, June 10 & 11, 1871, (WPCR), MF #803-5.

73. MH, FF, Aug. 4 & 5, 1873, (WPCR), MF #H-120b.

74. PJ, FF, Sept. 26, 1872, (WPCR), MF #803-5.

75. MH, FF, Dec. 16, 1874, (WPCR), MF #H-120b.

76. PJ, FF, Oct. 14, 1876, (WPCR), MF #803-5.

77. MH, FF, July 23, 1877, (WPCR), MF #H-120b.

78. MH, FF, Sept. 4, 1877, (WPCR), MF #H-120b.

79. LS, FF, Sept. 24, 28 & Dec. 4, 1867, (WPCR), MF #803-1.

80. PJ, FF, Aug. 13 & 24, 1874, (WPCR), MF #803-5.

81. Hunton, *John Hunton's Diaries*, Nov. 16 and 17, 1875, 101.

82. LS, FF, March 28, 1877, (WPCR) MF #803-1.

83. Telegrams Received (TR), FF, Sept. 27, 28 & May 16, 1878, (WPCR), MF #803-4.

84. TR, FF, Dec. 14 & 23, 1878, (WPCR), MF #803-15.

85. Elnora L. Frye, *Atlas of Wyoming Outlaws at the Territorial Penitentiary*, (Laramie, WY: Jelm Mountain Publications, 1990), 81.

86. LS, FF, March 5, 8, 26, & April 12, 1876, (WPCR), MF #803-1.

87. TSR, FF, Feb. 25, 1879, (WPCR), MF #803-4.

88. MH, FF, March 4, 1880, (WPCR), MF #H-120b.

89. MH, FF, Aug. 11, 1881, (WPCR), MF #H-120b; Field, *Fort Fetterman's Cemetery*, 18.

90. *Annual Report of the Secretary of War, 1877*, Vol. 1, Washington, D.C.: GPO, 1877, vii.

91. CCF 1867-1890, FF, May 18, 1874, (WPCR), MF # H-134.

92. LS, FF, May 25, 1874, (WPCR), MF #803-1.

93. LS, FF, Aug. 14, 1867, (WPCR), MF #803-1.

94. LS, FF, Oct. 12, 1868, (WPCR), MF #803-1.

95. Ibid. GO No. 11, DP, Oct. 12, 1868.

96. LS, FF, March 1, 1871, (WPCR), MF #803-1.

97. TSR, FF, July 25 & Aug. 15, 1871, (WPCR), MF #803-4.

98. MH, FF, Dec. 11, 1871, (WPCR), MF #H-120b.

99. MH, FF, Aug. 17, 1872, (WPCR), MF #H-120b.

100. Telegrams Sent, FF, June 2, 1880, (WPCR), MF #803-4.

101. LS, FF, June 30, 1875, (WPCR), MF #803-1.

102. LS, FF, June 20, 1874, (WPCR), MF #803-1.

103. Hunton, *John Hunton's Diaries*, Dec. 4-6, 1878, 103.

104. Hunton, *John Hunton's Diaries*, July 19- 27, 1879, 165-166.

105. LS, FF, Aug. 14 and Oct. 23, 1878, (WPCR), MF #803-2.

106. LS, FF, July 28, 1879, (WPCR), MF #803-2.

107. LS, FF, June 23, 1879, (WPCR), MF #803-2.

**7. Expanding the Fort**

1. MH, FF, June 30, 1871, (WPCR), MF #H-120b.

2. GO, FF, Jan. 28, 1869, GO #10, (WPCR), MF #803-6; TSR, FF, Feb. 9, 1869, (WPCR), MF #803-4.

3. GO, FF, March 25, 1869, (WPCR), GO #27, MF #803-6.

4. ROE, FF, Aug. 9, 1873 & Apr. 15, 1874, (WPCR), MF #803-5.

5. LS, FF, Aug. 31, 1874, (WPCR), MF #803-1.

6. MH, FF, Oct. 31, 1874, (WPCR), MF #H-120b.

7. LS, FF, Nov. 6, 1874, (WPCR), MF #803-1.

8. Circular Number 8, (SGO, May 1, 1875), 348.

9. ROE, FF, synopsis of July 1875, (WPCR), MF #803-5; PJ, FF, July 30, 1875, (WPCR), MF #803-5.

10. Circular Number 8, (SGO, May 1, 1875), 348.

11. PJ, FF, July 30, 1875, (WPCR), MF #803-5; ROE, FF, Aug. 1, 7, 21, 1875 & Sept. 15, 1875, (WPCR), MF #803-5; PQ LS, FF, Sept. 29, 1875, (WPCR), MF #803-10.

12. LS, FF, Aug. 20, 1876, (WPCR), MF #803-1; FF PQ LS, FF, Nov. 2, 1877, (WPCR), MF #803-11; Miscellaneous Quartermaster Transmittals, FF, Jan. 7, 1878, (WPCR), MF #803-11.

13. CCF, FF, Dec. 7 & 8, 1881 and March 16, 1882, (WPCR), MF #H-134.

14. Circular Number 4, *A Report on the Barracks and Hospitals of the United States Army*, (War Department, SGO, Washington D. C.: GPO), 351.

15. Circular Number 8, (SGO, May 1, 1875), 349.

16. PQ LS, FF, July 27, 1875, (WPCR), MF #803-10.

17. PQ LS, FF, Sept. 29, 1875, (WPCR), MF #803-10.

18. MH, FF, Sept. 12, 1870, (WPCR), MF #H-120b.

19. MH, FF, June 21, 1871, (WPCR), MF #H-120b.

20. MH, FF, Sept. 6, 1873, (WPCR), MF #H-120b.

21. CCF, FF, Jan. 6, 1880, (WPCR), MF #H-134.

22. LS, FF, Jan. 25, 1880, (WPCR), MF #803-2.

23. LS, FF, April 4, 1870, (WPCR), MF #803-1.

24. MH, FF, July 19, 1870, (WPCR), MF #H-120b.

25. Circular Number 4, *Report on the Barracks and Hospitals of the United States Army*, (Dec. 5, 1870), 351-352.

26. MH, FF, Jan. 25 and March 31, 1871, (WPCR), MF #H-120b.

27. MH, FF, March 22, 1873, (WPCR), MF #H-120b.

28. MH, FF, June 15, 1874, (WPCR), MF #H-120b.

29. Circular Number 8, SGO, May 1, 1875, 350.

30. Ibid.

31. ROE, FF, Sept. 5, 1879, (WPCR), MF #803-5.

32. MH, FF, Month of June 1876, (WPCR), MF #H-120b.

33. LS, FF, Dec. 4, 1876, (WPCR), MF #803-1.

34. Circular Number 4, *Report on the Barracks and Hospitals of the United States Army*, (SGO, 1870; reprinted New York, Sol Lewis, 1974).

35. FF building plans file, Office of the Quartermaster General, DP, 1880.

36. ROE, FF, Jan. 22, March 11, May 10, 11, & 12, 1875, MF #803-5, WPCR.

37. ROE, FF, July 11, 1870, (WPCR), MF #803-5. The racetrack is visible in a 1949 aerial photograph.

38. J.O. Ward, "Soldiering at Fetterman," *Frontier Times,* Vol. 44, No. 2 (Feb./ March, 1970), 10.

39. PJ, FF, July 17, 1870, (WPCR), MF #803-5.

40. MH, FF, Sept. 1, 1870, (WPCR), MF #H-120b.

41. LR, FF, Oct. 8, 1878, (WPCR), MF #803-14.

42. PJ, FF, May 27, 1874, (WPCR), MF #803-5.

43. LS, FF, June 9, 1874, (WPCR), MF #803-1.

44. FF LS 1867 – 1882, (WPCR), MF #803-1.

45. LS, FF, July 14, 1875, (WPCR), MF #803-1.

46. LS, FF, Dec. 2, 1875, (WPCR), MF #803-1; FF Endorsements, Aug. 2, 1880, (WPCR), MF #803-4.

47. MH, FF, Oct. 3, 1881, (WPCR), MF #H-120b.

48. ROE, FF, Sept. 5, 1879, (WPCR), MF #803-5.

49. CCF, FF, Nov. 21, 1872, (WPCR), MF #H-134.

50. LS, FF, Dec. 8, 1872, (WPCR), MF #803-1.

51. CCF, FF, April 12, 1877, (WPCR), MF #H-134.

52. PQ LS, FF, Sept. 5, 1877 & June 30, 1878, (WPCR), MF #803-10.

53. Circular Number 4, (SGO, Dec. 5, 1870), 351.

54. LS, FF, May 7, 1872, (WPCR), MF #803-1.

55. ROE, FF, Sept. 5, 1879, (WPCR), MF #803-5.

56. CCF, FF, Jan. 6, 1880, (WPCR), MF #H-134.

57. Circular Number 4, (SGO, Dec. 5, 1870), 351.

58. LS, FF, May 7, 1872, (WPCR), MF #803-1.

59. MH, FF, Oct. 25, 1873, (WPCR), MF #H-120b.

60. LS, FF, July 12, 1876, (WPCR), MF #803-1.

61. LS, FF, Nov. 7, 1876, (WPCR), MF #803-1.

62. LS, FF, Jan. 18, 1870, (WPCR), MF #803-1.

63. CCF, FF, Jan. 6, 1880, (WPCR), MF #H-134.

64. CCF, FF, Feb. 11, 1880, (WPCR), MF #H-134.

65. CCF, FF, May 11, 1878, (WPCR), MF #H-134.

66. PQ LS, FF, June 4, 11, 17, 1880, (WPCR), MF #803-10.

67. Circular Number 4, (SGO, Dec. 5, 1870), 351.

68. LS, FF, Oct. 2, 1869, (WPCR), MF #803-1.

69. LS, FF, Dec. 6, 1869, (WPCR), MF #803-1.

70. LS, FF, Feb. 4, 1870, (WPCR), MF #803-1.

71. PQ LS, FF, April 27, 1879, (WPCR), MF #803-10.

72. Circular Number 8, (SGO, May 1, 1875), 350.

73. MH, FF, May 10, 1874, (WPCR), MF #H-120b.

74. LS, FF, May 3, 1873, (WPCR), MF #803-1.

75. PJ, FF, June, 1875, (WPCR), MF #803-5.

76. ROE, FF, Sept. 5, 1879, (WPCR), MF #803-5.

77. LR, FF, Nov. 3, 1881, (WPCR), MF #803-14.

78. LS, FF, Sept. 15, 1879, (WPCR), MF #803-2.

79. Circular Number 4, (SGO, Dec. 5, 1870), 352.

80. MH, FF, May 11, 1869, (WPCR), MF #H-120b; LS, FF, March 1, 1870, (WPCR), MF #803-1.

81. LS, FF, Jan. 14, 1880, & May 7, 1880, (WPCR), MF #803-2; PQ LS, FF, Feb. 17, 1880, (WPCR), MF #803-10.

82. Records of the Quartermaster General, DP, building plat number 230, 1881, copy Wyoming State Archives.

83. Circular Number 8, (SGO, May 1, 1875), 349.

84. MH, FF, Oct. 31, 1873, (WPCR), MF #H-120b.

85. Ibid.

86. Letter from John Hunton to Mrs. Cyrus Beard, *Annals of Wyoming*, Vol. 4, No.2 (Oct. 1926), 315.

87. LS, FF, Nov. 4, 1868, (WPCR), MF #803-1.

88. PQ LS, FF, Jan. 2, 1875, (WPCR), MF #803-10.

89. MH, FF, June 7, 1878, (WPCR), MF #H-120b.

90. John Oliver Ward, "Soldiering at Fetterman," *Frontier Times*, Vol. 44, No. 2 (Feb.-March, 1970), 7-9.

91. GO, FF, July 24, 1878, (WPCR), MF #803-9.

92. PQ LS, FF, Sept. 7, 1878, (WPCR), MF #803-10.

93. ROE, FF, Inspection Report, Sept. 5, 1879, (WPCR), MF #803-5.

94. Circular Number 8, (SGO, May 1, 1875), 351.

95. Ibid.

96. MH, FF, May 7, 1874, (WPCR), MF #H-120b.

97. MH, FF, Jan. 20, 1875, (WPCR), MF #H-120b.

98. PQ LS, FF, Feb. 23, 1875, (WPCR), MF #803-10.

99. LS, FF, June 14, 1875, (WPCR), MF #803-1.

100. ROE, FF, June 26, 1875, (WPCR), MF #803-5; MH, FF, June 26, 1875, (WPCR), MF #H-120b.

101. PQ LS, FF, July 21, 1875, (WPCR), MF #803-10.

102. PJ, FF, July 30, 1875, (WPCR), MF #803-5.

103. MH, FF, Sept. 1875, (WPCR), MF #H-120b.

104. ROE, FF, Sept. 28, 1875, (WPCR), MF #803-5.

105. PJ, FF, Nov. 4, 1875, (WPCR), MF #803-5.

106. PQ LS, FF, Nov. 29, 1875, (WPCR), MF #803-10.

107. LS, FF, June 21, 1876, (WPCR), MF #803-1.

108. PQ LS, FF, Oct. 19, 1876, (WPCR), MF #803-10.

109. PQ LS, FF, May 7, 1877, (WPCR), MF #803-10.

110. MH, FF, Jan. 1879, (WPCR), MF #H-120b.

111. PQ LS, FF, Feb. 24, 1880, (WPCR), MF #803-10; ROE, FF, Sept. 5, 1879, (WPCR), MF #803-5.

112. MH, FF, Oct. 1879, MF #H-120b, WPCR.

113. Circulars, FF, Dec 30, 1880, (WPCR), MF #803-10.

114. *Bill Barlow's Budget*, Vol. 3, No. 42, Wednesday 1889.

## 8. Fort Fetterman Becomes a Town 1882-1885

1. MH, FF, Nov. 10, 1881, (WPCR), MF #H-120b.

2. LS, FF, Nov. 16, 1881, (WPCR), MF #803-2.

3. CCF, FF, May 11, 1882, (WPCR), MF #H-134.

4. TSR, FF, May 18, 1882, (WPCR), MF #803-4.

5. GO, FF, GO No. 54, May 16, 1882, (WPCR), MF #803-10.

6. Correspondence between the National Archives (NA) and author, Aug. 25, 1971.

7. Correspondence between Honorable S.W. Downey of Wyoming and Secretary of War Robert T. Lincoln, May 19 and July 31, 1882. NA.

8. Hunton, *John Hunton's Diaries*, Vol. 4, 1882, 218.

9. Robert B. David, *Malcolm Campbell, Sheriff*, (Casper, WY: Wyomingana, Inc., S. E. Boyer & Company, 1932), 89-96

10. Correspondence between Frank Gore and Thomas Rowley, Feb. 23, 1940, author's collection.

11. Abe Abraham to Edward Rowley, Jan. 29, 1940, author's collection.

12. Abe Abraham to Edward Rowley, Jan. 29, 1940, author's collection.

13. Field, *Fort Fetterman's Cemetery*, 23.

14. David, *Malcolm Campbell, Sheriff*, 77-78.

15. Ibid., 116.

16. Ibid., 116-119; Field, *Fort Fetterman's Cemetery*, p. 21.

17. Abe Abrahams to Edward Rowley, March 6, 1940, author's collection.

18. Frank Gore to Thomas Rowley, Feb. 23, 1940, author's collection.

19. Memoirs of Mr. Ed Schloss, June 25, 1934, author's collection.

20. Abe Abrahams to Edward Rowley, Feb. 4, 1940, author's collection.

21. Field, *Fort Fetterman's Cemetery*, 22.

22. Frank Gore to Thomas Rowley, Feb. 23, 1940, author's collection.

23. David, *Malcolm Campbell, Sheriff*, p. 77.

24. Abe Abrahams to Edward Rowley, Feb. 4, 1940, author's collection.

25. "The notorious Jack Sanders shot at Ft. Fetterman by his Partner, Billy Bacon," *Big Horn Sentinel*, Dec. 12, 1885.

26. Dec. 3, 1885, Cheyenne *Democratic Leader*, Wyoming State Archives, Cheyenne, Wyoming.

27. C.W. (Charlie) Horr to Wyoming State Engineer L. C. Bishop, May 4, 1950; Hunton, *John Hunton's Diaries*, 216-218.

28. Hunton, *John Hunton's Diaries*, 78-79.

29. *Bill Barlow's Budget* Vol 1, No. 7, Wednesday, July 21, 1886. Merris Barrow used the pen name of Bill Barlow.

30. *Cheyenne Mirror,* Dec. 10, 1886, WPHS research files, Cheyenne, Wyoming.

31. David, *Malcolm Campbell, Sheriff*, 89-96.

**9. The Rise and Fall of "Drybone" 1885–1890**

1. Ben Merchant Vorpahl, *My Dear Wister: The Frederic Remington-Owen Wister Letters*, (Palo Alto, CA: American West Publishing Company, 1972), 17-20. The town of Drybone appears in several of Wister's works, including his famous *The Virginian*. The chapter of *Lin McLean* called "Destiny at Drybone" was first published as a short story called "Burial of the Biscuit Shooter."

2. Owen Wister, *Lin McLean* (New York: Harper & Brother, A.C. Burt Company, 1907), 264 & 267.

3. *Bill Barlow's Budget,* 1907, Anniversary Edition, Douglas, WY.

4. *Cheyenne Mirror*, Sept. 22, 1886, WPHS research files, Cheyenne, Wyoming.

5. *Bill Barlow's Budget,* , Wednesday, June 9, 1886, Vol. 1, No. 1.

6. *Bill Barlow's Budget*, Wednesday, June 16, 1886, Vol. 1, No. 2.

7. *Army & Navy Journal* (July 17, 1886), 1048. Corporal F.Y. Black, of Troop I, Fifth Cavalry, briefly described Fetterman City in 1885 as his regiment journeyed from Fort McKinney, Wyoming Territory to Fort Supply, Indian Territory.

8. *Bill Barlow's Budget*, Wednesday, July 7, Vol. 1, No. 5, 1886.

9. *Bill Barlow's Budget*, Wednesday, July 14, 1886, Vol. 1, No. 6.

10. *Bill Barlow's Budget*, Wednesday, Aug. 18, 1886, Vol. 1, No. 11.

11. *Cheyenne Mirror*, Aug. 27, 1886, WPHS research files, Cheyenne, Wyoming.

12. *Bill Barlow's Budget*, Wednesday, Aug. 25, 1886, Vol. 1, No. 12..

13. *Bill Barlow's Budget*, Wednesday, Oct. 20, 1886, Vol. 1, No. 20.

14. *Bill Barlow's Budget*, Wednesday, Oct. 27, 1886, Vol. 1, No. 21.

15. *Bill Barlow's Budget*, Wednesday, Dec. 1, 1886, Vol. 1, No. 26.

16. *Bill Barlow's Budget*, Wednesday, Dec. 8, 1886, Vol. 1, No. 27.

17. *Bill Barlow's Budget*, Wednesday, Aug. 18, 1886, Vol. 1, No. 11.

18. *Bill Barlow's Budget*, Wednesday, Sept. 8, 1886, Vol. 1, No. 14.

19. Field, *Fort Fetterman's Cemetery*, 23.

20. David, *Malcolm Campbell, Sheriff*, 78.

21. Vorpahl, *My Dear Wister*, 172.

22. Wister, *Lin McLean*, 277-300.

23. *Cheyenne Mirror*, Oct. 20, 1886, WPHS research files, Cheyenne, Wyoming.

24. *Bill Barlow's Budget*, Wednesday, March 16, 1887, Vol. 1, No. 41.

25. *Bill Barlow's Budget*, Wednesday, April 20, 1887, Vol. 1, No. 46.

26. *Cheyenne Mirror*, Dec. 10, 1886, WPHS research files, Cheyenne, Wyoming.

27. *Bill Barlow's Budget*, Wednesday, Jan. 5, 1886, Vol. 1, No. 31.

28. *Bill Barlow's Budget*, Wednesday, July 20, 1887, Vol. 2, No. 7.

29. *Bill Barlow's Budget*, 1907, Anniversary Edition, 4.

30. *Cheyenne Mirror*, Dec. 23, 1886, WPHS research files, Cheyenne, Wyoming.

31. *Bill Barlow's Budget*, Wednesday, Jan. 5, 1886, Vol. 1, No. 31.

32. *Bill Barlow's Budget*, Wednesday, Sept. 1, 1886, Vol. 1, No. 13.

33. *Bill Barlow's Budget*, Wednesday, Sept. 15, 1886, Vol. 1, No. 15.

34. *Bill Barlow's Budget*, Wednesday, Feb. 2, 1887, Vol. 1, No. 35.

35. *Bill Barlow's Budget*, Wednesday, Feb. 9, 1887, Vol. 1, No. 36.

36. *Bill Barlow's Budget*, Wednesday, March 2, 1887, Vol. 1, No. 39.

37. *Cheyenne Mirror*, Aug. 27, 1886, WPHS research files, Cheyenne, Wyoming.

38. *Cheyenne Mirror*, Sept. 30, 1886, WPHS research files, Cheyenne, Wyoming.

39. *Bill Barlow's Budget*, Wednesday, June 30, 1886, Vol. 1, No. 4.

40. *Cheyenne Mirror*, Sept. 30, 1886, WPHS research files, Cheyenne, Wyoming.

42. *Bill Barlow's Budget*, Wednesday, June 9, 1886, Vol. 1, No. 1.

42. *Bill Barlow's Budget*, Wednesday July 7, 1886, Vol. 1, No. 5.

43. *Cheyenne Mirror*, Oct. 8, 1886, WPHS research files, Cheyenne, Wyoming.

44. *Cheyenne Mirror*, Aug. 27, 1886, WPHS research files, Cheyenne, Wyoming.

45. *Bill Barlow's Budget*, Wednesday, July 21, 1886, Vol. 1, No. 7.

46. Field, *Fort Fetterman's Cemetery*, 26.

47. *Bill Barlow's Budget*, Wednesday, Feb. 2, 1887, Vol. 1, No. 35.

48. *Bill Barlow's Budget*, Wednesday, July 21, 1886, Vol. 1, No. 7.

49. *Bill Barlow's Budget*, Wednesday, Sept. 5, 1888, Vol. 3, No. 14.

50. Hunton, *John Hunton's Diary,* Vol. 4, 1882, 208

51. *Bill Barlow's Budget,* Wednesday, Jan. 12, 1887, Vol. 1, No. 32.

52. *Bill Barlow's Budget,* Wednesday, Feb. 2, 1887, Vol. 1, No. 35.

53. *Bill Barlow's Budget,* Wednesday, April 25, 1888, Vol. 2, No. 47.

54. *Bill Barlow's Budget,* Wednesday, June 16, 1886, Vol. 1, No. 2.

55. *Cheyenne Mirror,* Oct. 20, 1886, WPHS research files, Cheyenne, Wyoming.

56. *Bill Barlow's Budget,* Wednesday, Jan. 12, 1887, Vol. 1, No. 32.

57. *Bill Barlow's Budget,* Wednesday, March 30, 1887, Vol. 1, No. 43.

58. *Bill Barlow's Budget,* Wednesday, June 15, 1887, Vol. 2, No. 2.

59. *Bill Barlow's Budget,* Wednesday, Jan. 12, 1887, Vol. 1, No. 32.

60. *Bill Barlow's Budget,* Wednesday, Dec. 7, 1887, Vol. 2, No. 27.

61. *Cheyenne Mirror,* Dec. 23, 1886, WPHS research files, Cheyenne, Wyoming.

62. Ibid.

63. *Bill Barlow's Budget,* Wednesday, July 7, 1886, Vol. 1, No. 5.

64. *Cheyenne Mirror,* Sept. 9, 1886, WPHS research files, Cheyenne, Wyoming.

65. *Cheyenne Mirror,* Dec. 10, 1886, WPHS research files, Cheyenne, Wyoming.

66. *Bill Barlow's Budget,* Wednesday, Oct. 20, 1886, Vol. 1, No. 20.

67. *Bill Barlow's Budget,* Wednesday, July 13 and 20, 1887, Vol. 2, Nos. 6 and 7.

68 Wister, *Lin McLean,* 266.

69. *Bill Barlow's Budget,* Wednesday, Nov. 3, 1886, Vol. 1, No. 22.

70. *Bill Barlow's Budget,* Wednesday, June 16, 1886, Vol. 1, No. 2.

71. *Bill Barlow's Budget,* Wednesday, Feb. 2, 1887, Vol. 1, No. 35.

72. *Bill Barlow's Budget,* Wednesday, June 15, 1887, Vol. 2, No. 2.

73. *Bill Barlow's Budget,* Wednesday, June 8, 1887, Vol. 2, No. 1.

74. *Bill Barlow's Budget,* Wednesday, Aug. 11, 1886, Vol. 1, No. 10.

75. *Bill Barlow's Budget,* Wednesday, May 4, 1887, Vol. 1, No. 48.

76. *Cheyenne Mirror,* Oct. 20, 1886, WPHS research files, Cheyenne, Wyoming.

77. *Bill Barlow's Budget,* Vol. 1, No. 32, Wednesday, Jan. 12, 1887.

78. *Bill Barlow's Budget,* Wednesday, June 13, 1888, Vol. 3, No. 2.

79. David, *Malcolm Campbell, Sheriff,* 302.

## Appendix A: Biographies of Prominent Fort Fetterman Citizens

1. Wyoming Death Index, File No. 1930, Registration No. 931, (WPCR).

2. C.W. (Charlie) Horr to Wyoming State Engineer L. C. Bishop, May 4, 1950; Hunton, *John Hunton's Diaries,* 216-218.

3. Bill Barlow's Budget, Wednesday, July 21, 1886, Vol. 1, No. 7.

4. Pexton, *Pages from Converse County's Past,* 13.

5. *Cheyenne Mirror*, Dec. 10, 1886, WPHS research files, Cheyenne, Wyoming.

6. Margaret Prine "Merris C. Barrow: Sagebrush Philosopher and Journalist," *Annals of Wyoming*, Vol. 24, No. 1 (Jan. 1952), 53-71.

7. *Bill Barlow's Budget*, Anniversary Edition, 1907, 8.

8. *Bill Barlow's Budget*, Wednesday, April 27, 1887, Vol. 1, No. 47.

9. Albert B. Bartlett, *History of Wyoming* Vol. 3, 625 (Chicago: S. J. Clarke Publishing Company) 1918.

10. Pexton, *Pages from Converse County's Past*, 91-93.

11. "Pioneer People of Douglas and Converse County, Wyoming 1886", *Douglas Diamond Jubilee Days Committee*, July 4-8, 1962, 6-8.

12. Pexton, *Pages from Converse County's Past*, 137.

13. *Douglas Budget*, Wednesday, Aug. 14, 1901, Vol. 16, No. 10.

14. Bartlett, *History of Wyoming*, Vol. 3, 106-107.

15. Ruth Grant, *Pages from Converse County's Past*, 393.

16. Bartlett, *History of Wyoming* Vol. 3, 578-579.

17. *Bill Barlow's Budget*, Wednesday Jan. 3, 1912, Vol. 3, No. 30.

18. *Bill Barlow's Budget*, Wednesday Jan. 3, 1912, Vol. 25, No. 30.

19. Pexton, *Pages from Converse County's Past*, 543.

20. *Douglas Budget*, Thursday, June 20, 1963. Article reprinted from the Feb. 10, 1897 issue of the *Douglas Budget*, Douglas, Wyoming.

21. "Pioneer People of Douglas and Converse County, Wyoming 1886", *Douglas Diamond Jubilee Days Committee*, July 4-8, 1962, 37.

22. *Bill Barlow's Budget*, Wednesday, Oct. 5, 1887, Vol. 2, *Douglas Budget*, Douglas, Wyoming.

23. "Pioneer People of Douglas and Converse County, Wyoming 1886," *Douglas Diamond Jubilee Days Committee*, July 4-8, 1962, 37.

## Appendix B: Children Born at Fetterman as a Military Post
1. FF MH, June 10, 1869, MF #H-120b.
2. FF MH, March 31, 1871, MF #H-120b.
3. FF MH, Nov. 4, 1871, MF #H-120b.
4. FF MH, Oct. 10, 1874, MF #H-120b.
5. FF MH, Nov. 15, 1874, MF #H-120b.
6. FF MH, April 5, 1875, MF #H-120b.
7. FF MH, Nov. 13, 1876, MF #H-120b.
8. FF MH, Aug. 14, 1877, MF #H-120b.
9. FF MH, Oct. 12, 1877, MF #H-120b.

10. FF MH, Feb. 15, 1878, MF #H-120b.

11. FF MH, Jan. 18, 1879, MF #H-120b

12. FF MH, Feb. 1, 1879, MF #H-120b.

13. FF MH, March 1, 1879, MF #H-120b.

14. FF MH, March 30, 1879, MF #H-120b.

15. FF MH, Sept. 6, 1879, MF #H-120b.

16. FF MH, Sept. 26, 1879, MF #H-120b.

17. FF MH, Oct. 16, 1879, MF #H-120b.

18. FF MH, Oct. 16, 1879, MF #H-120b.

19. FF MH, Nov. 17, 1879, MF #H-120b.

20 FF MH, Nov. 29, 1879, MF #H-120b.

21. FF MH, Nov. 29, 1879, MF #H-120b.

22. FF MH, Dec. 2, and 12, 1880, MF #H-120b.

23. FF MH, Nov. 19, 1881, MF #H-120b.

**Appendix D: Biographies of Selected Officers at Fort Fetterman**

1. Francis B. Heitman, *Historical Register and Dictionary of the United States Army, September 29, 1789 to March 2, 1903* (Washington, D.C.: GPO, 1903; reprinted Urbana, IL: University of Illinois Press, 1965), Vol. 1, 324.

2. Heitman, *Historical Register*, 282-283.

3. Heitman, *Historical Register*, 293-294.

4. Heitman, *Historical Register*, 312.

5. Heitman, *Historical Register*, 321-322; Charles Springer, *Soldiering in Sioux Country: 1865* (San Diego, CA: Frontier Heritage Press, 1971), 73.

6. Heitman, *Historical Register*, 257-258.

7. Heitman, *Historical Register*, 340.

8. Heitman, *Historical Register*, 383.

9. Heitman, *Historical Register*, 392.

10. Heitman, *Historical Register*, 399.

11. Heitman, *Historical Register*, 482.

12. Colonel Harry N. Cootes and Chaplain Ralph C. Deibert, *A History of the Third United States Cavalry; Dediciated to the Officers and Men of the Regiment of Mounted Riflemen*, (Harrison, PA: Telegraph Press, 1933), 80.

13. Heitman, *Historical Register*, 646-647.

14. Heitman, *Historical Register*, 695.

15. Heitman, *Historical Register*, 755.

16. Heitman, *Historical Register*, 803.

17. Heitman, *Historical Register*, 825.

18. Heitman, *Historical Register*, 962.

19. Heitman, *Historical Register*, 984.

20. Heitman, *Historical Register*, 988.

21. Heitman, *Historical Register*, 1013.

22. Heitman, *Historical Register*, 1017; Records of the War Department, DP, LS, FF 1867–1882, Wyoming State Department of Commerce, Archives & Historical Division, MF #803-1.

23. Heitman, *Historical Register*, 1019.

24. Heitman, *Historical Register*, 1059.

# Bibliography

**Periodicals & Quarterly Journals**

"Anniversary Edition, 1907." *Bill Barlow's Douglas (Wyoming) Budget.* 21st anniversary special edition, 1907.

*Bill Barlow's Douglas (Wyoming) Budget* June 9, 1886–Dec. 26, 1888.

*Cheyenne Mirror* 1886.

Ellison, Robert S. "Historic Fort Fetterman." *The Midwest Review* 7, No. 8 (Casper, WY: Industrial Relations, Midwest Refining Co., Aug. 1926).

Jones, Brian. "John Richard, Jr. and the Killing at Fetterman." *Annals of Wyoming,* Vol. 43, No. 2 (1971).

"Letter from John Hunton to Mrs. Cyrus Beard." *Annals of Wyoming,* Vol. 4, No. 2 (Oct. 1926).

Parker, Watson. "The Majors and the Miners: The Role of the U. S. Army in the Black Hills Gold Rush." *Journal of the West* Vol. XI, No. 1 (Jan., 1972).

"Pioneer People of Douglas and Converse County Wyoming." Douglas, WY: Douglas Diamond Jubilee Days Committee, July 4, 1962.

Prine, Margaret. "Merris C. Barrow: Sagebrush Philosopher and Journalist." *Annals of Wyoming* Vol. 24, No. 1 (January, 1952).

Robrock, David P. "A History of Fort Fetterman, Wyoming 1867–1882." *Annals of Wyoming* Vol.48, No. 1 (Spring 1976).

"75th Anniversary Edition." *Douglas (Wyoming) Budget.* (1961).

Ward, John Oliver, "Soldiering at Fetterman." *Frontier Times* Vol. 44, No. 2 (Feb.–March 1970).

## Books & Pamphlets

Bartlett, Albert B. *History of Wyoming*. Chicago: S. J. Clarke Publishing Company, 1918.

Blake, Lillian Hogerson. *Charles John Hogerson, A Wyoming Pioneer*. The Wyoming Society of the National Society of the Colonial Dames of America, Vol. III, 1965.

Bourke, John G. *On the Border With Crook*. Lincoln, NE: The University of Nebraska Press, 1971.

———. *Mackenzie's Last Fight with The Cheyennes: A Winter Campaign in Wyoming*. Governor's Island, N. Y. H., 1890. Reprinted Bellevue, Nebraska: Old Army Press, 1970.

Brown, Dee. *Fort Phil Kearny*. Lincoln, NE: University of Nebraska Press, 1971.

Caperton, Thomas J. and Fry, LoRheda. *Old West Army Cookbook, 1865–1900*. Museum of New Mexico 1974, reprinted from *El Palacio* Vol. 80, No. 4.

Colonel Harry N. Cootes and Chaplain Ralph C. Deibert, *A History of the Third United States Cavalry; Dediciated to the Officers and Men of the Regiment of Mounted Riflemen*, Harrison, PA: Telegraph Press, 1933.

David, Robert B. *Finn Burnett, Frontiersman*. Glendale, CA: The Arthur H. Clark Co., 1937.

———. *Malcolm Campbell, Sheriff*. Casper, WY: Wyomingana, Inc., S. E. Boyer & Company, 1932.

Field, Sharon Lass. *Fort Fetterman's Cemetery*. Cheyenne, WY: self-published, 1970.

Finerty, John F. *War-Path and Bivouac*. Chicago: The Lakeside Press, 1955.

Frye, Elnora L. *Atlas of Wyoming Outlaws at the Territorial Penitentiary*. Laramie, WY: Jelm Mountain Publications, 1990.

Hebard, Grace Raymond. *The Pathbreakers from River to Ocean*. Chicago: The Lakeside Press, 1913.

Hedren, Paul L. *Fort Laramie in 1876*. Lincoln, NE: University of Nebraska Press, 1988.

*Pages From Converse County's Past*. Heritage Book Committee, Wyoming Pioneer Association. Casper, WY: Wyoming Historical Press, 1986.

Heitman, Francis B. *Historical Register and Dictionary of the United States Army* (2 vols.) Washington, D. C.: Government Printing Office, 1903. Reprint Urbana, IL: University of Illinois Press, 1965.

Hooker, William T. *The Bullwhacker.* Edited by Howard R. Priggs. New York: World Book Co., 1924.

Hunton, John. *John Hunton's Diaries.* Edited by L. G. Flannery. Lingle, WY:, Guide-Review Press, 1956.

Knight, Oliver. *Life and Manners in the Frontier Army.* Norman, OK: University of Oklahoma Press, 1978.

Murray, Robert A. *Military Posts in the Powder River Country of Wyoming, 1865–1894.* Lincoln, NE: University of Nebraska Press, 1968.

Parker, Watson. *Gold in the Black Hills.* Norman, OK: University of Oklahoma Press, 1966.

*Record of Engagements with Hostile Indians within the Military Division of the Missouri, from 1868 to 1882.* Washington D.C.: Government Printing Office, 1882. Reprinted, Bellevue, NE: Old Army Press, 1969.

Rickey, Don Jr. *Forty Miles a Day on Beans and Hay.* Norman, OK: University of Oklahoma Press, 1966.

Springer, Charles H. *Soldiering in Sioux Country: 1865.* Edited by Benjamin Franklin Cooling III. San Diego, CA: Frontier Heritage Press, 1971.

Summerhayes, Martha. *Vanished Arizona: Recollections of the Army Life of a New England Woman.* Lincoln, NE: University of Nebraska Press, 1979.

Trenholm, Virginia Cole. *Footprints on the Frontier.* Douglas, WY: Douglas Enterprise Co., 1945.

Utley, Robert M. *Frontier Regulars: The United States Army and the Indian Wars, 1866–1890.* New York: Macmillian Publishing Co., Inc., 1973.

Vaughn, J. W. *Indian Fights: New Facts on Seven Encounters.* Norman, OK: University of Oklahoma Press, 1966.

——. *The Reynolds Campaign on Powder River.* Norman, OK: University of Oklahoma Press, 1961.

———. *With Crook at the Rosebud.* Harrisburg, PA: Stackpole, 1956.

Vodges, Ada. *Ada Vodges' Diary.* Original in collection of the Huntington Library, San Marino, CA.

Vorpahl, Ben Merchant. *My Dear Wister: The Frederic Remington-Owen Wister Letters.* Palo Alto, CA: American West Publishing Company, 1972.

Wister, Owen. *Lin McLean.* New York: A. L. Burt Company, 1907.

**Government Documents**

Hieb, David L. *Fort Laramie National Monument, Wyoming.* National Park Service Historical Handbook Series No. 20, Washington, D. C.: 1954. Reprint, 1961.

Sanborn, John B. to N. G. Taylor, Commissioner of Indian Affairs, Washington, D. C., February 22, 1869. Letters Received, Office of Indian Affairs, 1869.

*Report of the Secretary of War, 1867–1868.* Serial 1324. 40th Congress, Second Session, Washington D. C.: Government Printing Office.

*Report of the Secretary of War, 1877.* Vol 1. Washington D. C.: Government Printing Office.

Circular Number 8. Washington D. C.: Surgeon General's Office, War Department, 1875. Reprintrd. New York: Sol Lewis, 1974.

Circular Number 4. *Report on the Barracks and Hospitals of the United States Army.* Washington D. C.: Surgeon General's Office, War Department, 1870. Reprinted. New York: Sol Lewis, 1974.

Greene, Jerome. *Historic Furnishing Study of the Fort Laramie Restored 1876 Bakery.* Denver, CO: Denver Service Center, Historic Preservation Team, National Park Service, Department of the Interior, 1974.

U. S. Adjutant General's Office. *Chronological List of Actions, etc., With Indians from January 15, 1837 to January, 1891.* Washington D. C.: Government Printing Office. Reprinted. Bellevue, NE: Old Army Press, 1979.

Hayden, Dr. F. V. *U. S. Geological Survey of Wyoming and Contiguous Territory, 1870.* Washington D. C.: Government Printing Office.

Correspondence between the Honorable S. W. Downey of Wyoming and Secretary of War, Robert T. Lincoln, May 19 and July 31, 1882. National Archives.

Wyoming Death Index. File No. 1930. Wyoming State Archives.

National Archives and Records Service, Washington D. C. Microfilm copies provided by the Wyoming State Archives, Cheyenne, WY. Post Letters Sent July 1867–June 1878. Telegrams September 1867–November 1868. Index to letterpress book October 6, 1877–June 1878. Microfilm roll 803-1.

——. Letters sent: June 1878–1882. Endorsements 1867–April 21, 1874. Microfilm roll 803-2.

——. Endorsements April 2, 1874–July 10, 1880. Microfilm roll 803-3.

——. Endorsements July 1880–March 1882. Special orders April 1868 –November 1868. Telegrams sent & received 1868–1882. Guard Details January 28–July 21, 1874. Orders for supplies October 1874–November 1875. Rosters May 1873. Microfilm roll 803-4.

——. Requisitions 1875. Post Journals 1868–1876. Clothing account book of Indian Scouts 1874. Burial Record 1868–1876. Consolidated Morning Reports 1867. Accounts Post Funds 1867–1870. Records post school 1873–1874. Guard Details 1875. Ration accounts 1876–1877. Roster of Officers for Details 1876–1877. Register of Civilians 1878–1880. Communications Sent 1880–1881. Guard Reports 1868–1869. List of Commissioned and Non-Commissioned Officers 1878–1885. Post Orders 1867–1882. WY. Microfilm roll 803-5.

——. Special Orders May 9, 1868–November 5, 1869. General Orders January 1868–January 1869. Post Circulars June 1868–October 1869. Microfilm roll 803-6.

——. Post Circulars November 6, 1869–November 1876. Special Orders November 1869–May 12, 1874. General Orders February 1870–May 1, 1874. Microfilm roll 803-7.

——. Special Orders May 15, 1874–June 20, 1876. General Orders 1874–1876. Microfilm roll 803-8.

——. Special Orders September 14, 1879–January 12, 1882. Post Circulars February 20, 1879–March 20, 1882. General Orders 1881–January 7, 1882. Register of Letters Sent May 1, 1878–July 16, 1880. Microfilm roll 803-9.

——. Special Orders June 20, 1876–September 12, 1879. Post Circulars May 1877 & July 1881. General Orders 1877–March 9, 1881. Post Orders June 23, 1881. Microfilm roll 803-10.

———. Letters Sent August 29–April 7, 1877. Miscellaneous Transmittals October 4, 1876–April 7, 1878. Copies of letters of Post Quartermaster 1875–1880. Microfilm roll 803-11.

———. Quartermaster Reports June 30, 1877–November 3, 1877. Post Commissary of Subsistence Reports 1876–1880. Register of Letters Received 1868–1869. Microfilm roll 803-12.

———. Letters Received 1868–1882. Letters Received from Department of the Platte July 18, 1881–March 21, 1882. Morning Reports-Quartermaster 1876–1878. Civilian Employee Time Books 1877–1880. Telegrams 1877–1879. Microfilm roll 803-13.

———. Incoming Letters & Telegrams February 14, 1876–1881. Microfilm roll 803-14.

———. Telegrams November 24, 1878–June 1, 1879. Orders January 9, September 5, 1878. Microfilm roll 803-15.

———. Consolidated Correspondence File 1867–1890. Microfilm roll H-134.

# Index

Abney, James M., 157, 191-192

Abrahams, Abe, 149-155, 191

Alder Gulch, 15

Allen, James, 73

Altman, Mr., 147-148, 178, 194

American Horse, 83

Anderson, T.M., 146

Andrews, D.H., 165

Andrews, William H., 81

Antelope Creek, 185

Antelope Springs, 47

Anvil Ranch, 167

Arnold, John, 167

Augur, Christopher Colon, 21, 23, 54-55

B.C. Tommy, 184

Babcock, Private, 69

Bacon Park, 157, 192

Bacon, Billy, 149-158, 165, 191-192

Bacon, Frances, 156-157, 191-192

Bahr, Conrad, 70, 201

Baily, Lou, 174

bakery, 32-33, 96, 137

Bannock, MT, 15

Barber, Amos, 149-150, 159-160, 164-167, 181-182, 188, 192

Barker, Joe, 179

Barlow, Bill (*See* Barrow, Merris C.)

Barrow, Helen, 193

Barrow, Merris C., 144, 162-163, 165-168, 176, 178, 186, 193, 199-200

Barrow, Minnie Glorence Combs, 193

Barrow, Robert, 193

Bartlett, S.A., 99

Bauer, Louis P., 139-140

Beaman, I.W., 99

Belknap, William W., 77

Belle Fourche River, 82

Benjamin Ranch, 201

Benjamin, H.A., 113

Bessemer, WY, 180

Big Horn Mountains, 16, 47, 50, 80, 83

*Big Horn Sentinel*, 155

Big Piney Creek, 20

Bighorn River, 16, 19

*Bill Barlow's Budget*, 144, 157, 162-163, 167-168, 173-176, 180-182, 186, 188, 193 (*See also Douglas Budget*)

Bird, Tom, 199

Bisbee, Captain, 125

Black Coal, 108

Black Hills, 21, 75-77, 82, 84

Black, Joe, 174

Blair, H.T., 174

Blaisdell, Mr., 185

Blue Front (*See* Metcalf & Williams Store)

Bolln, George, 177-179, 193-194

Bolln, Henry, 194

Bolln, Paulene Muegel, 178, 194

Borker, Mr., 182

Boswell, N.K., 194

Bourke, Lieutenant, 79

Bourke, Private Thomas, 53

Bowie, Alex, 165

Box Elder Creek, 24, 26, 41, 60, 73, 138

Bozeman Trail, 16-21, 23, 37, 49-50, 54, 145, 149, 189 (*See also* Montana Road)

Bozeman, John, 16-17

Bozeman, MT, 15

Brave Bear, 58, 62

Brennen, O.J., 166

Breslin, Patrick H., 103

Bridger, James, 16, 38, 42, 75

Bridger, James (not mountain man), 108-109

Broglin, Lieutenant, 65

Brown, Rufus, 54, 100

Bubb, John W., 80, 205

Buckley, Dick, 155

Buffalo, WY, 154-155, 162, 199

Bureau of Indian Affairs, 75

Bury, James H., 165, 173-175, 179, 194

Bury, Jennie Dater, 194

Bury, Mary, 194

Bushnell, C.C., 201

Cain, Post Commander, 203

California, 15, 17, 37

Callaghan, John, 110

Cameron, Cornelius, 105

Camp Carlin, 37, 55

Camp Cloud Peak, 81

Camp Hallack, 98

Camp McKinney, 112

Camp, C.T., 173

Campbell, Charley, 195

Campbell, Dan, 148-149

Campbell, I.N., 127

Campbell, Jack, 107

Campbell, Malcolm, 73, 106, 148-150, 152, 157-158, 168-169, 182, 189, 194-195

Cantonment Reno, 47, 98 (*See also* Fort McKinney)

Capps, Red, 135, 148-149

Carlton, Caleb H., 31-32, 56, 89, 91, 98, 139, 205-206

Carn, A.C, 141

Carrington, C.P., 99

Carrington, Henry B., 18-20

Casper, WY, 187, 194-195

Cattle Kate (*See* Wilson, Ella)

Cazabon, Frenchy, 157

cemetery, 138, 168, 178, 182

Centennial Campaigns, 47, 69-87, 205, 208-209

Chadron, NE, 161-162

Chambers, Alexander, 58, 60-63, 74, 79, 81, 97, 123, 203, 206-207, 215

Chambers, William, 108

Chandler, Zachariah, 77

Chase, George, 201

Chaves, Vivian "Picaqune", 71

*Cheyenne Democratic Leader*, 155

Cheyenne Depot, 37

*Cheyenne Mirror*, 162, 166, 173-174, 176-177, 182-183

Cheyenne River, 107

Cheyenne, WY, 41, 47, 55, 84, 87, 97, 147, 154, 157, 182, 191, 192-194

Cheyenne-Deadwood stage road, 156

Civil War, 15-16, 35, 197

Clarke, F.M., 174

Clay, Judge, 174, 186

Clay, Mr., 109

Clear Fork Creek, 47

Coates, Edwin M., 38, 40, 47, 81, 97, 99, 139-140, 203, 207

Cobb, Charles, 66, 100-102, 126, 153-155, 187

Coleman, Corporal, 72

Commercial Bank and Trust, 196

company barracks, 31, 32-33, 115, 117-119, 161

Connor, Patrick E., 17-18, 207-208

Conrad, Francis, 67

Conrad, Reverend, 174

Cooke, Philip, 20-21, 208

corral, stables, and shops, 31-32, 97, 113, 115, 128-130

Cotter, Private, 201

Coutant, C.G., 144

Cox, Alex, 165, 173

Craw, Minnie, 174

Crawford, Emmet, 104

Crazy Horse, 19, 79-80, 83

Crazy Woman's Fork, 83

Crook, George, 47, 77, 79-83, 107, 125, 208-209

Crosby, Harry, 150

Cross, George, 195-196

Cross, Julia, 196

Cross, Margaret, 195-196

Crow Creek, 37

Cully, Mr., 106

Custer, George A., 55, 75-76, 79, 80-82

Dague, Private, 99, 201

Daily, William, 195

Dakota Territory, 16, 21, 83

Daley, James, 106

Daniel, Abe, 199

Dater, Philip, 165

David, Robert B., 52, 168-169

Davis, Bill, 107

Davis, John, 105

Dayton, Thomas, 106

Deadwood, 83, 107, 199

Deer Creek, 24, 26, 30, 55, 63, 73, 77, 111, 187

DeLay, Mr., 139-140

Department of the Platte, 23-24, 26, 30, 40, 56, 63, 72, 79, 80, 129, 137, 146

Dewees, G.B., 54

Diamond, Thomas, 152

Dick's Place, 161, 180-182, 196

Dickinson, Mr., 101

Dodge, Richard Irving, 76, 111

Doggett, Mr., 173

Doolan, Bridget, 201

Dost, G.H., 110

Dougherty, Lieutenant, 53

*Douglas Budget*, 193 (*See Bill Barlow's Budget*)

Douglas, WY, 52, 158, 166-167, 173-174, 176, 177-189, 191-200

Drew, George A., 74, 209

Drybone (*See* Fetterman, WY)

Duck Creek Ranch, 199

Dull Knife, 60, 83

Dye, William McEntire, 23-27, 43, 45, 50, 89, 91, 100-101, 103, 105, 110, 203, 209

E S Ranch, 150
Eads, William, 15
Ecoffey, Jules, 127
Egan, James, 80, 209-210
Eighteenth Infantry, 18, 27-28, 38, 53, 105
Elgin, Dick, 148-149
Elk Mountain, 197
Elkhorn Creek, 84-87
Elliot, Henry, 99
Emery, Russell B., 69-70
Erben, Eula E., 192
Erwin, John, 107

Faulkner, Archie, 165, 180-182, 196
Fenex, John, 150
Ferguson, Private, 103
ferry, 43-44, 58, 61-62, 81
    Bridger's Ferry, 74, 77, 87
Fetterman Coal Mines, 183
Fetterman Fight, 19, 24, 50
Fetterman Hotel, 120, 168, 173-175, 181, 194
Fetterman, William J., 19-20, 24, 50-51
Fetterman, WY, 21, 159-189
Fifth Cavalry, 82-83, 107, 199
Fisher Stage Company, 42
Fisher, Isaac, 20
Fisher, Lieutenant, 111
Ford, A.S., 99
Fort Laramie Treaty (See Peace Treaty of 1868)
Forts:
    Fort Abraham Lincoln, 75, 79

Fort Benton, 15
Fort Bridger, 37
Fort C.F. Smith, 19, 66
Fort Caspar, 16, 21, 27-29, 33, 45, 53, 118, 122
Fort Connor, 17-19 (See also Fort Reno)
Fort Custer, 42
Fort D.A. Russell, 32, 37, 41, 105, 145-146, 199
Fort Fred Steele, 37, 39, 70
Fort Hall, 15
Fort John Buford (See Fort Sanders)
Fort Laramie, 16, 18-20, 23-24, 26, 30, 38, 40-41, 43, 44-45, 49-50, 53-54, 56, 60, 63, 65-66, 68, 69-70, 72, 76, 82, 84, 104, 106, 108, 110, 112, 197, 199
Fort McKinney, 37, 42, 47, 107, 162
Fort Mitchell, NE, 21
Fort Phil Kearny, 19-20, 24
Fort Randall, 50, 56
Fort Reno, 17-19, 28, 47, 53-54, 80, 110, 139, 199
Fort Robinson, 76
Fort Sanders, 37-38, 145
Fort Washakie, 146, 199
Fort Yankton, 79
Fourteenth Infantry, 71-72, 82, 83, 102-103, 105, 203
Fourth Artillery, 82-83
Fourth Cavalry, 82
Fourth Infantry, 23, 28, 40, 54, 67, 69-70, 79-80, 81-82, 83, 91-92, 98-99, 101, 103, 105-106, 108, 110, 125, 134, 139, 145, 201, 203
Fryer, Robert, 111
Furey, John V., 80, 82

Gallegos, Raphel, 105
Garver, C.M., 176
Gibbon, John, 79
Gifford, R., 99
Gill, John, 192
Gill, Margaret, 192
Gime, Cully, 107
Glenrock, WY, 187, 199
Goodrich, Geo., 153
Goodynoontz, Norvill, 167
Goose Creek, 81-82
Goose Egg Ranch, 148-149
Gordon, Johnny, 156-157, 191
Gordon, Major, 100
Gore, Frank, 149, 152, 157, 192
Gould, Frank, 110
Graham, Clint, 195
Grant, U.S., 20, 50, 60, 77
Grass, 56, 58, 62
Grasshopper Creek, 15
Greggs, Thomas J., 54-55
Grouard, Frank, 80
Grover, Cuvier, 210
Grummond, George W., 20
guardhouse, 115, 133-136, 161
Guthrie, W.E., 165

Hadley, George, 106
Halpole, R.V., 42
Hampton, Jesse, 73
Handy, Charles, 201
Harnett, Mattie, 177
Harney's Reservation, 55
Harper, Abraham, 54
Harper, George, 74
Harper, Joseph, 54
Harper, Samuel, 54

Harrington, Ella, 106
Hartsuff, Albert, 80
Hayden, F. V., 99-100
Hazen's Reservation, 55
Heck Reel Fight (*See* Indian Fight on
    the Elkhorn)
Helena, MT, 15
Henry, Guy V., 81, 210-211
Himnan, Samuel, 75
Hines, "Missou", 186
Hoffman, Joseph, 105
Hog Ranch, 147-158, 164
Hogerson, Charles, 201
Horse, Private, 102
Horseshoe Creek, 41, 45, 70, 84, 87
Horseshoe Station, 30
hospital, 29-30, 99-100, 115-119,
    122-125, 164, 188, 201
    Fort Fetterman Hospital Association,
    161, 164-168, 188, 192
Houghton, M.D., 144
Hubbard, Phares C., 179-180
Hunter, G.K., 201
Hunton, John, 40, 111-113, 138,
    147, 157, 192

Idaho, 15
Idelman Bros., 182
Idelman, Phil, 182
Independence Rock, 107
Indian Fight on the Elkhorn, 84-86
Indian Tribes
    Arapaho, 49-50, 52, 54-55, 63, 65,
    69-70, 73, 108
    Cheyenne, 19-20, 49-57, 61, 63-
    65, 68, 69, 71-72, 74, 78-80, 83-84
    Comanche, 50-51
    Crow, 49, 62, 66, 68, 80

Kiowa, 50-51, 55
Kiowa-Apache, 50
Pawnee, 82
Shoshoni, 49, 80
Sioux, 17-20, 50-68, 69-72, 75-80, 82, 111, 125
    Hunkpapa, 49
    Lower Yanktonai, 17
    Minneconjou, 49, 71
    Oglala, 49
    Santee, 49
    Teton, 17, 49
    Upper Yanktonai, 17
Inez, WY, 183
Inyan Kara Mountain, 75
Irish Pete, 85

Jackson, William Henry, 33, 99-103
James, Frank, 107
James, M.E. "Smoky", 174
Jamison, Sheriff, 178
Jaycox, Mary, 174
Jaycox, William, 186-187
Jenney, Walter P., 76
Johnson, E.C., 166-167
Johnson, Private, 70
Jordan, A.C., 42, 127-128
Jordon, Joseph, 105

Kane, Harrison, 149, 151
Kansas, 49
Keeffe, Joseph, 40, 44
Keller, John W., 92
Kelley, Sam, 107
Kendrick, John, 179
King, C.H., 185

King, Charles, 98
Kinney, Nathaniel C., 19
Krause, David, 72

LaBonte Creek, 24, 26, 38, 52, 69, 71-72, 86, 156-157, 191
LaBonte Ranch, 195
Lamb, Private, 139
LaPrele Canyon, 70, 99
LaPrele Creek, 16, 23-24, 27, 30, 38, 40-42, 71-72, 74, 89, 97, 99, 103, 106, 111, 138, 141, 196-198
*Laramie Boomerang*, 193
*Laramie Daily Times*, 193
Laramie Peak, 23, 38, 53, 72
Laramie Range, 23, 138
Laramie River, 16, 84, 156
Laramie, WY, 37, 106, 141, 157, 193
Last Chance Gulch, 15
Latta, Mr., 133
laundress, 28, 98-99, 115-117, 137-138
Lawrence, John, 149-152
Leary, Patrick, 101
Leighton, A., 127-128
Levasseur, Lea Marie, 195-196
*Lin McLean*, 159-161, 169-172
Litchfield, H.G., 24, 27, 30
Little Bighorn River, 81
Little Box Elder Creek, 26, 138
Little Medicine Creek, 41
Lodge Trail Ridge, 20
Luhn, Gerhard, 81, 122, 141-143, 201, 211
Lusk, WY, 184
Lynn, Ed, 181-182
Mackenzie, Ranald, 83-84

Mackin, C., 23, 124

Madison, Judge, 174

magazine and ordnance storehouse, 29, 115, 136-137, 161, 186, 189

manifest destiny, 17

Mann, Jim, 107

Manypenny, George, 77

Martin, Private, 104-105

Mason, C.W., 146, 203

Mason, John S., 40, 44, 74, 97, 111-113, 117, 124, 127-128, 136, 140, 141, 203, 211-212

Mason, Thomas J., 104-105

Maverick Bank, 176

McCallister, John A., 70

McDonald, C.S., 194

McDonald, Michael "Pat", 73

McFarland, William, 108-109

McFoley, Reverend, 99

McGaughlin, Sergeant, 106

McGrath, Matt, 199

McGrew, James, 108

McGuiness, Private, 92

McKenna, George, 70

McKinney, John A., 83

McMillen, Mr., 73

McReynolds, Mr., 186

Meanea, F.A., 179

Meat Market, 161, 180-181, 196

Mecum, Judge, 182

Medicine Bow River, 41

Medicine Bow road, 42

Medicine Bow Station, 109, 112

Medicine Bow, WY, 40-42, 70, 79, 81

Medicine Lodge Creek, 49

Meinhold, Charles, 75

Merival, Frank, 42

Merival, Joe, 41-42, 71, 111

Metcalf & Williams Store, 161, 175-177, 180

Metcalf, George W., 176-177, 196-197, 199

Metcalf, Susie Webel, 177, 196

Miller, Lew, 194

Miller, Louis, 148-149

Miller, Sam, 166

Mills, Anson, 83

Mississippi River, 17, 35

Missouri River, 15, 18, 50, 56, 75-76

Mitchell, Dan, 187

Mitchell, S. Weir, 159

Monroe, Francis Le Baron, 23, 60, 123

Montana, 15-16, 49-50, 79, 83

Montana Road, 16-17 (*See also* Bozeman Trail)

Moore, Lee, 148-149, 165

Morrissey, Mr., 106

Moses, Richard, 180-182, 187, 196

Mosley, Mr., 185

Mousseau, M.A., 54

Mularkey, James A., 71-72

Nearing, Ned, 161, 164, 166, 173, 175, 179-181, 183, 187

Nebraska, 49, 72, 193

Nevada, 37

Nichols, E.K., 102, 128

Nichols, William, 173-175, 194

Nickerson, Captain, 79

Nineteenth Infantry, 203

Ninth Infantry, 79, 82-83

Noble, Priscilla, 194

Nolan, James, 101

O'Brian, John D., 201

O'Brien, John J., 212

O'Hara, Mr., 201

Odd Fellows, 199

officers' quarters, 81-82, 115, 117-121, 164, 183, 185, 189

Ogallala Sheep and Cattle Company, 199

Old Bear, 71-72

Old-Man-Afraid-of-His-Horses, 17-18, 55-56, 58, 66, 70

Oregon Trail, 15-16, 21, 23, 37, 41, 44

Orin Junction, WY, 42

Ottens, John, 87

Overland Stage, 44

Owens, W.O., 187

Packer, Alfred, 157, 194

Palmer, Innis N., 26

parade ground, 31, 104, 115-117, 161

Parks, William H., 181-182

Parrott, Big Nose George, 107

Pathfinder Dam, 180

Patterson, Alfred Jr., 201

Patterson, Henry W., 65, 201

Patterson, Louisa Davison, 201

Payne, James H., 106

peace treaties

    Medicine Lodge treaties, 50

    Treaty of 1865, 17-18

    Treaty of 1866, 18

    Treaty of 1868, 21, 49-68, 75, 77-78

Peacock, Frank, 108-109

Pease, Mr., 177-178

Pennsylvania Volunteers, 197

Persimmon Bill (See Chambers, William)

Peterson, Harold, 179-180

Phillips, John "Portugee", 20

Piney Creek, 19

Platte River, 15-16, 21, 23, 26-27, 30, 37, 42-44, 50-55, 58, 61, 69-72, 74, 77, 80, 87, 97, 105-106, 113, 140-141, 145, 147-149, 156, 161, 189

Point of Rocks, 38

Pollard, Mr., 156, 191

Pony Express, 17, 35

Poole, D.C., 197

Pope, John, 18

post headquarters, 115-119, 122

post trader's store and quarters, 42, 115, 126-128, 161

Potter, Mary, 168

Pourier, Baptiste, 67, 80

Powder River, 16-19, 47, 50, 53-55, 60, 62, 66-67, 74, 79-80, 107

Powder River Expedition, 83-84

Powell, George, 84, 87, 197, 201

Powell, James, 20

Powell, Maggie Skogland, 197, 201

Powell, William H., 82, 145-146, 203, 212-213

Pumpkin Buttes, 107

quartermaster and commissary storehouse, 43, 78, 130-133

Rabbit Creek, 83

Rae, Robert, 69-70

railroad, 17, 21, 35-38, 184-186, 187-189, 199

    Central Pacific Railroad, 35

    Fremont, Elkhorn and Missouri Valley Railroad, 161, 184-186, 188

        Pioneer Townsite Company, 184-186

Union Pacific Railroad, 37-38, 50, 54-55, 70, 79, 147, 162, 194, 197

Wyoming Central Railroad, 192

Randall, George M., 79

Rastaetter, Charles, 165, 179, 194

Rawlins, WY, 107

Raynolds, W.F., 75

recreation areas, 125-126

Red Canyon, 38

Red Cloud, 17-19, 49-50, 53, 56-58, 60-63, 66, 69-70

Red Cloud Agency, 72, 80

Red Dog, 60-62

Red Leaf, 56

Red Shirt, 62

Reed, Tom, 107

Reel, Heck, 84, 87

Reid, C., 178

Remington, Frederic, 169-170

Reno Creek, 20

Reshaw, John (*See* Richard, John Jr.)

Reynolds, Joseph J., 79-80, 213

Richard, Joe, 60, 65

Richard, John Jr., 60, 65-68

Richard, John Sr., 65

Richard, Louis, 80

Richardson, Reverend, 174

Robinson, Henry E., 81

Robinson, Levi H., 72-73

Rock Creek, 162, 182, 197

Rock Creek Station, 38-42, 74

Rock Creek–Fetterman road, 38, 41

Roe, Mr., 106

Rosebud Creek, 80-81, 125

Royal, William B., 79

Ruggles, George D., 56, 109

Russell, Sergeant, 201

Ryan, Ellen, 99

S. M. Fetterman Belle, 184

Sage Creek Ranch, 199

Sampson, W.C., 165, 167, 175, 181, 194

Sanders, Corporal, 69-70

Sandy, McKinney (*See* James, Frank)

Sanford, John B., 66

Saunders, John "Jack", 149-155, 165, 192

Saunders, Viola, 151-154, 165

Sawmill, 53, 115, 138-140

Sawyer, James A., 16-17

Schaus, Julius, 168

Schaus, Sophia, 168

Schloss, Ed, 152

Schmidt, H., 99

Seade, M.V., 174

Searight, Mr., 148-149

Searle, Herman S., 27, 38

Second Cavalry, 20, 54-55, 70, 72, 79, 82, 83, 203

Seventh Cavalry, 79, 81

Seventh Infantry, 205

74 Ranch, 166

Sheldon, K.W., 201

Sheridan, Phil, 77-78, 80, 82

Sherman, Sylvester, 84-86

Sherman, William T., 50-51, 55

Sioux City, IA, 16

Six Mile Ranch, 106, 201

Slaymaker, Ellen Howard, 168-170, 173, 197

Slaymaker, Flora Hobbs, 197

Slaymaker, Samuel, 168-170, 174, 197-198

Slim Buttes, 83, 125
Smith, Charles H., 110
Smith, E.C., 201
Smith, Edward P., 77
Snider, Deputy, 107
Sorrel Horse, 50
South Dakota, 50, 75
Sparhawk Opera House, 126, 182-183
Sparhawk, Frank H., 179, 182-183
Sparks, Frederick, 110
Spencer, James H., 201
Spotted Tail Agency, 108
Spring Canyon, 38, 41
Spring Creek, 38
stagecoach lines, 17
Standing Elk, 18
Stanton, Mr., 174
Stanton, William, 79
Stevenson, James, 99
Stewart, James, 38
Sullivan, Andy, 195
Sullivan, Joe, 195
Sullivan, Patrick, 108
Sullivan, Private, 69, 105-106
Swartz, John, 157

Taylor, D.B., 18
Taylor, John, 101
*Tecumseh Chieftain*, 193
Teitenheimer, Carl, 215
telegraph, 17, 27, 30, 35, 69
    Overland Telegraph Line, 44
    Western Union Telegraph Co., 35,
    44
Ten Eyck, Tenodor, 20
Terry, Alfred, 79
Teschmacher, H.E., 165

Third Cavalry, 72-73, 77, 79, 82, 83,
    104-106, 109, 118, 201, 203
Thirtieth Infantry, 205
Thirty-third Infantry, 197
Thomas, Cyrus, 99
Three Circle Ranch, 186
Throstle, Mr., 84-86
Tillotson, Ephraim, 42, 102, 127-128,
    133, 147, 178, 213
Tobey, John M., 63
Tumbull, C.T., 99
Twenty-second Infantry, 197
Twenty-seventh Infantry, 20, 24
Twenty-third Infantry, 79, 82-83

Utah, 18
Uva, WY, 156, 191

Valley House, 168, 173-174
Van Meter, J.H., 173, 175
Van Norman, Dr., 167
Van Vliet, Frederick, 72-73, 109, 213-
    214
Veitenheimer, Carl, 39
Verden, J. Crook, 166
Vinson, H.H., 107
Virginia City, MT, 15-16
Vodges, Ada, 56-68, 70-71, 89-94,
    96-97, 100, 105
Vodges, Anthony Wayne, 56, 58, 89,
    94, 214
Vorpahl, Ben Merchant, 169-170
VR Ranch, 166

Wagon Hound Creek, 157
Walker, Tom, 148
Wallace, Frank, 150
Wallace, James E., 174

Walsh, Hospital Steward, 106

War Department, 18, 42, 77, 87, 146-147

Ward, John O., 106, 126-127, 139-140, 201

Ward, Mrs. John, 109, 201

Warden, George Francis (*See* Parrott, Big Nose George)

Warren, Francis E., 192

Warren, G.K., 75

Warren, Newton, 76

Washington, D.C., 49, 60-61, 62, 105

water system, 115, 140-144

Watkins, Dr., 154

Watson, Ella (*See* Wilson, Ella)

Wattles, Mr., 185

Weaver, W.S., 165

Webel, C.C.P., 147-148, 182, 194

Webster, George O., 81, 140, 214

Wells, Almond B., 103

Wells, Eugene, 91, 93, 214-215

Wentworth, Private, 70

Werner, Mary Anna Pfiefer, 179, 199

Werner, William, 178-179, 189, 198-199

Wessells, Henry W., 27-32, 38, 45, 53, 89, 106, 203, 215

Wheatley, James, 20

Wheaton, Charles, 197

Wheelock, Frank, 199

Wheelock, Benjamin, 184, 199

Wheelock, Joe, 199

White, John, 15

White, Private, 92

Widdowfield, Robert, 107

Williams, Elizabeth Ragsdale, 199-200

Williams, John T., 174, 176-177, 180, 187, 196-197, 199-200

Williams, Nathan, 73

Williams, Private, 110

Williams, Reverend, 200

Wilson, Alex, 195

Wilson, Benjamin, 106

Wilson, Dr., 167

Wilson, Ella, 150

Wilson, Robert, 66, 92, 100-102, 108, 126

Winchell, Mr., 75

Wister, Owen, 21, 159-161, 168-172, 184, 189

Wolcott, Frank, 111, 113, 159

Wood, Private, 134

Woodward, George A., 201, 203, 215-216

Worner, Catharina Straur, 198

Worner, Franz Ignaz, 198

Worner, William *See* Werner, William

Wyoming House, 168, 173

Wyoming National Guard, 197

Wyoming Stock Grower's Association, 157

*Wyoming Tribune*, 193

Yates, F.D., 100

Yeager, Bob, 106

Yellow Bear, 68

Yellow Robe, 80

Yestman, Lieutenant, 45

Young-Man-Afraid of-His-Horses, 59

AUTHOR THOMAS A. LINDMIER was raised in Douglas, Wyoming near the site of historic Fort Fetterman. He holds a B.A. in history from the University of Wyoming. Upon completing college, Tom began a career in historic site development, interpretation, and management.

Currently he is the superintendent of South Pass City State Historic Site and serves on the board of directors for the Wyoming Pioneer Museum State Historic Site in Douglas. Tom is a generalist in western history with a strong interest in military, ranching, transportation, and general western expansion.

He first began researching and studying Fort Fetterman while a senior in high school as part of an independent study program for honor students. The resulting research paper set him off on a journey of over thirty years of additional research. While a student at the University of Wyoming, he worked four summers as the groundskeeper at Fort Fetterman State Historic Site. Since then, while working for State of Wyoming at various historic sites, he has maintained his lifelong love for the history of Fort Fetterman and the area.

❧ NOTES ON THE PRODUCTION OF THE BOOK ❧


This book was simultaneously released in two editions.

A *limited edition* of only 200 copies was Smyth sewn,
bound in Tartan Red Corinth, and embossed with copper foil.
Each copy is signed by the author and hand numbered.
This edition was issued with no dust jacket.

The *softcover trade edition* is covered with twelve-point stock, printed
in four colors, and coated with a special gloss finish.

The text of both editions is from the Garamond Family by Adobe.
Display type is Garamond Expert by Adobe and
Border Dingbats 1 by SMC.

The book is printed on sixty-pound Thor Recycled White,
an acid-free, recycled paper
by Thomson-Shore.